T0202614

XML and JSON Recipes for SQL Server

A Problem-Solution Approach

Alex Grinberg

Apress®

XML and JSON Recipes for SQL Server

Alex Grinberg
Richboro, Pennsylvania, USA

ISBN-13 (pbk): 978-1-4842-3116-6   ISBN-13 (electronic): 978-1-4842-3117-3
https://doi.org/10.1007/978-1-4842-3117-3

Library of Congress Control Number: 2017962636

Managing Director: Welmoed Spahr
Editorial Director: Todd Green
Acquisitions Editor: Jonathan Gennick
Development Editor: Laura Berendson
Technical Reviewer: Michael Coles
Coordinating Editor: Jill Balzano
Copy Editor: Karen Jameson
Compositor: SPi Global
Indexer: SPi Global
Artist: SPi Global

Distributed to the book trade worldwide by Springer Science+Business Media New York, 233 Spring Street, 6th Floor, New York, NY 10013. Phone 1-800-SPRINGER, fax (201) 348-4505, e-mail orders-ny@springer-sbm.com, or visit www.springeronline.com. Apress Media, LLC is a California LLC and the sole member (owner) is Springer Science + Business Media Finance Inc (SSBM Finance Inc). SSBM Finance Inc is a **Delaware** corporation.

For information on translations, please e-mail rights@apress.com, or visit http://www.apress.com/rights-permissions.

Apress titles may be purchased in bulk for academic, corporate, or promotional use. eBook versions and licenses are also available for most titles. For more information, reference our Print and eBook Bulk Sales web page at http://www.apress.com/bulk-sales.

Any source code or other supplementary material referenced by the author in this book is available to readers on GitHub via the book's product page, located at www.apress.com/9781484231166. For more detailed information, please visit http://www.apress.com/source-code.

Printed on acid-free paper

This book is dedicated to my parents and Chante Silva.
You have left a light forever in our hearts and will not be forgotten.

Contents

About the Author xix

About the Technical Reviewer xxi

Acknowledgments xxiii

▪Part I: XML in SQL Server 1

▪Chapter 1: Introducing XML 3

Stepping into XML 3

    Sample Database 4

    Understanding XML 4

    Entitizing XML Characters 6

    Exploring the XML Data Type 7

1-1. Creating an Untyped XML Column 8

    Problem 8

    Solution 8

    How It Works 10

1-2. Creating an XML Schema in Visual Studio 11

    Problem 11

    Solution 11

    How It Works 13

1-3. Creating an XML Schema from SSMS 14

    Problem 14

    Solution 15

    How It Works 16

1-4. Binding XML to a Schema Collection 18

    Problem 18

    Solution 18

    How It Works 19

1-5. Creating a Typed XML Column 20

    Problem 20

    Solution 21

    How It Works 21

Summary 22

■Chapter 2: Building XML 23

Fixing the "Unable to show XML" Error 24

2-1. Converting Relational Data to a Simple XML Format 26

    Problem 26

    Solution 26

    How It Works 26

2-2. Generating XML Data with Table Names as Element Names 28

    Problem 28

    Solution 28

    How It Works 30

2-3. Generating Element-Centric XML 30

    Problem 30

    Solution 31

    How It Works 31

2-4. Adding a Root Element 32

    Problem 32

    Solution 32

    How It Works 33

2-5. Including Elements with NULL Values in Your XML Data............... 33

Problem 33

Solution..33

How It Works..34

2-6. Including Binary Data in Your XML.. 34

Problem 34

Solution..34

How It Works..35

2-7. Generating Nested Hierarchical XML Data..................................... 36

Problem 36

Solution..36

How It Works..38

2-8. Building Custom XML.. 38

Problem 38

Solution..38

How It Works..40

2-9. Simplifying Custom XML Generation 45

Problem 45

Solution..45

How It Works..46

2-10. Adding Special Nodes to Your XML 48

Problem 48

Solution..48

How It Works..49

Summary.. 51

Chapter 3: Manipulating XML Files 53

3-1. Storing XML Result in a File from SQL 53

Problem 53

Solution 53

How It Works 55

3-2. Creating XML from an SSIS Package 59

Problem 59

Solution 59

How It Works 72

3-3. Loading XML from a Stored Procedure 72

Problem 72

Solution 72

How It Works 75

3-4. Loading XML from SSIS Package 78

Problem 78

Solution 78

How It Works 90

3-5. Implementing a CLR Solution 92

Problem 92

Solution 92

How It Works 96

Summary 99

Chapter 4: Shredding XML 101

4-1. Shredding XML with Internal ENTITY Declarations 101

Problem 101

Solution 101

How It Works 102

4-2. Migrating OPENXML into XQuery 108

Problem 108

Solution 108

How It Works 109

4-3. Shredding XML from a Column 113

Problem 113

Solution 113

How It Works 114

4-4. Dealing with Legacy XML Storage 116

Problem 116

Solution 117

How It Works 118

4-5. Navigating Typed XML Columns 120

Problem 120

Solution 120

How It Works 122

4-6. Retrieving a Subset of Your XML Data 123

Problem 123

Solution 123

How It Works 124

4-7. Finding All XML Columns in a Table 127

Problem 127

Solution 127

How It Works 129

4-8. Using Multiple CROSS APPLY Operators 132

Problem 132

Solution 132

How It Works 133

Summary 134

■Chapter 5: Modifying XML 135

5-1. Inserting a Child Element into Your XML 135

Problem 135

Solution.. 135

How It Works.. 136

5-2. Inserting a Child Element into an Existing XML Instance
with Namespace 137

Problem 137

Solution.. 137

How It Works.. 138

5-3. Inserting XML Attributes 140

Problem 140

Solution.. 140

How It Works.. 141

5-4. Inserting XML Attribute Conditionally... 143

Problem 143

Solution.. 143

How It Works.. 144

5-5. Inserting a Child Element with Position Specification 144

Problem 144

Solution.. 144

How It Works.. 146

5-6. Inserting Multiple Elements 146

Problem 146

Solution.. 146

How It Works.. 147

5-7. Updating an XML Element Value 148

Problem 148

Solution... 148

How It Works.. 149

5-8. Updating XML Attribute Value 150

Problem 150

Solution... 150

How It Works.. 151

5-9. Deleting an XML Attribute 151

Problem 151

Solution... 151

How It Works.. 152

5-10. Deleting an XML Element.. 153

Problem 153

Solution... 153

How It Works.. 154

Summary.. 156

■Chapter 6: Filtering XML... 157

6-1. Implementing the exist() Method 157

Problem 157

Solution... 157

How It Works.. 158

6-2. Filtering an XML Value with the exist() Method 160

Problem 160

Solution... 160

How It Works.. 161

6-3. Finding All Occurrences of an XML Element Anywhere Within an XML Instance 164

Problem 164

Solution 164

How It Works 166

6-4. Filtering by Single Value 167

Problem 167

Solution 167

How It Works 168

6-5. Filtering XML by T-SQL Variable 168

Problem 168

Solution 168

How It Works 169

6-6. Comparing to a Sequence of Values 170

Problem 170

Solution 170

How It Works 171

6-7. Matching a Specified String Pattern 171

Problem 171

Solution 172

How It Works 172

6-8. Filtering a Range of Values 174

Problem 174

Solution 174

How It Works 175

6-9. Filtering by Multiple Conditions 175

Problem 175

Solution 175

How It Works 176

6-10. Setting a Negative Predicate 177

    Problem 177

    Solution... 177

    How It Works... 178

6-11. Filtering Empty Values 178

    Problem 178

    Solution... 179

    How It Works... 180

Summary.. 182

Chapter 7: Improving XML Performance 185

7-1. Creating a Primary XML Index 185

    Problem 185

    Solution... 185

    How It Works... 187

7-2. Creating a Secondary PATH Type Index.................................. 193

    Problem 193

    Solution... 193

    How It Works... 195

7-3. Creating a Secondary VALUE Type Index................................ 196

    Problem 196

    Solution... 196

    How It Works... 198

7-4. Creating a Secondary PROPERTY Type Index......................... 200

    Problem 200

    Solution... 200

    How It Works... 202

7-5. Creating a Selective XML Index 202

　Problem 202

　Solution... 203

　How It Works... 205

7-6. Optimizing a Selective XML Index... 210

　Problem 210

　Solution... 210

　How It Works... 211

7-7. Creating a Secondary Selective XML Index 213

　Problem 213

　Solution... 213

　How It Works... 214

7-8. Modifying Selective XML Indexes 215

　Problem 215

　Solution... 215

　How It Works... 217

Wrapping up 218

■Part II: JSON in SQL Server 219

■Chapter 8: Constructing JSON 221

JSON Introduction 221

8-1. Building JSON with AUTO Mode... 225

　Problem 225

　Solution... 225

　How It Works... 226

8-2. Handling NULL When JSON Build... 230

　Problem 230

　Solution... 230

　How It Works... 231

8-3. Escaping the Brackets for JSON Output 232

Problem 232

Solution 232

How It Works 232

8-4. Adding ROOT Key Element to JSON 233

Problem 233

Solution 233

How It Works 233

8-5. Gaining Control over JSON Output 234

Problem 234

Solution 234

How It Works 235

8-6. Handling Escape Characters 239

Problem 239

Solution 239

How It Works 240

8-7. Dealing with CLR Data Types 241

Problem 241

Solution 242

How It Works 243

Summary 244

■Chapter 9: Converting JSON to Row Sets 245

9-1. Detecting the Columns with JSON 245

Problem 245

Solution 245

How It Works 247

9-2. Returning a Subset of a JSON Document 249

Problem 249

Solution.. 249

How It Works... 250

9-3. Returning a Scalar Value from JSON 251

Problem 251

Solution.. 251

How It Works... 252

9-4. Troubleshooting a Returned NULL.............................. 254

Problem 254

Solution.. 254

How It Works... 254

9-5. Converting JSON into a Table.............................. 255

Problem 255

Solution.. 255

How It Works... 256

9-6. Processing JSON Nested Sub-Objects................................ 259

Problem 259

Solution.. 259

How It Works... 262

9-7. Indexing JSON.. 263

Problem 263

Solution.. 263

How It Works... 264

Summary... 267

■ **Chapter 10: Modifying JSON**..**269**

10-1. Adding a New Key-Value Pair to JSON......................................269

Problem 269

Solution...269

How It Works...270

10-2. Updating Existing JSON 270

Problem 270

Solution...270

How It Works...271

10-3. Deleting from JSON 271

Problem 271

Solution...271

How It Works...271

10-4. Appending a JSON Property...273

Problem 273

Solution...273

How It Works...274

10-5. Modifying with Multiple Actions..274

Problem 274

Solution...274

How It Works...275

10-6. Renaming a JSON Key 275

Problem 275

Solution...275

How It Works...276

10-7. Modifying a JSON Object 277

   Problem 277

   Solution 277

   How It Works 277

10-8. Comparing XML vs. JSON 279

   Problem 279

   Solution 279

   How It Works 283

Wrapping Up 285

Index 287

About the Author

Alex Grinberg has more than 20 years of IT experience. His primary focus is on the latest Microsoft technologies, including .NET (VB and C#), SSRS, and SSIS. He provides tuning, optimization, analysis, and development services toward creating new applications; converting legacy applications into newer technologies such as SQL Server, VB.NET, and C#; and toward onsite training. Alex is a senior DBA architect at Cox Automotive Inc. He provides consulting services for the New York City, Philadelphia, and Delaware areas.

About the Technical Reviewer

Michael Coles is a database architect and developer working out of New Jersey. He has authored several books and published dozens of articles on SQL Server development topics. Michael holds multiple Microsoft certifications and has been recognized as a Microsoft MVP for his work with SQL Server and for his contributions to the SQL community.

Acknowledgments

For a number of years I had been dreaming about writing a book to share my knowledge. Finally, this dream came true. However, to write a book is not a single-person effort. There are many people who helped me to deliver this book to the reader. I would like to thank the Apress team – Jonathan Gennick, Jill Balzano, and Laura Berendson who motivated me and provided valuable advice to move forward with the book.

My big appreciation and respect to technical reviewer Michael Coles, who provided me with plenty of recommendations to make this book better and more comprehensively cover the recipes, especially for the XML part. Also, I would like to thank Alessandro Alpi, who consulted with me for the JSON part.

I got tremendous help from Cox Automotive colleagues, especially Cary Dickerson, who provided me with the powerful server to test the recipes that allows me to demonstrate and compare the recipe's performance as they run in the production environment. Thanks to Michael Neuburger and Mathew Silva for their support during the book-writing period. My sincerest apologies if I missed anyone, but there were a lot of you!

I also would like to thank my friends Said Salomon and Vince Napoli for encouraging and supporting me.

Of course, my deepest special thanks to my family - wife Ludmila and daughters Anna and Katherine, who suffered minimal attention from me during the book-writing process, but still supported me throughout the project and patiently waited for the book to be completed.

Thanks very much to all of you! It was a pleasure to work with you!

Alex Grinberg

PART I

XML in SQL Server

CHAPTER 1

■ ■ ■

Introducing XML

Welcome and thank you for reading *XML and JSON Recipes for SQL Server*. In the modern world of information technology, keeping data stored and manipulated reliably and efficiently is one of the first priorities. In the last decade, SQL Server has evolved into a sophisticated Enterprise RDBMS tool, and it is still growing by providing more functionalities to store and manipulate data reliably. eXtensible Markup Language (XML) is one of the technologies that SQL Server implements not only for data manipulation but also for many internal usages, such as Execution Plans, Extended Events, DDL trigger Eventdata() function, and behind construction for SQL Server Business Intelligence Tools (SSIS, SSRS, SSAS). In Part 1 of this book, I will cover and provide the recipes on how to work with the SQL Server XML data type; discuss and demonstrate real type scenarios to load, build, and shred the XML; and present how daily tasks can be simplified by implementing XML technologies. In this book, I will primarily be focusing on technology rather than theory.

Stepping into XML

To work with XML, we need to understand this technology, especially for SQL Server. XML is similar to HTML (Hypertext Markup Language). XML and HTML contain markup elements to describe the contents of the file or page for HTML. The big difference between them is that HTML contains predefined elements (tags), while XML's elements and attributes are not predefined and based on described data within the files.

Several more important differences between HTML and XML:

- XML is key sensitive while HTML is not.

- XML opened element must be closed. HTML can have an opened element without a closed element. For example, *<DATA>Display Text* will compile for HTML and will return an error for XML.

■ **Caution**   SQL Server, by default, is not case sensitive. However, XML is case sensitive, and all XQuery Path Language (XPath) functions and node tests are case sensitive (all lowercase). They will return an error when entered with any case other than lowercase.

© Alex Grinberg 2018
A. Grinberg, *XML and JSON Recipes for SQL Server*,
https://doi.org/10.1007/978-1-4842-3117-3_1

Sample Database

All code samples for Part I in this book utilize the SQL Server AdventureWorks sample database, unless otherwise specified and referenced separately in the text. The AdventureWorks database URL is https://github.com/Microsoft/sql-server-samples/releases/tag/adventureworks2014. I would highly recommend downloading and installing the AdventureWorks sample database to run the samples presented.

Understanding XML

Before working with XML, we need to explain the difference between the two types of node-centric XML formats supported by SQL Server:

1. Element-centric

2. Attribute-centric

Both elements and attributes can contain data. However, SQL Server has specialized functionality and features for each format generating or shredding (shredding is a process to convert XML into rows-columns format) attribute-centric or element-centric data. In the element-centric format, values are contained within the opening and closing tags of an element, for example, *<elementName>*. The attribute-centric format relies on attributes of an element in the element's opening tag. They are assigned a value by the equal sign, and the values are wrapped in double quotes, for example, *<elementName attribute="value">*. For instance, the sample SQL query in Listing 1-1 returns two rows, with the result shown in Figure 1-1.

Listing 1-1. Simple SQL query

```
SELECT TOP (2) Category.Name AS CategoryName,
        Subcategory.Name AS SubcategoryName,
        Product.Name,
        Product.ProductNumber AS Number,
        Product.ListPrice AS Price
FROM   Production.Product Product
        INNER JOIN Production.ProductSubcategory Subcategory
                ON Product.ProductSubcategoryID = Subcategory.Product
                SubcategoryID
        LEFT JOIN Production.ProductCategory Category
                ON Subcategory.ProductCategoryID = Category.Product
                CategoryID
WHERE Product.ListPrice > 0
        AND Product.SellEndDate IS NULL
ORDER BY CategoryName, SubcategoryName;
```

CategoryName	SubcategoryName	Name	Number	Price
Accessories	Bike Racks	Hitch Rack - 4-Bike	RA-H123	120.00
Accessories	Bike Stands	All-Purpose Bike Stand	ST-1401	159.00

Figure 1-1. *Result data set from sample SQL query*

This is an example of what the relational data from Figure 1-1 might look like in an element-centric XML format. Notice that all values are presented as XML elements in this format demonstrated in Listing 1-2.

Listing 1-2. Showing element-centric XML

```
<Category>
  <Category xmlns="http://schemas.microsoft.com/sqlserver/2004/07/Chapter01/
ProductSchema">
    <CategoryName>Accessories</CategoryName>
    <Subcategory>
      <SubcategoryName>Bike Racks</SubcategoryName>
      <Product>
        <Name>Hitch Rack - 4-Bike</Name>
        <Number>RA-H123</Number>
        <Price>120.0000</Price>
      </Product>
    </Subcategory>
    <Subcategory>
      <SubcategoryName>Bike Stands</SubcategoryName>
      <Product>
        <Name>All-Purpose Bike Stand</Name>
        <Number>ST-1401</Number>
        <Price>159.0000</Price>
      </Product>
    </Subcategory>
  </Category>
</Category>
```

Converted relational data from Figure 1-1 might look like an attribute-centric XML format demonstrated in Listing 1-3.

Listing 1-3. Showing attribute-centric XML

```
<Category CategoryName="Accessories">
  <Subcategory SubcategoryName="Bike Racks">
    <Product Name="Hitch Rack - 4-Bike" Number="RA-H123" Price="120.0000" />
  </Subcategory>
  <Subcategory SubcategoryName="Bike Stands">
    <Product Name="All-Purpose Bike Stand" Number="ST-1401" Price="159.0000" />
  </Subcategory>
</Category>
```

Comparing the element-centric XML data in Listing 1-2 to the attribute-centric XML data in Listing 1-3, several differences can be clearly defined:

- Element-centric XML is bigger (in number of characters) than attribute-centric XML.

- Element-centric XML supports element hierarchy.

- Element-centric XML can represent SQL NULLs with the xsi:nil attribute (xsi:nil will covered in Chapter 2, Recipe 2-5 "Handling Elements with NULL Values").

We will provide a deeper analysis and show additional differences, use cases, and demonstrations in Chapter 2, "Building XML."

Entitizing XML Characters

XML elements are defined by left- and right-angled brackets (less-than and greater-than signs, "<" and ">"). XML attribute values are wrapped in double quotation marks. Data containing these special characters that are not part of the XML markup can cause issues during XML parsing. To resolve these potential conflicts, XML defines a set of special character sequences, known as *predefined entities*, which all XML parsers must honor. The character sequences, which include the double quotation mark, ampersand, apostrophe, less-than sign, and greater-than sign, and their associated XML entities are listed in Table 1-1.

Table 1-1. *Listing Predefined Entities in XML*

Character	Entity Reference	Description
"	&quot;	double quotation mark
&	&amp;	ampersand
'	&apos;	apostrophe (apostrophe-quote)
<	&lt;	less-than sign
>	&gt;	greater-than sign

The process when predefined entities are replaced with entity references is known as *entitizing*. To demonstrate entitizing, I took the XML in Listing 1-4 then typed (copy/paste) into a Notepad.

Listing 1-4. Sample XML with predefined entities

```
<char>
  <ToXML Entity="Entity ampersand &amp;; in XML data." />
  <ToXML Entity="Entity less-than sign &lt;; in XML data." />
  <ToXML Entity="Entity greater-than sign &gt;; in XML data." />
  <ToXML Entity="Entity apostrophe &apos;; in XML data." />
  <ToXML Entity="Entity quotation mark &quot;; in XML data." />
</char>
```

I then saved the file with an .xml extension. For instance, I call the file XML_Entity. xml. When the file is created, I simply double-click on the file or open it in Internet Explorer. As a result, the entity references will display as normal characters, as shown in Figure 1-2.

```
<char>
    <ToXML Entity="Entity ampersand &; in XML data."/>
    <ToXML Entity="Entity less-than sign <; in XML data."/>
    <ToXML Entity="Entity greater-than sign >; in XML data."/>
    <ToXML Entity="Entity apostrophe '; in XML data."/>
    <ToXML Entity="Entity quotation mark "; in XML data."/>
</char>
```

Figure 1-2. Sample with XML entities expanded

Exploring the XML Data Type

XML support within the Microsoft SQL Server database was first introduced in SQL Server 2000. XML can consist of very long strings of data; therefore, it is very rare to encounter XML data that will not fit in a VARCHAR(8000) or NVARCHAR(4000) Unicode column. Since much XML data won't fit into these data types, SQL Server 2000 suggested that DBAs and Developers utilize TEXT, and in some cases IMAGE, data types. Many found dealing with these data types to be a nightmare, as they were difficult to work with. Also, when dealing with XML on 2000 you had to utilize the COM-based stored procedures.

With the release of SQL Server 2005, the XML data type was provided, which made it significantly easier to work with XML data, and the XML data can be stored in its native format. The result of the XML data type returns a clickable hyperlink format when the output is set to *Result To Grid* in SSMS. To review XML content, you can just click on the hyperlink and SSMS will display the XML result in a separate XML document tab. The XML document tab does not allow you to connect to SQL Server instances or execute any SQL statements.

The XML data type is a convenient and well-designed data type that allows you to store data and documents in the XML format. In some cases, other large SQL Server data types can be used to store XML data, such as NVARCHAR(MAX), VARCHAR(MAX), or VARBINARY(MAX). The old data types IMAGE, NTEXT, and TEXT can do the job as well but are not as user friendly to work with.

For example, when XML data is stored as a document, and you do not need to query this data in its entirety, you can use the NVARCHAR(MAX), VARCHAR(MAX), VARBINARY(MAX). The best argument for using a LOB data type to store XML is when you need to store the exact representation of the XML, since the XML data type will store the content you provide, but it might alter insignificant whitespace and the order of attributes is not guaranteed. Take a look at msdb.dbo.sysssispackages table where the packagedata column stores server-side SSIS packages. SQL Server utilizes the IMAGE data type (I would not recommend following Microsoft in this case) to store the SSIS package code. For those who have never looked at SSIS code, it is XML data. Therefore, when I need to query SSIS (I had several reasonable requests for such a task), I converted the packagedata column to VARBINARY(MAX) and then cast it to and XML data type instance, as shown in Listing 1-5.

Listing 1-5. Converting IMAGE data type into XML data type

```
SELECT CAST(CAST(packagedata as VARBINARY(MAX)) AS XML) AS SSISPackage
FROM msdb.dbo.sysssispackages;
```

■ **Caution**   Legacy Large Object Binary data types IMAGE, NTEXT, and TEXT should not be considered for any column implementation. Books Online do not reference these data types because they are deprecated. However, some system tables still have it; even Microsoft announced that IMAGE, NTEXT, and TEXT data types would be deprecated in the year 2008.

The XML data type has the following limitations:

- The storage is limited to 2.1 GB.
- It cannot be used as a table Primary Key.
- It cannot be sorted by the ORDER BY clause.
- It cannot be compared in the WHERE clause.
- It cannot be used in the GROUP BY clause.
- It cannot be a parameter to any scalar built-in functions except ISNULL, COALESCE, DATALENGTH, CAST, TRY_CAST, CONVERT, CHOOSE, and IIF functions.
- The columns with XML data type cannot be part of a linked server query.
- XML columns can only be indexed via an XML index; for clustered and nonclustered table indexes, XML columns can be included with the INCLUDE clause.

The XML data type has two forms:

- *Untyped XML* (the default), is an XML data type instance that does not have an associated XML schema.
- *Typed XML* is an XML data type instance with an XML schema bound to it.

1-1. Creating an Untyped XML Column
Problem

You want to define an untyped XML column in a table.

Solution

Define the designated column as XML data type upon creation. The example in Listing 1-6 demonstrates syntax on how to create a simple untyped XML column.

Listing 1-6. Syntax for creating an untyped XML column

```
CREATE TABLE dbo.UntypedXML
(
        UntypedXML_ID INT IDENTITY(1, 1) NOT NULL PRIMARY KEY,
        UntypedXMLData XML
);
```

The example in Listing 1-7 demonstrates how insert a new row into to the table we created in Listing 1-6.

Listing 1-7. Inserting a new row with XML data

```
INSERT INTO dbo.UntypedXML
(
        UntypedXMLData
)
SELECT N'<Category>
  <Category xmlns="http://schemas.microsoft.com/sqlserver/2004/07/Chapter01/
  ProductSchema">
    <CategoryName>Accessories</CategoryName>
    <Subcategory>
      <SubcategoryName>Bike Racks</SubcategoryName>
      <Product>
        <Name>Hitch Rack - 4-Bike</Name>
        <Number>RA-H123</Number>
        <Price>120.0000</Price>
      </Product>
    </Subcategory>
    <Subcategory>
      <SubcategoryName>Bike Stands</SubcategoryName>
      <Product>
        <Name>All-Purpose Bike Stand</Name>
        <Number>ST-1401</Number>
        <Price>159.0000</Price>
      </Product>
    </Subcategory>
  </Category>
</Category>';
```

The example in Listing 1-8 demonstrates how to declare an XML data type variable and then insert it into the table we previously created.

Listing 1-8. Inserting new row via XML variable

```
DECLARE @xml XML = N'<char>
  <ToXML Entity="Entity ampersand &amp;; in XML data." />
  <ToXML Entity="Entity less-than sign &lt;; in XML data." />
  <ToXML Entity="Entity greater-than sign &gt;; in XML data." />
```

```
<ToXML Entity="Entity apostrophe &apos;; in XML data." />
<ToXML Entity="Entity quotation mark &quot;; in XML data." />
</char>';

INSERT INTO dbo.UntypedXML
(
        UntypedXMLData
)
SELECT @xml;
```

■ **Note**   When we declare a variable as XML data type then assign XML to the variable, SQL Server implicitly converts character data to XML data type. That applies to VARCHAR, NVARCHAR, and VARBINARY data types.

The example in Listing 1-9 demonstrates how to create a stored procedure with an XML data type parameter, which inserts into the table when it is called.

Listing 1-9. Stored procedure to insert XML data into a table

```
CREATE PROCEDURE dbo.usp_Insert_UntypedXML
        @UntypedXML XML
AS
INSERT INTO dbo.UntypedXML
(
        UntypedXMLData
)
SELECT @UntypedXML;
GO
```

How It Works

When an XML schema is not bound to the column, variable, or stored procedure parameter, the object created is untyped XML. However, untyped XML instances still require the XML data it contains to follow the XML format per the W3C standard. When a column is created as an untyped XML instance, the parser will verify incoming data to ensure that the XML data is "well-formed," or a fragment (with no root element) that otherwise follows the rules for well-formedness. For example, all opened elements are closed, the opened and closed elements are matched to each other, and no invalid characters are found. Untyped XML objects are useful when the following applies:

- No XML schema exists for the data.

- The XML documents and data consist of different elements and attributes, but still need to be stored in the same XML enabled column. Listings 1-7 and 1-8 demonstrate this case.

- An application verifies and then sends well-formed XML or XML fragments to a table.

After a table with an untyped XML column is created, you can expand the table and then expand columns under Object Explorer. The column list appears, showing the XML data type distinguished with a dot inside parentheses, indicating that this is an untyped XML column as shown in Figure 1-3.

```
□ ▤ dbo.UntypedXML
  □ ▢ Columns
      ⚷ UntypedXML_ID (PK, int, not null)
      ▤ UntypedXMLData (XML(.), null)
```

Figure 1-3. Untyped XML column in Table Designer

1-2. Creating an XML Schema in Visual Studio
Problem

You want to obtain or generate an XML schema to constrain the data in a typed XML column.

Solution

To generate an XML schema using Microsoft Visual Studio, you need to use a version from 2008 or newer. SQL Server Data Tools will work as well since it uses the Microsoft Visual Studio Shell. You will then need an XML file. If you have the XML data, for instance, created as a result from the FOR XML clause (more on this in Chapter 2), then save the XML data as a file with extension *.xml*.

To load the XML file:

1. Start MS Visual Studio.

2. Go to the File menu.

3. Select the Open option.

4. Click File (shortcut CTRL + O). The dialog Open File will appear.

5. Navigate to the XML file storage location.

6. Click the Open button, as shown in Figure 1-4.

11

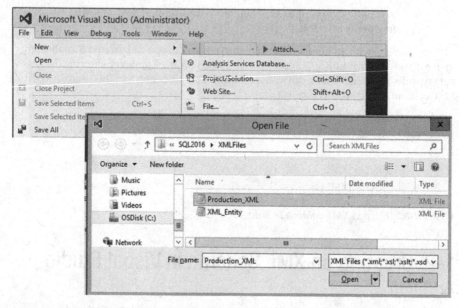

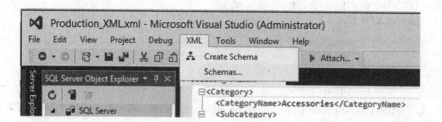

Figure 1-4. *Opening an XML file in Visual Studio*

Once the file is loaded, Visual Studio will recognize the XML file format and change the Menu options to add the XML Menu Options. To generate an XML schema, complete the following steps:

1. Select the XML menu.

2. Click on Create Schema option, shown in Figure 1-5.

Figure 1-5. *Creating the XML Schema*

The XML schema will be created in a separate tab. You can copy the XML schema contents, or save the *.xsd* file (shortcut CTRL + S) for future use, as shown in Figure 1-6.

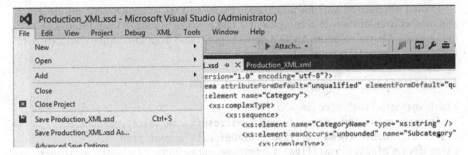

Figure 1-6. Saving XML schema as an .xsd file

How It Works

The era of creating your XML schemas manually is over, from my point of view. There are many ways to generate an XML schema automatically. In this recipe, I demonstrated two methods to automatically create an XML schema. Both methods are based on Microsoft products:

- MS Visual Studio (2008 and up)
- MS SQL Server (2005 and up)

For simplicity, I am reusing the XML data from Listing 1-2, as reproduced in Listing 1-10.

Listing 1-10. Sample XML

```
<Category>
  <Category xmlns="http://schemas.microsoft.com/sqlserver/2004/07/Chapter01/
  ProductSchema">
    <CategoryName>Accessories</CategoryName>
    <Subcategory>
      <SubcategoryName>Bike Racks</SubcategoryName>
      <Product>
        <Name>Hitch Rack - 4-Bike</Name>
        <Number>RA-H123</Number>
        <Price>120.0000</Price>
      </Product>
    </Subcategory>
    <Subcategory>
      <SubcategoryName>Bike Stands</SubcategoryName>
      <Product>
        <Name>All-Purpose Bike Stand</Name>
        <Number>ST-1401</Number>
        <Price>159.0000</Price>
      </Product>
    </Subcategory>
  </Category>
</Category>
```

13

When you have an XML file and need to create an XML schema from it, the easiest and most convenient way to accomplish this task is to use Microsoft Visual Studio, as demonstrated in the solution. An XML schema generated from the sample data XML data is shown in Listing 1-11.

Listing 1-11. XML schema generated by Visual Studio

```
<?xml version="1.0" encoding="utf-8"?>
<xs:schema xmlns:tns="http://schemas.microsoft.com/sqlserver/2004/07/
Chapter01/ProductSchema" attributeFormDefault="unqualified"
elementFormDefault="qualified" targetNamespace="http://schemas.microsoft.
com/sqlserver/2004/07/Chapter01/ProductSchema" xmlns:xs="http://www.
w3.org/2001/XMLSchema">
  <xs:element name="Category">
    <xs:complexType>
      <xs:sequence>
        <xs:element name="CategoryName" type="xs:string" />
        <xs:element maxOccurs="unbounded" name="Subcategory">
          <xs:complexType>
            <xs:sequence>
              <xs:element name="SubcategoryName" type="xs:string" />
              <xs:element name="Product">
                <xs:complexType>
                  <xs:sequence>
                    <xs:element name="Name" type="xs:string" />
                    <xs:element name="Number" type="xs:string" />
                    <xs:element name="Price" type="xs:decimal" />
                  </xs:sequence>
                </xs:complexType>
              </xs:element>
            </xs:sequence>
          </xs:complexType>
        </xs:element>
      </xs:sequence>
    </xs:complexType>
  </xs:element>
</xs:schema>
```

1-3. Creating an XML Schema from SSMS
Problem

You want to generate an XML schema from within SQL Server Management Studio (SSMS).

Solution

An alternate way to create an XML schema is using the SQL Server FOR XML clause with the XMLSCHEMA directive. The reason for demonstrating this option is to show an alternative way to generate an XML schema with FOR XML clause result.

To generate an inline XSD (XML Schema Definition) XML schema in SQL Server you need to add a FOR XML clause with XMLSCHEMA keyword to your query (the FOR XML clause will be covered in greater detail in Chapter 2, "Building XML"). Optionally the schema name can be specified inside XMLSCHEMA keyword parentheses. For example, to add the ProductSchema schema to your XSD schema, specify the following: *XMLSCHEMA('http://schemas.microsoft.com/sqlserver/2004/07/Chapter01/ProductSchema')*, as shown in Listing 1-12.

Listing 1-12. Creating XML schema query

```
SELECT TOP (2) Category.Name AS CategoryName,
       Subcategory.Name AS SubcategoryName,
       Product.Name,
       Product.ProductNumber AS Number,
       Product.ListPrice AS Price
FROM   Production.Product Product
       INNER JOIN Production.ProductSubcategory Subcategory
               ON Product.ProductSubcategoryID = Subcategory.
ProductSubcategoryID
       LEFT JOIN Production.ProductCategory Category
               ON Subcategory.ProductCategoryID = Category.Product
               CategoryID
WHERE Product.ListPrice > 0
       AND Product.SellEndDate IS NULL
ORDER BY CategoryName, SubcategoryName
FOR XML AUTO, ELEMENTS, XMLSCHEMA('http://schemas.microsoft.com/
sqlserver/2004/07/Chapter01/ProductSchema'), ROOT('Category');
```

To extract the XSD schema you need to perform the following steps:

- Run your SQL statement with the XMLSCHEMA keyword.

- Click on the query result to open the XML with schema in XML Editor, as shown in Figure 1-7.

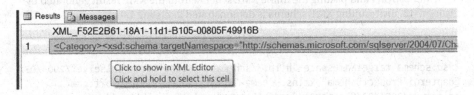

Figure 1-7. *Showing result in XML Editor*

- The XML Editor will show both the XSD part and the XML part. We will be focusing on the <xsd:schema> element.

- Copy from the opening <xsd:schema> tag to the closing </xsd:schema> tag.

- Open a new SSMS window paste the copied part, as shown in Figure 1-8.

```
<Category>
   <xsd:schema targetNamespace="ProductSchema" xmlns:schema="ProductSchema" xmlns:xsd="http://www
      <xsd:import namespace="http://schemas.microsoft.com/sqlserver/2004/sqltypes" schemaLocation=
   <xsd:element name="Category">
      <xsd:complexType>
         <xsd:sequence>
            <xsd:element name="CategoryName" minOccurs="0">
               <xsd:simpleType sqltypes:sqlTypeAlias="[AdventureWorks2012].[dbo].[Name]">
                  <xsd:restriction base="sqltypes:nvarchar" sqltypes:localeId="1033" sqltypes:sqlCom
                     <xsd:maxLength value="50" />
                  </xsd:element>
            <xsd:element name="Price" type="sqltypes:money" />
         </xsd:sequence>
      </xsd:complexType>
   </xsd:element>
   </xsd:schema>
   <Category xmlns="ProductSchema">
   <CategoryName>Accessories</CategoryName>
   <Subcategory>
      <SubcategoryName>Bike Racks</SubcategoryName>
      <Product>
         <Name>Hitch Rack - 4-Bike</Name>
```

Figure 1-8. *Extracting XSD schema part*

How It Works

The FOR XML clause with the XMLSCHEMA keyword provides a mechanism to add your XML Schema to your XML result. When the namespace needs to be associated with the XML result then the namespace declaration should be specified after the XMLSCHEMA keyword in parentheses. For example:

```
XMLSCHEMA('http://schemas.microsoft.com/sqlserver/2004/07/Chapter01/
ProductSchema'), ROOT('Category')
```

After copying and pasting the inline XML schema from the XML result generated by Listing 1-13, the resulting XML schema is demonstrated in Listing 1-14.

Listing 1-13. The XML schema from the FOR XML clause result

```
<xsd:schema targetNamespace="http://schemas.microsoft.com/sqlserver/2004/07/
Chapter01/ProductSchema" xmlns:schema="http://schemas.microsoft.com/
sqlserver/2004/07/Chapter01/ProductSchema" xmlns:xsd="http://www.
w3.org/2001/XMLSchema" xmlns:sqltypes="http://schemas.microsoft.com/
sqlserver/2004/sqltypes" elementFormDefault="qualified">
```

```xml
<xsd:import namespace="http://schemas.microsoft.com/sqlserver/2004/
sqltypes" schemaLocation="http://schemas.microsoft.com/sqlserver/2004/
sqltypes/sqltypes.xsd" />
<xsd:element name="Category">
  <xsd:complexType>
    <xsd:sequence>
      <xsd:element name="CategoryName" minOccurs="0">
        <xsd:simpleType sqltypes:sqlTypeAlias="[AdventureWorks2012].
        [dbo].[Name]">
          <xsd:restriction base="sqltypes:nvarchar" sqltypes:
          localeId="1033" sqltypes:sqlCompareOptions="IgnoreCase
          IgnoreKanaType IgnoreWidth" sqltypes:sqlSortId="52">
            <xsd:maxLength value="50" />
          </xsd:restriction>
        </xsd:simpleType>
      </xsd:element>
      <xsd:element ref="schema:Subcategory" minOccurs="0"
      maxOccurs="unbounded" />
    </xsd:sequence>
  </xsd:complexType>
</xsd:element>
<xsd:element name="Subcategory">
  <xsd:complexType>
    <xsd:sequence>
      <xsd:element name="SubcategoryName">
        <xsd:simpleType sqltypes:sqlTypeAlias="[AdventureWorks2012].
        [dbo].[Name]">
          <xsd:restriction base="sqltypes:nvarchar"
          sqltypes:localeId="1033" sqltypes:sqlCompareOptions="IgnoreCa
          se IgnoreKanaType IgnoreWidth" sqltypes:sqlSortId="52">
            <xsd:maxLength value="50" />
          </xsd:restriction>
        </xsd:simpleType>
      </xsd:element>
      <xsd:element ref="schema:Product" minOccurs="0"
      maxOccurs="unbounded" />
    </xsd:sequence>
  </xsd:complexType>
</xsd:element>
<xsd:element name="Product">
  <xsd:complexType>
    <xsd:sequence>
      <xsd:element name="Name">
        <xsd:simpleType sqltypes:sqlTypeAlias="[AdventureWorks2012].
        [dbo].[Name]">
          <xsd:restriction base="sqltypes:nvarchar"
          sqltypes:localeId="1033" sqltypes:sqlCompareOptions="IgnoreCa
          se IgnoreKanaType IgnoreWidth" sqltypes:sqlSortId="52">
```

```
          <xsd:maxLength value="50" />
        </xsd:restriction>
      </xsd:simpleType>
    </xsd:element>
    <xsd:element name="Number">
      <xsd:simpleType>
        <xsd:restriction base="sqltypes:nvarchar"
        sqltypes:localeId="1033" sqltypes:sqlCompareOptions="IgnoreCa
        se IgnoreKanaType IgnoreWidth" sqltypes:sqlSortId="52">
          <xsd:maxLength value="25" />
        </xsd:restriction>
      </xsd:simpleType>
    </xsd:element>
    <xsd:element name="Price" type="sqltypes:money" />
  </xsd:sequence>
</xsd:complexType>
    </xsd:element>
</xsd:schema>
```

You might have noticed the difference in the XML schema generation and contents between Visual Studio and SQL Server Management Studio. Creating an XML Schema via SQL Server tends to create a much larger XML schema. However, both variants deliver an XML schema that can be used with the XML Schema Collection to validate XML data against.

1-4. Binding XML to a Schema Collection

Problem

You have an XML schema that you want to bind to a table's column to create a typed XML column.

Solution

To make an XML schema eligible to be bound to a table's column, XML variable, or XML stored procedure's parameter, the XML Schema Collection needs to be created, as shown in Listing 1-14. To demonstrate the process, I am reusing the XML Schema from Listing 1-11.

Listing 1-14. Creating the XML Schema Collection

```
CREATE XML SCHEMA COLLECTION dbo.TypedXML_VisualStudio
AS
N'<?xml version="1.0"?>
<xs:schema xmlns:tns="http://schemas.microsoft.com/sqlserver/2004/07/
Chapter01/ProductSchema" attributeFormDefault="unqualified"
elementFormDefault="qualified" targetNamespace="http://schemas.microsoft.
```

```
com/sqlserver/2004/07/Chapter01/ProductSchema" xmlns:xs="http://www.
w3.org/2001/XMLSchema">
  <xs:element name="Category">
    <xs:complexType>
      <xs:sequence>
        <xs:element name="CategoryName" type="xs:string" />
        <xs:element maxOccurs="unbounded" name="Subcategory">
          <xs:complexType>
            <xs:sequence>
              <xs:element name="SubcategoryName" type="xs:string" />
              <xs:element name="Product">
                <xs:complexType>
                  <xs:sequence>
                    <xs:element name="Name" type="xs:string" />
                    <xs:element name="Number" type="xs:string" />
                    <xs:element name="Price" type="xs:decimal" />
                  </xs:sequence>
                </xs:complexType>
              </xs:element>
            </xs:sequence>
          </xs:complexType>
        </xs:element>
      </xs:sequence>
    </xs:complexType>
  </xs:element>
</xs:schema>';
GO
```

How It Works

The syntax for creating the XML Schema Collection is fairly simple. When the XML schema is generated, the schema contents need to be added to an SQL Server XML Schema Collection object. The syntax to create the schema collection (shown in Listing 1-14) has several components:

- CREATE XML SCHEMA COLLECTION - declarative statement

- dbo - relational schema (if not provided then the SQL Server default will be assumed)

- XML Schema Collection name - any SQL Server valid unique name

- AS <schema_contents> - The XML Schema contents that can be constant, or scalar variable in xml, nvarchar, varchar, or varbinary data type

To create an XML SCHEMA COLLECTION one of the following server- or database-level permissions are required:

- CONTROL (server level)

- ALTER ANY DATABASE (server level)

- ALTER (database level)

- CONTROL (database level)

- ALTER ANY SCHEMA and CREATE XML SCHEMA COLLECTION (database level)

After successful creation, your new XML Schema Collection can be found in the SSMS Object Explorer under Programmability, Types, XML Schema Collection, as shown in Figure 1-9.

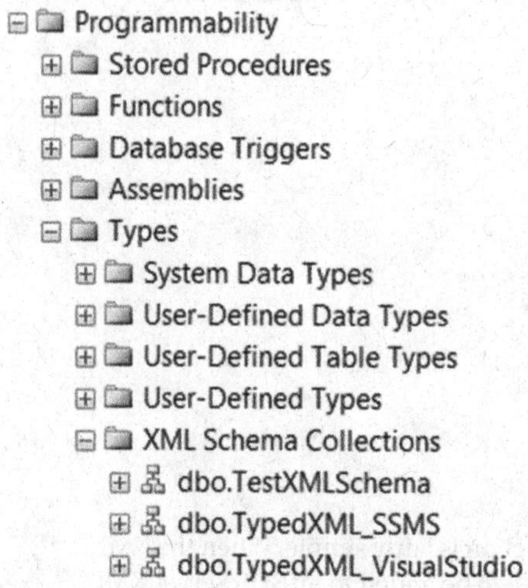

⊟ 🗀 Programmability
  ⊞ 🗀 Stored Procedures
  ⊞ 🗀 Functions
  ⊞ 🗀 Database Triggers
  ⊞ 🗀 Assemblies
  ⊟ 🗀 Types
    ⊞ 🗀 System Data Types
    ⊞ 🗀 User-Defined Data Types
    ⊞ 🗀 User-Defined Table Types
    ⊞ 🗀 User-Defined Types
    ⊟ 🗀 XML Schema Collections
      ⊞ 🔏 dbo.TestXMLSchema
      ⊞ 🔏 dbo.TypedXML_SSMS
      ⊞ 🔏 dbo.TypedXML_VisualStudio

Figure 1-9. Finding the XML Schema Collection

■ **Note**   When the XML Schema Collection is bound to one or more columns, no changes can be applied to the XML Schema Collection. To modify or drop the XML Schema Collection you need to unbind it from the column(s) first.

1-5. Creating a Typed XML Column
Problem

You have created an XML Schema Collection, and now you want to bind it to a column to create a typed XML column.

Solution

When the XML Schema Collection is successfully created, the code to bind your XML Schema to a newly created table is shown in Listing 1-15.

Listing 1-15. Creating new table with typed XML column

```
CREATE TABLE dbo.TypedXML_VS
(
        TypedXML_ID INT IDENTITY(1, 1) NOT NULL PRIMARY KEY,
        TypedXMLData XML(TypedXML_VisualStudio)
);
GO
```

You can bind the XML Schema Collection to an existing XML column with the ALTER TABLE ... ALTER COLUMN statement, as demonstrated in Listing 1-16.

Listing 1-16. Binding XML Schema Collection to the column

```
ALTER TABLE TypedXML_VS
ALTER COLUMN TypedXMLData XML (TypedXML_VisualStudio);
```

How It Works

The mechanism to bind an XML Schema Collection to an XML column is straightforward. The XML Schema Collection name needs to be identified as part of the XML data type, in parentheses. The syntax is: *column_name XML (XML_SCHEMA_COLLECTION_NAME)*. For the new table, the XML Schema Collection can be bound to a column in the CREATE TABLE DDL command (Listing 1-15). When the table contains an untyped XML column, the ALTER TABLE command will complete the task (Listing 1-16).

When the XML Schema Collection is bound to a column, the XSD itself cannot be modified or deleted. However, the table with the typed XML column can be dropped. To disconnect the XSD from the column, you need to execute an ALTER TABLE DDL command, where the XML data type does not have parentheses, as shown in Listing 1-17.

Listing 1-17. Disconnecting the XSD from the column

```
ALTER TABLE TypedXML_VS
ALTER COLUMN TypedXMLData XML;
```

After the XSD is unbound, the XML column becomes untyped.
A couple of questions and answers about a typed XML.
Why do I want to do this and what is the benefit?

- Ability to validate an XML data per the XML schema.

- Take advantage of storage and query optimizations based on type information.

- Better advantage of type information within a compilation of the queries.

21

What happens to XML data I insert into a typed XML column?

- Each insert validates by the XML schema; when validation fails, then SQL Server raises an error and insert fails.

What happens if I have XML already existing in the table and apply an XML schema to it?

- If a table with the XML column has existing XML, then bind XML schema to the table fails when the XML does not conform to the XML schema.

Summary

SQL Server 2000 first introduced XML functionality in the SQL database. Since that time, XML technology has evolved into a comprehensive information technology platform. SQL Server 2005 was delivered with the XML data type. In this chapter, you received an introduction to XML. I explained the difference between the element and attribute, which is very important to differentiate for future chapters. I defined and explained XML schemas and introduced two ways how to generate an XML Schema. From my point of view, with the availability of modern technology, there is no need to create the XML Schema manually, since it is a complex and time-consuming process. Save your time, and if you are dealing with the Microsoft tools MS Visual Studio, SQL Server Data Tools, and SSMS, either one can generate the XML Schema automatically.

The next chapter of the book demonstrates how to build an XML out of a result set.

CHAPTER 2

■■■

Building XML

XML is represented in SQL Server using a complex data type that has special syntax and well-defined format. It can be used when we need to construct XML-formatted output or shred existing XML into relational format. In this chapter I will provide recipes for building XML from a result set based on one or more tables, and for formatting and presenting the result as XML output.

Introduced in SQL Server 2000, the FOR XML clause has evolved dramatically to become a comprehensive solution for building XML output. FOR XML has to be the last clause in a SELECT statement and has to appear after an ORDER BY clause when the sorting has a place within a query.

The FOR XML clause has the following modes:

- RAW – Returns simple XML from one or more tables, in which each row is represented with a <row> element. Attribute-centric XML is generated by default, which means each of the row's non-null column values are represented as attributes of the <row> element. If, however, you specify the ELEMENTS directive, each of the row's column values is represented as an element nested within the <row> element. RAW mode does not support nested element structure.

- AUTO – Returns simple XML structure from one or more tables. AUTO mode is similar to RAW mode, except that it supports nested elements when two or more tables are joined in the query's FROM clause.

- EXPLICIT – Allows you to explicitly construct the XML. EXPLICIT mode acceses the XML in a *universal table* format behind the scenes. This is a well-defined rowset format thay is very similar to shredded XML. Constructing XML using EXPLICIT mode requires a specific syntax to define the "shape" of the XML result; therefore this mode can be complex to use. SQL Server 2008 introduced PATH mode as a simplified alternative to EXPLICIT mode.

- PATH – Provides a simpler way to explicitly construct XML with a mix of elements and attributes. This is a great alternative to the EXPLICIT mode.

© Alex Grinberg 2018
A. Grinberg, *XML and JSON Recipes for SQL Server*,
https://doi.org/10.1007/978-1-4842-3117-3_2

When you specify the FOR XML clause, you can also provide the following directives, which control formatting options of the FOR XML clause modes:

- ELEMENTS – Returns element-centric XML. The default is attribute-centric results, and this option applies to RAW, AUTO, and PATH modes only.

- BINARY BASE64 - Retrieves binary data in Base-64-encoded format.

- TYPE - Returns the result as an XML data type instance.

- ROOT – Extends the XML result with top-level (root) element, which is a requirement of "well-formed" XML.

- XSINIL - Returns the element name within the XML result when the value is NULL. The element is returned with an xsi:nil attribute set to "true," like this: <element xsi:nil = "true"/>.

- ABSENT – Opposite of the XSINIL directive. The ABSENT directive is the default. When used, it specifies that NULLs should be eliminated from the XML result.

- XMLSCHEMA – Extends the XML result with an inline W3C XML Schema (XSD).

Fixing the "Unable to show XML" Error

To review XML results of a query in SQL Server Management Studio (SSMS), you can simply click on the hyperlinked XML result displayed in the Results pane. The XML result will display in a new SSMS XML editor window. When we are dealing with very large result sets, however, the XML might exceed the default limit for XML data (2 MB) and throw a System.OutOfMemoryException with the message "Unable to show XML," as shown in Figure 2-1.

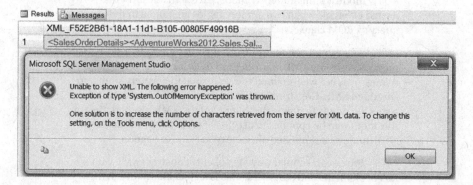

Figure 2-1. *"Unable to show XML" error message*

The error message recommends increasing the number of characters retrieved from the server for XML data. As indicated, this option is available from the Options item in the Tools menu. The default maximum for XML data is 2 MB. To change this setting go to Tools in the menu bar and select Options... on the menu. Once you are in the Options dialog, do the following:

1. Expand Query Results.

2. Expand SQL Server.

3. Click Result to Grid.

4. In the right pane, use the drop-down to change the Maximum Characters Retrieved for XML data. The available settings are: 1 MB, 2 MB, 5 MB, or Unlimited.

5. Click OK to save your settings. Figure 2-2 shows the Options dialog.

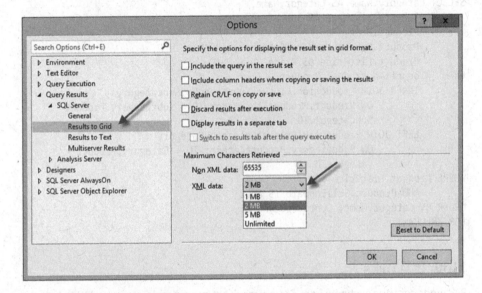

Figure 2-2. Changing XML data settings

If you would like to change the maximum size of your XML results for the current query only, and do not want to save the SSMS settings permanently, click on the Query menu and select Query Options.... Navigate to the Grid settings under Results and change the Maximum Characters Retrieved XML data option as in the previous recipe.

2-1. Converting Relational Data to a Simple XML Format

Problem

You want to convert a query result set to a simple XML format.

Solution

SQL Server provides the FOR XML clause to format query results as XML data. RAW mode generates a simple XML format. For example, Listing 2-1 demonstrates RAW mode in a FOR XML clause.

Listing 2-1. Demonstrating RAW mode within a FOR XML clause

```
SELECT Category.Name AS CategoryName,
       Subcategory.Name AS SubcategoryName,
       Product.Name,
       Product.ProductNumber AS Number,
       Product.ListPrice AS Price
FROM   Production.Product Product
       INNER JOIN Production.ProductSubcategory Subcategory
              ON Product.ProductSubcategoryID = Subcategory.Product
              SubcategoryID
       LEFT JOIN Production.ProductCategory Category
              ON Subcategory.ProductCategoryID = Category.Product
              CategoryID
WHERE Product.ListPrice > 0
       AND Product.SellEndDate IS NULL
ORDER BY CategoryName, SubcategoryName
FOR XML RAW;
```

How It Works

RAW mode converts each row from a query result set into a simple, structured XML element. By default, RAW mode returns a <row> element for each data row, and all values are mapped to attributes with the same column names (or column aliases, if specified) as the source SQL query. This XML structure is commonly referred to as *attribute-centric* XML. Listing 2-2 shows sample RAW mode output.

Listing 2-2. Sample RAW mode output

```
<row CategoryName="Components" SubcategoryName="Brakes" Name="Front Brakes"
Number="FB-9873" Price="106.5000" />
<row CategoryName="Components" SubcategoryName="Brakes" Name="Rear Brakes"
Number="RB-9231" Price="106.5000" />
```

```
<row CategoryName="Components" SubcategoryName="Pedals" Name="LL Road Pedal"
Number="PD-R347" Price="40.4900" />
<row CategoryName="Components" SubcategoryName="Cranksets" Name="LL
Crankset" Number="CS-4759" Price="175.4900" />
```

■ **Caution**   Attribute-centric XML has a limitation, in that it requires unique attribute names to be mapped to each element. Therefore, the SQL query must provide a unique name for each column, in much the same way that you must provide unique column names when creating an SQL view. Element-centric XML, however, does not have this limitation.

In a production environment, the default <row> element is generally not suitable or business applicable to send to a client in your XML data. To replace a <row> element with another element name that is friendlier and more business appropriate in your generated XML data, RAW mode can accept a user-defined element name (a *row tag name*). You can specify this row tag name in parentheses following the FOR XML RAW clause, like this: FOR XML RAW('ElementName'). Listing 2-3 demonstrates how to replace the default element name with a user-defined name, and Listing 2-4 shows the XML result.

Listing 2-3. Demonstrating the row tag name option of the FOR XML RAW clause

```
SELECT Category.Name AS CategoryName,
       Subcategory.Name AS SubcategoryName,
       Product.Name,
       Product.ProductNumber AS Number,
       Product.ListPrice AS Price
FROM   Production.Product Product
       INNER JOIN Production.ProductSubcategory Subcategory
               ON Product.ProductSubcategoryID = Subcategory.Product
               SubcategoryID
       LEFT JOIN Production.ProductCategory Category
               ON Subcategory.ProductCategoryID = Category.Product
               CategoryID
WHERE Product.ListPrice > 0
       AND Product.SellEndDate IS NULL
ORDER BY CategoryName, SubcategoryName
FOR XML RAW('Product');
```

Listing 2-4. Result of FOR XML RAW query with row tag name specified

```
<Product CategoryName="Components" SubcategoryName="Brakes"
Name="Front Brakes" Number="FB-9873" Price="106.5000" />
<Product CategoryName="Components" SubcategoryName="Brakes"
Name="Rear Brakes" Number="RB-9231" Price="106.5000" />
<Product CategoryName="Components" SubcategoryName="Pedals"
Name="LL Road Pedal" Number="PD-R347" Price="40.4900" />
<Product CategoryName="Components" SubcategoryName="Cranksets" Name="LL
Crankset" Number="CS-4759" Price="175.4900" />
```

27

2-2. Generating XML Data with Table Names as Element Names

Problem

You would like to simply construct XML results from a Single Table with element names in the XML result that indicate the source table.

Solution

AUTO mode is very similar in functionality to RAW mode when the source query references a single table. The only difference is that AUTO mode names each element representing a row with the name of the table as specified in the source query. That is to say, when the query has a schema and table name, like Production.Product, each row element will be `<Production.Product>`. Listing 2-5 demonstrates AUTO mode for a single table.

Listing 2-5. Building XML with FOR XML AUTO for a single table

```
SELECT Product.Name,
       Product.ProductNumber AS Number,
       Product.ListPrice AS Price
FROM   Production.Product
WHERE Product.ListPrice > 0
       AND Product.SellEndDate IS NULL
ORDER BY Product.Name
FOR XML AUTO;
```

Listing 2-6 shows the XML result of this query.

Listing 2-6. Results of FOR XML AUTO for a single table

```
<Production.Product Name="Front Brakes" Number="FB-9873" Price="106.5000" />
<Production.Product Name="Rear Brakes" Number="RB-9231" Price="106.5000" />
<Production.Product Name="LL Road Pedal" Number="PD-R347" Price="40.4900" />
<Production.Product Name="LL Crankset" Number="CS-4759" Price="175.4900" />
```

■ **Note**   The W3C XML standard allows the use of periods (.) in element and attribute names.

AUTO mode, unlike RAW mode, does not support a row tag name option. Therefore, you must provide a table alias to change the row tag element name. Listing 2-7 demonstrates how to use an alias to change the element name in AUTO mode.

Listing 2-7. Changing the element name by aliasing a table with FOR XML AUTO

```
SELECT Product.Name,
       Product.ProductNumber AS Number,
       Product.ListPrice AS Price
FROM   Production.Product AS Product
WHERE Product.ListPrice > 0
       AND Product.SellEndDate IS NULL
ORDER BY Product.Name
FOR XML AUTO;
```

Listing 2-8 shows the XML result of the FOR XML AUTO query with the aliased source table name.

Listing 2-8. Result of single-table FOR XML AUTO query with source table aliased

```
<Product Name="Front Brakes" Number="FB-9873" Price="106.5000" />
<Product Name="Rear Brakes" Number="RB-9231" Price="106.5000" />
<Product Name="LL Road Pedal" Number="PD-R347" Price="40.4900" />
<Product Name="LL Crankset" Number="CS-4759" Price="175.4900" />
```

When two or more tables are joined in the source query of a FOR XML AUTO query, the XML takes a different shape. The XML result is nested multiple levels deep with each level of nested node named for the tables in the FROM clause in the order in which they are named. As shown in Listing 2-9, construct the XML based on three tables.

Listing 2-9. Using the FOR XML AUTO clause to construct XML data with multiple joined tables

```
SELECT Category.Name AS CategoryName,
       Subcategory.Name AS SubcategoryName,
       Product.Name,
       Product.ProductNumber AS Number,
       Product.ListPrice AS Price,
       SellEndDate
FROM   Production.Product Product
       INNER JOIN Production.ProductSubcategory Subcategory
           ON Product.ProductSubcategoryID = Subcategory.Product
           SubcategoryID
       LEFT JOIN Production.ProductCategory Category
           ON Subcategory.ProductCategoryID = Category.Product
           CategoryID
WHERE Product.ListPrice > 0
       AND Product.SellEndDate IS NULL
ORDER BY CategoryName, SubcategoryName
FOR XML AUTO;
```

The XML result of this query is formatted as follows:

1. <Category> is the top-level element.

2. <Subcategory> is a child of the <Category> element.

3. <Product> is the child of the <Subcategory> element.

The hierarchical XML results of the FOR XML AUTO query with multiple joined tables is shown in Figure 2-3.

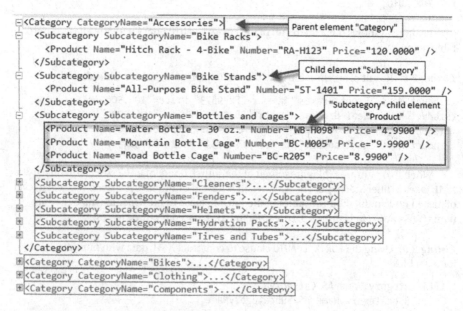

Figure 2-3. *Hierarchical XML result when FOR XML AUTO mode is applied to multiple joined tables in a query*

How It Works

AUTO mode provides an easy way to build XML. The SQL query engine analyzes your query structure and builds a hierarchy using the names provided in the query to generate element and attribute names — this is why this mode is called "AUTO." As demonstrated in the Solution section, when FOR XML AUTO is implemented, the SQL Server engine returns hierarchical XML.

2-3. Generating Element-Centric XML
Problem

Both RAW and AUTO modes return attribute-centric XML by default. However, you want to generate element-centric XML data when business rule requires it.

Solution

The FOR XML clause with the ELEMENTS option returns the XML result in element-centric format. Listing 2-10 shows how to add the ELEMENTS directive to the FOR XML AUTO clause.

Listing 2-10. FOR XML AUTO query with ELEMENTS directive

```
SELECT Product.Name,
       Product.ProductNumber AS Number,
       Product.ListPrice AS Price
FROM   Production.Product AS Product
WHERE Product.ListPrice > 0
       AND Product.SellEndDate IS NULL
ORDER BY Product.Name
FOR XML AUTO, ELEMENTS;
```

The results of the FOR XML AUTO query with ELEMENTS directive is shown in Listing 2-11.

Listing 2-11. Results of FOR XML AUTO query with ELEMENTS directive

```
<Product>
  <Name>Chain</Name>
  <Number>CH-0234</Number>
  <Price>20.2400</Price>
</Product>
<Product>
  <Name>Classic Vest, L</Name>
  <Number>VE-C304-L</Number>
  <Price>63.5000</Price>
</Product>
```

How It Works

The ELEMENTS option formats your XML result with columns nested as sub-elements of each row element. This format is known as element-centric XML. The ELEMENTS option can be specified with the FOR XML clause's RAW, AUTO, and PATH modes. FOR XML EXPLICIT mode does not support the ELEMENTS directive.

The ELEMENTS directive must be separated from the RAW, AUTO, and PATH mode keyword by a comma. For example: FOR XML AUTO, ELEMENTS.

This simple change allows you to return the XML in an element-centric format instead of the default attribute-centric format.

2-4. Adding a Root Element

Problem

You would like to add a root (top-level) element to your generated XML.

Solution

The ROOT option wraps your XML result in a top-level root element of your choosing. Listing 2-12 demonstrates how to add a ROOT directive to the query.

Listing 2-12. Adding the ROOT directive to a FOR XML AUTO query

```
SELECT Product.Name,
       Product.ProductNumber AS Number,
       Product.ListPrice AS Price
FROM  Production.Product AS Product
WHERE Product.ListPrice > 0
       AND Product.SellEndDate IS NULL
ORDER BY Product.Name
FOR XML AUTO, ELEMENTS, ROOT;
```

Listing 2-13 shows the result of the FOR XML AUTO query with both the ELEMENTS and ROOT directives.

Listing 2-13. Snippet of well-formed XML generated with ELEMENTS and ROOT directives

```
<root>
  <Product>
    <Name>All-Purpose Bike Stand</Name>
    <Number>ST-1401</Number>
    <Price>159.0000</Price>
  </Product>
  <Product>
    <Name>AWC Logo Cap</Name>
    <Number>CA-1098</Number>
    <Price>8.9900</Price>
  </Product>
  <Product>
    <Name>Bike Wash - Dissolver</Name>
    <Number>CL-9009</Number>
    <Price>7.9500</Price>
  </Product>
  ...
</root>
```

How It Works

The ROOT option specifies that your XML result will be wrapped in a single top-level root element. By default, the ROOT directive generates a top-level element named <root>. However, the default name <root> can also be replaced with a user-defined value in parentheses. For example: FOR XML AUTO, ELEMENTS, ROOT('Products'). When the root element name is specified, the XML result uses the name you specify as the top-level root element. In the previous example, the root element will be named <Products>.

2-5. Including Elements with NULL Values in Your XML Data

Problem

By default, the XML that SQL Server generates excludes any columns with NULLs. You would like to specifically include columns containing NULLs.

Solution

The XSINIL option of the ELEMENTS directive forces the XML result to include elements in which the source columns contain NULLs. Listing 2-14 demonstrates how to add an XSINIL option to your query.

Listing 2-14. Adding an XSINIL option to the FOR XML query

```
SELECT Product.Name,
       Product.ProductNumber AS Number,
       Product.ListPrice AS Price,
       SellEndDate
FROM   Production.Product AS Product
WHERE Product.ListPrice > 0
ORDER BY Product.Name
FOR XML AUTO, ELEMENTS XSINIL, ROOT('Products');
```

Listing 2-15 displays the result of using the XSINIL option.

Listing 2-15. Snippet of results of the XSINIL option query

```
<Products xmlns:xsi="http://www.w3.org/2001/XMLSchema-instance">
  ...
  <Product>
    <Name>Bike Wash - Dissolver</Name>
    <Number>CL-9009</Number>
    <Price>7.9500</Price>
    <SellEndDate xsi:nil="true" />
  </Product>
```

```
<Product>
  <Name>Cable Lock</Name>
  <Number>LO-C100</Number>
  <Price>25.0000</Price>
  <SellEndDate>2013-05-29T00:00:00</SellEndDate>
</Product>
...
</Products>
```

In the sample results, product number CL-9009 has a SellEndDate of NULL in the database, so it is represented with an xsi:nil attribute set to "true." Product number LO-C100, however, has a non-NULL SellEndDate value, so it has no xsi:nil attribute.

How It Works

The ELEMENTS directive supports two options:

1. XSINIL – this option forces the XML result to generate elements for NULL values in the source data.

2. ABSENT – this option leaves any elements that contain NULL values in the source data out of your XML result. This is the default option for the ELEMENTS directive, and does not need to be specified explicitly.

The XSINIL and ABSENT options are considered part of the ELEMENTS directive, and they can be specified as such, when needed. Therefore, unlike directives, the XSINIL and ABSENT options are separated from their ELEMENTS directive by a space, not a comma.

2-6. Including Binary Data in Your XML
Problem

You want to include the contents of a binary column in your XML data.

Solution

You may run into a situation in which you are querying a column that contains binary data, and you want the binary data to be included in your XML result. Consider Listing 2-16, which is a query that attempts to return binary data in XML format.

Listing 2-16. Failing query to retrieve binary data in XML format

```
SELECT LargePhotoFileName,
       LargePhoto
FROM   Production.ProductPhoto
FOR XML AUTO, ELEMENTS;
```

When you try to execute this query it raises an error:

FOR XML AUTO requires primary keys to create references for 'LargePhoto'. Select primary keys, or use BINARY BASE64 to obtain binary data in encoded form if no primary keys exist.

This query fails because you did not include a primary key column in your result set. Changing the query as shown in Listing 2-17 will resolve the issue.

Listing 2-17. Working query to retrieve binary data in XML format

```
SELECT LargePhotoFileName,
       LargePhoto,
       ProductPhotoID
FROM  Production.ProductPhoto
FOR XML AUTO, ELEMENTS;
```

However, instead of the expected binary data, a reference to the primary key row is returned, as shown in Listing 2-18.

Listing 2-18. Snippet of results of binary data query with reference to primary key row

```
<Production.ProductPhoto>
  <LargePhotoFileName>racer02_black_large.gif</LargePhotoFileName>
  <LargePhoto>dbobject/Production.ProductPhoto[@ProductPhotoID='70']/
  @LargePhoto</LargePhoto>
  <ProductPhotoID>70</ProductPhotoID>
</Production.ProductPhoto>
```

To include an actual representation of your binary data in your XML result, simply apply the BINARY BASE64 directive to your FOR XML clause. This directive forces the XML result to include binary data in Base64-encoded format. Listing 2-19 demonstrates the BINARY BASE64 directive of the FOR XML clause.

Listing 2-19. Using the BINARY BASE64 directive of the FOR XML clause

```
SELECT LargePhotoFileName,
       LargePhoto
FROM  Production.ProductPhoto
FOR XML AUTO, ELEMENTS, BINARY BASE64;
```

How It Works

The BINARY BASE64 directive encodes binary data in Base-64 format. When the query returns a column of the varbinary data type, the BINARY BASE64 directive of the FOR XML clause returns your binary data in Base-64-encoded in your XML result.

Each FOR XML mode acts on the binary data in your result set using specific rules:

- AUTO mode returns a reference to a binary column and row when the primary key is included in your query result.

- RAW and EXPLICIT modes will raise an error when the query has a column with binary data.

- Only PATH mode does not raise an error, and returns the XML result with binary data when the BINARY BASE64 directive is not specified.

For example, execute the following query:

```
SELECT LargePhotoFileName, LargePhoto
FROM  [Production].[ProductPhoto]
FOR XML PATH;
```

And this query:

```
SELECT LargePhotoFileName, LargePhoto
FROM  [Production].[ProductPhoto]
FOR XML AUTO, ELEMENTS, BINARY BASE64;
```

Both queries will return the same result. However, I would strongly recommend including a BINARY BASE64 directive to all FOR XML modes when the binary data is part of the result set. This is because you need to retrieve an actual datum, not the reference to the data, as it could happen when the primary key is listed in the SELECT clause.

2-7. Generating Nested Hierarchical XML Data
Problem
You want to nest the results of an XML-generating subquery into your outer XML-generating query, to create more complex hierarchical XML data.

Solution
You might want run into a situation that requires generating hierarchical XML that can be generated via SQL correlated subqueries. As an example, a product category in the AdventureWorks database can have multiple related subcategories. Assume that you want to generate an XML result that lists all product categories, each with its product subcategories nested within it.

Your first pass at a SQL query might look like Listing 2-20.

Listing 2-20. First attempt at creating hierarchical XML with a correlated subquery

```
SELECT Category.Name AS CategoryName,
    (
            SELECT Subcategory.Name AS SubcategoryName
            FROM Production.ProductSubcategory Subcategory
            WHERE Subcategory.ProductCategoryID = Category.Product
            CategoryID
```

```
        FOR XML AUTO
    ) Subcategory
FROM Production.ProductCategory Category
FOR XML AUTO, ROOT('Categories');
```

The result of this query results in XML entities like < and > throughout your XML data, as shown in Figure 2-4, instead of the expected properly nested XML elements. This is because the XML being generated in the correlated subquery is treated as a string data type instead of proper XML data.

```
CategoryName="Accessories" Subcategory="&lt;Subcategory S      ucategoryName=&quot;Bike Stands&quot;/&gt;&lt;S
CategoryName="Bikes" Subcategory="&lt;Subcategory Subcate     ategoryName=&quot;Road Bikes&quot;/&gt;&lt;Subc
CategoryName="Clothing" Subcategory="&lt;Subcategory Sub      ategoryName=&quot;Caps&quot;/&gt;&lt;Subcategory
CategoryName="Components" Subcategory="&lt;Subcategory Sub.    ategoryName=&quot;Bottom Brackets&quot;/&gt;&l
```

Figure 2-4. Results of first attempt at creating hierarchical XML data

How can you return the query in XML format? You want proper tags, and not the XML > and < entities.

To force the result set to be retuned in proper XML format, add the TYPE directive to your FOR XML clauses. Listing 2-9 demonstrates this option. Listing 2-21 shows the generated XML.

Listing 2-21. Implementing the TYPE directive

```
SELECT Category.Name AS CategoryName,
    (
        SELECT Subcategory.Name AS SubcategoryName
        FROM Production.ProductSubcategory Subcategory
        WHERE Subcategory.ProductCategoryID = Category.Product
        CategoryID
        FOR XML AUTO, TYPE
    ) Subcategory
FROM Production.ProductCategory Category
FOR XML AUTO, ELEMENTS, TYPE, ROOT('Categories');
```

The results of this updated query with the TYPE directive is shown in Listing 2-22.

Listing 2-22. Snippet of nested hierarchical XML generated with nested subquery and TYPE directive.

```
<Categories>
  <Category CategoryName="Accessories">
    <Subcategory>
      <Subcategory SubcategoryName="Bike Racks" />
      <Subcategory SubcategoryName="Bike Stands" />
      <Subcategory SubcategoryName="Bottles and Cages" />
      <Subcategory SubcategoryName="Cleaners" />
      <Subcategory SubcategoryName="Fenders" />
```

```
      <Subcategory SubcategoryName="Helmets" />
      <Subcategory SubcategoryName="Hydration Packs" />
      <Subcategory SubcategoryName="Lights" />
      <Subcategory SubcategoryName="Locks" />
      <Subcategory SubcategoryName="Panniers" />
      <Subcategory SubcategoryName="Pumps" />
      <Subcategory SubcategoryName="Tires and Tubes" />
    </Subcategory>
  </Category>
  ...
</Categories>
```

How It Works

By default, the FOR XML clause returns an nvarchar(max) data type result. The XML generated by the subquery is retuned as character data, instead of the required XML format. When SQL Server converts XML data to character format, it properly entitizes certain special characters, like the "<" and ">" characters (< and >, respectively.) The TYPE directive forces SQL to return the XML results in proper XML format, without entitizing the contents. The TYPE directive can be used with all FOR XML modes.

2-8. Building Custom XML
Problem

You want fine-grained control to customize the format of your generated XML.

Solution

In previous recipes we focused on the RAW and AUTO modes that return either element-centric or attribute-centric XML, and automatically generate names based on the source table and column names (or aliases). But what if you want more control over your element-centric or attribute-centric XML results? EXPLICIT mode gives you more control over your XML result. Listing 2-23 demonstrates a query to generate your XML result with a custom-defined structure.

Listing 2-23. Using EXPLICIT mode to control the format of your XML result

```
SELECT 1          AS Tag,
       0          AS Parent,
       Prod.Name  AS [Categories!1!Category!ELEMENT],
       NULL       AS [Subcategories!2!Subcategory!ELEMENT],
       NULL       AS [Product!3!ProductName!ELEMENT],
       NULL       AS [Product!3!Color!ELEMENTXSINIL],
       NULL       AS [Product!3!Shelf],
       NULL       AS [Product!3!Bin],
       NULL       AS [Product!3!Quantity]
```

```
FROM Production.ProductCategory Prod

UNION ALL

SELECT 2 AS Tag,
       1 AS Parent,
       Category.Name,
       Subcategory.Name,
       NULL,
       NULL,
       NULL,
       NULL,
       NULL
FROM Production.ProductCategory Category
       INNER JOIN Production.ProductSubcategory Subcategory
       ON Category.ProductCategoryID = Subcategory.ProductCategoryID

UNION ALL

SELECT 3  AS Tag,
       2  AS Parent,
       ProductCategory.Name,
       Subcategory.Name,
       Product.Name,
       Product.Color,
       Inventory.Shelf,
       Inventory.Bin,
       Inventory.Quantity
FROM Production.Product Product
       INNER JOIN Production.ProductInventory Inventory
       ON Product.ProductID = Inventory.ProductID
       INNER JOIN Production.ProductSubcategory Subcategory
       ON Product.ProductSubcategoryID = Subcategory.ProductSubcategoryID
       INNER JOIN Production.ProductCategory
       ON Subcategory.ProductCategoryID = Production.ProductCategory.
       ProductCategoryID
ORDER BY [Categories!1!Category!ELEMENT],
       [Subcategories!2!Subcategory!ELEMENT],
       [Product!3!ProductName!ELEMENT]
FOR XML EXPLICIT, ROOT('Products');
```

How It Works

EXPLICIT mode is one of the most complex FOR XML modes to use. All elements and attributes need to be provided explicitly, and each child block must be linked to the parent explicitly as well. When comparing EXPLICIT mode other modes, such as RAW and AUTO, the queries with the EXPLICIT mode are much lengthier. The benefit of EXPLICIT mode, however, is that it provides much greater control over the shape of the XML generated by the query result.

To better understand how EXPLICIT mode works, I'll walk you through an example. Let's start with a base T-SQL query, like the one shown in Listing 2-24, which shows SQL that we would like to convert to an XML structure.

Listing 2-24. SQL query we would like to convert to XML format

```
SELECT ProductCategory.Name Category,
       Subcategory.Name Subcategory,
       Product.Name ProductName,
       Product.Color,
       Inventory.Shelf,
       Inventory.Bin,
       Inventory.Quantity
FROM Production.Product Product
       INNER JOIN Production.ProductInventory Inventory
       ON Product.ProductID = Inventory.ProductID
       INNER JOIN Production.ProductSubcategory Subcategory
       ON Product.ProductSubcategoryID = Subcategory.ProductSubcategoryID
       INNER JOIN Production.ProductCategory
       ON Subcategory.ProductCategoryID = Production.ProductCategory.
       ProductCategoryID
```

ORDER BY ProductCategory.Name, Subcategory.Name, Product.Name; The SQL in Listing 2-24 returns the product list based on categories and subcategories. Therefore, we need to make a decision and ask some questions:

1. How do we want the XML structured?

2. How many sibling levels does the XML need to have?

3. Which columns will be mapped to elements and which should be attributes?

4. Do we need to preserve elements with NULL values?

In Figure 2-5 we show the results of the query in Listing 2-24, and begin the process of drawing a road map for the XML result we want. Figure 2-5 demonstrates a sample of a road map that will help us build the query using EXPLICIT mode.

Level 1 - Top Element. Child of root.	Level 2 – Child of Level 1.	Elements			Attributes		
Category	Subcategory	ProductName	Color	Shelf	Bin	Quantity	
Accessories	Lights	Headlights - Weatherproof	NULL	N/A	0	216	
Accessories	Lights	Taillights - Battery-Powered	NULL	N/A	0	144	
Accessories	Locks	Cable Lock	NULL	N/A	0	252	
Accessories	Panniers	Touring-Panniers, Large	Grey	N/A	0	72	
Accessories	Pumps	Minipump	NULL	N/A	0	288	
Accessories	Pumps	Mountain Pump	NULL	N/A	0	324	
Accessories	Tires and Tubes	HL Mountain Tire	NULL	L	5	267	
Accessories	Tires and Tubes	HL Mountain Tire	NULL	R	5	232	

Level 3 – Child of Level 2.

Figure 2-5. *Results of query in Listing 2-23*

Using this figure as a guide, we will define a logical structure that will model our target XML structure. This logical structure is shown in Listing 2-25.

Listing 2-25. Proposed logical XML structure

```
<Products>
  <Categories>
    <Category> ELEMENT </Category>
    <Subcategories>
      <Subcategory> ELEMENT </Subcategory>
      <Product Shelf = Attribute Bin = Attribute Quantity = Attribute>
        <ProductName> ELEMENT </ProductName>
        <Color> ELEMENT XSINIL </Color>
      </Product>
    </Subcategories>
  </Categories>
</Products>
```

Following the road map in Figure 2-5 and the logical XML structure of Listing 2-25, the resulting XML structure will be composed of five nested levels, which will contain:

- <Products> is the root element.

- <Categories> is a container data element that holds each <Category> element and all its related <Subcategory> elements directly.

- <Category> is a direct child of the <Categories> element and will contain the category name. The <Subcategories> element is a sibling of the <Category> element, and also a direct child of the <Categories> element. This is a container element for subcategory-specific data related to the sibling <Category> element.

- <Subcategory> is a direct child of the <Subcategories> element. This element holds the name of the current subcategory. The <Product> element represents an individual product within a subcategory. This element is a direct child of the <Subcategories> element and a sibling of the <Subcategory> element. The <Product> element will have multiple attributes assigned to it, and it acts as a container for product-specific data elements.

- <ProductName> is a data element that contains a product's name. The <Color> element contains a product's color, when available. The <Color> element is identified as XSINIL, which means we want this element to appear in the result even when the source column is NULL. The <ProductName> and <Color> elements are siblings, and both are direct children of the <Product> element.

The next step is to build the query. The syntax for EXPLICIT mode has certain rules and specifications that you will need to follow:

1. The query can have one or more SELECT statement blocks, with UNION ALL linking all of them together.

2. Each SELECT statement block must contain two integer type columns named Tag and Parent, respectively, as the first two columns in the query. These columns define the structural relationship between the parent and child levels. For example, Listing 2-23 has multiple nested levels and the SELECT clause establishes the hierarchy, as shown in the code snippet in Listing 2-26.

Listing 2-26. Code snippet, Tag, and Parent columns define the XML hierarchy

```
SELECT 1 AS Tag,
       0 AS Parent,
.
.
.
UNION ALL

SELECT 2 AS Tag,
       1 AS Parent,
.
.
.
UNION ALL

SELECT 3 AS Tag,
       2 AS Parent,
.
.
.
```

In the first SELECT query, the Parent column starts the hierarchy, with a value of 0. The Tag column specifies the hierarchy level. In the second SELECT query the Tag value becomes the Parent and increments to the next number. This flip-flop mechanism is applied to each hierarchical level.

3. The next important rule establishes an XML structure. In EXPLICIT mode, each column must be defined within the first SELECT block, and EXPLICIT mode has a special syntax for this. In Listing 2-23, you can see that all columns after the Tag and Parent columns have a very specific style of alias, which must be formatted as: [ElementName!TagNumber!AttributeName!Directive].

An example from our query in Listing 2-23 is [Categories!1!Category!ELEMENT]. This particular alias defines the structure for the <Category> element of our XML, which contains the category name. Here is the breakdown of this alias:

- *Categories* –a generic identifier for the element name.

- *1* –the tag number of the element, representing the nested XML level. A value of 1 implies this is the top element (excluding the root).

- *Category* –the value attribute's name, unless an ELEMENT directive is specified, in which case it is used as an element name.

- *ELEMENT* –this directive specifies element-centric representation. Attribute-centric is the default, therefore there is no need to specify an attribute-centric representation. If the ELEMENTXSINIL is used, the element will be included even when the source value is NULL.

- Each alias section is separated by an exclamation point(!), this naming convention is required as part of the rule. Because each alias contains special characters ("!"), they must be quoted. Here are some other aliases from Listing 2-23:

- *[Subcategories!2!Subcategory!ELEMENT]* – Child of Categories element (tag 2), represent Subcategory values, element-centric

- *[Product!3!ProductName!ELEMENT]* – Child of Subcategories element (tag 3), represent ProductName value, element-centric

- *[Product!3!Color!ELEMENTXSINIL]* – Child of Subcategories (tag 3), represent Color value, element-centric with XSINIL directive

- *[Product!3!Shelf]* – Child of Subcategories (tag 3), represent Shelf value, attribute-centric.

- *[Product!3!Bin]* – Child of Subcategories (tag 3), represent Bin value, attribute-centric

- *[Product!3!Quantity]* – Child of Subcategories (tag 3), represent Quantity value, attribute-centric

4. The ElementName portion of the aliases must be the same within a given TagNumber, even if the values are retrieved from different tables. For example, an ElementName of Product must be used consistently for TagNumber 3, as shown here:

```
[Product!3!ProductName!ELEMENT] - table Product, column Name
[Product!3!Color!ELEMENTXSINIL] - table Product, column Color
[Product!3!Shelf] - table Inventory column Shelf
[Product!3!Bin] -.table Inventory column Bin
[Product!3!Quantity] - table Inventory column Quantity
```

5. The SELECT blocks of your source query must all conform to SQL's UNION ALL operator rule. Each SELECT statement must have the same number of columns. When the column is not needed, it must be filled with NULL values.

6. Sorting is an important consideration for EXPLICIT mode. The ORDER BY clause finalizes the XML hierarchy. Therefore, the sorting order needs to follow the parent-child sequence. The column names in an ORDER BY clause must be the same as aliases in the top SELECT query. For example:

```
ORDER BY [Categories!1!Category!ELEMENT],
         [Subcategories!2!Subcategory!ELEMENT],
         [Product!3!ProductName!ELEMENT]
```

It is clear that implementing EXPLICIT mode is significantly more complex than implementing the other modes we've covered so far; however, EXPLICIT mode provides the user with full control over the XML generation process. Unlike other modes, this FOR XML mode can be extended with internal directives that allow the user to control each individual XML element and attribute. Table 2-1 lists the directives for the EXPLICIT mode.

Table 2-1. Listing the EXPLICIT mode directives

Directive	Definition	Syntax Example
ID, IDREF, IDREFS	Enables intra-document links and is similar to the primary key and foreign key relationships in relational databases.	[Product!3!ProductList !IDREFS]
CDATA	If the directive is set to CDATA, the contained data is not entity encoded, but is put in the CDATA section. The CDATA attributes must be nameless.	[Product!3!!CDATA]
HIDE	Hides the node. This is useful when you retrieve values only for sorting purposes, but you do not want them in the resulting XML.	[Product!3!Shelf!HIDE]
ELEMENT	Generates an element instead of an attribute.	[Product!3!ProductName !ELEMENT]
ELEMENTXSINIL	Generates an element with an xsi:nil="true" attribute for NULLs. Similar to XSINIL directive.	[Product!3!Color!ELEME NTXSINIL]
XML	Generates an element, just like the element directive. The difference is that the xml directive does not encode entities.	[Product!3!Color!XML]
XMLTEXT	If the xmltext directive is specified, the column content is wrapped in a single tag that is integrated with the rest of the document.	[Parent!1!!XMLTEST]

2-9. Simplifying Custom XML Generation

Problem

EXPLICIT mode allows fine-grained control of your generated XML format, but is complex to utilize. You want to generate custom-formatted XML, but you want an alternative that is easier to use, but achieves results similar to EXPLICIT mode.

Solution

PATH mode can provide XML results that are similar to the results generated by the XML using EXPLICIT mode. However, the mechanism used to generate the PATH mode XML is much simpler than the EXPLICIT mode, which is a big positive. One of the limitations of PATH mode is that it does not have as many directive options as EXPLICIT mode.
Listing 2-27 demonstrates the query from Recipe 2-9, implemented with PATH mode.

45

Listing 2-27. Generating custom XML generation with PATH mode

```
SELECT ProductCategory.Name AS "Category/CategoryName",
        Subcategory.Name AS "Category/Subcategory/SubcategoryName",
        Inventory.Shelf AS "Category/Subcategory/Product/ProductName/
        @Shelf",
        Inventory.Bin AS "Category/Subcategory/Product/ProductName/@Bin",
        Inventory.Quantity AS "Category/Subcategory/Product/ProductName/@
        Quantity"
        Product.Name AS "Category/Subcategory/Product/ProductName",
        Product.Color AS "Category/Subcategory/Product/Color",
FROM Production.Product Product
        INNER JOIN Production.ProductInventory Inventory
        ON Product.ProductID = Inventory.ProductID
        INNER JOIN Production.ProductSubcategory Subcategory
        ON Product.ProductSubcategoryID = Subcategory.ProductSubcategoryID
        INNER JOIN Production.ProductCategory
        ON Subcategory.ProductCategoryID = Production.ProductCategory.
        ProductCategoryID
ORDER BY ProductCategory.Name, Subcategory.Name, Product.Name
FOR XML PATH('Categories'), ELEMENTS XSINIL, ROOT('Products');
```

How It Works

Compare Listing 2-23, illustrating EXPLICIT mode and Listing 2-27 illustrating PATH
mode. It is clear that the PATH mode does not utilize multiple SELECT statements and
UNION ALL to generate nested XML data. Instead the XML hierarchy is defined by XML
Path Language (XPath)-style column aliases, where steps in the path are separated by
forward slashes.

To generate XML using PATH mode, follow these rules:

1. The position should reflect the expected XML hierarchy,
    that is, the child elements listed under parent elements. For
    example:

    ```
    SELECT ProductCategory.Name AS "Category/CategoryName",
            Subcategory.Name AS "Category/Subcategory/
    SubcategoryName",
    ```

2. Each child level is established in the XPath alias, by separating
    them from the parent element with a slash, and adding the
    child element name. For example:

    ```
    Name AS "Category/CategoryName",
    Name AS "Category/Subcategory/SubcategoryName",
    Name AS "Category/Subcategory/Product/ProductName",
    ```

3. When an "@" symbol is present in the alias, it renders the value as an attribute; otherwise it defines an element. This snippet shows the "@" in action, defining attributes in the XML output:

```
SELECT ...
        Inventory.Shelf AS "Category/Subcategory/
        Product/ProductName/@Shelf",
        Inventory.Bin AS "Category/Subcategory/
        Product/ProductName/@Bin",
        Inventory.Quantity AS "Category/Subcategory/
        Product/ProductName/@Quantity",
        ...
```

4. The ORDER BY clause does not have the same effect in PATH mode as it does in EXPLICIT mode, and therefore it can be omitted altogether. However, it is good practice to sort the query according to the XML structure. For example:

```
ORDER BY ProductCategory.Name, Subcategory.Name, Product.Name
```

5. A suggested naming convention is to provide the PATH with an element name inside the parentheses. By default, the PATH mode generates a <row> element, but that is not the best XML design. For example:

```
FOR XML PATH('Categories')
```

6. When the XSINIL directive is implemented in the PATH mode, then this directive is automatically applied to all XML elements. However, in the EXPLICIT mode, the ELEMENTXSINIL directive only affects the element that the directive specifies.

7. Specifying the root element is good XML design practice. I would highly recommend utilizing the ROOT('ElementName') option in all XML queries.

Wrapping up this recipe, I recommend analyzing your prospect XML then making a choice of whether to use EXPLICIT or PATH mode. Both modes have advantages and disadvantages: EXPLICIT mode is more complex to use, but it gives you better control over the XML output. PATH mode is the opposite in the sense that it is easy to write the code; however, you have a bit less control over the elements and attributes.

2-10. Adding Special Nodes to Your XML
Problem

You would like to add special nodes to your generated XML data, such as comments, processing instructions, or custom text.

Solution

The FOR XML clause PATH mode supports XML Path Language (XPath) node tests. The XPath syntax supports a subset of node test names that act as functions. These functions add specific types of nodes to the resulting XML output. Listing 2-28 is a query demonstrating multiple XPath node tests.

Listing 2-28. Demonstrating XPath node tests

```
SELECT ProductCategory.Name AS "Category/CategoryName",
       N'Sales started ' + convert(nvarchar(12), Product.SellStartDate,
       101) AS "Category/comment()",
       N'The record for product number ' + Product.ProductNumber AS
       "processing-instruction(xml:file)",
       (
                SELECT DISTINCT Location.Name "text()", N', cost rate $',
                       Location.CostRate "text()"
                FROM Production.ProductInventory Inventory
                       INNER JOIN Production.Location Location
                       ON Inventory.LocationID = Location.LocationID
                WHERE Product.ProductID = Inventory.ProductID
                FOR XML PATH('LocationName'), TYPE
       ) AS "Locations/node()",
       Subcategory.Name AS "Category/Subcategory/SubcategoryName",
       Product.Name AS "Category/Subcategory/Product/ProductName",
       Product.Color AS "Category/Subcategory/Product/Color",
       Inventory.Shelf AS "Category/Subcategory/Product/ProductName/
       @Shelf",
       Inventory.Bin AS "Category/Subcategory/Product/ProductName/@Bin",
       Inventory.Quantity AS "Category/Subcategory/Product/ProductName/
       @Quantity"
FROM Production.Product Product
       INNER JOIN Production.ProductInventory Inventory
       ON Product.ProductID = Inventory.ProductID
       INNER JOIN Production.ProductSubcategory Subcategory
       ON Product.ProductSubcategoryID = Subcategory.ProductSubcategoryID
INNER JOIN Production.ProductCategory
       ON Subcategory.ProductCategoryID = Production.ProductCategory.
       ProductCategoryID
ORDER BY ProductCategory.Name, Subcategory.Name, Product.Name
FOR XML PATH('Categories'), ELEMENTS XSINIL, ROOT('Products');
```

> **■ Caution** XPath node test names are case sensitive. Therefore, all node test names must be entered in lowercase, otherwise SQL will raise an error. For example when the function *text()* is typed as *Text()*, an error similar to the following is thrown: *Msg 6850, Level 16, State 1 … Column name 'Text()' contains an invalid XML identifier as required by FOR XML; …*

How It Works

When XPath node tests are used in PATH mode, they add a special node to your XML result. The node test is always located at the end of an XPath column alias. For example, in the *"Category/comment()"* path or the *"processing-instruction(xml:file)"* path. Additionally, the node test can be used as the column alias alone, without a hierarchy path. Table 2-2 lists the supported FOR XML PATH XPath node tests.

Table 2-2. XPath node tests

Node type	Node Returns	Node Example
comment()	Returns a comment node.	element/comment() selects all the comment nodes that appear after the context node.
node()	Returns a node of any type. Usfull to add subset XML to result.	element/node() selects all the nodes that appear before the context node.
processing-instruction (name)	Returns a processing instruction node.	processing instruction (PI Name) selects all the processing instruction nodes within the context node.
text()	Returns a text node. Useful to combine more than one column into one XML element.	element/text() selects the text nodes that are children of the context node.

Reviewing the code in Listing 2-28, we see the following:

1. To generate a comment under the <CategoryName> element, the path is provided in the alias with the *comment()* node test. The resulting XML maps the data row into the special comment tag <!--comment--> in your XML result. From our sample code:

```
N'Sales started' + convert(nvarchar(12), Product.
SellStartDate, 101) AS "Category/comment()"
```

49

2. The *processing-instruction(name)* node test must have a target name inside its parentheses. If the target name is not provided, an error will be thrown. This function creates a special XML node of the format *<?name ?>*. For example:

```
N'The record for product number ' + Product.
ProductNumber AS "processing-instruction(xml:file)"
```

3. The *text()* node test is very helpful when you need to concatenate multiple columns into a single element. For example:

```
SELECT DISTINCT Location.Name "text()", ', cost rate $',
        Location.CostRate "text()"
```

4. The *node()* node test is useful when you need to insert values in the XML data type. In Listing 2-28, the correlated subquery performs two actions. Firstly, it concatenates the location and cost rate columns; secondly, it produces an XML result, because the product can have more than one associated location. Figure 2-6 demonstrates all the XPath node test functions in one XML result.

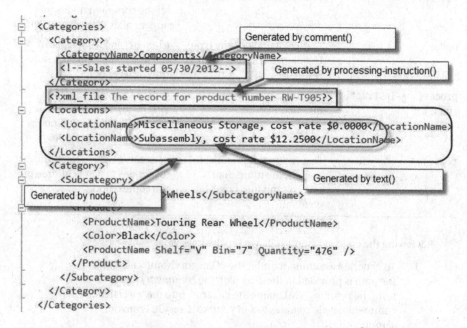

```
<Categories>
  <Category>
    <CategoryName>Components</CategoryName>       Generated by comment()
    <!--Sales started 05/30/2012-->
  </Category>                                     Generated by processing-instruction()
  <?xml_file The record for product number RW-T905?>
  <Locations>
    <LocationName>Miscellaneous Storage, cost rate $0.0000</LocationName>
    <LocationName>Subassembly, cost rate $12.2500</LocationName>
  </Locations>
  <Category>
    <Subcategory>                                 Generated by text()
      Generated by node()    >Wheels</SubcategoryName>
      <Product>
        <ProductName>Touring Rear Wheel</ProductName>
        <Color>Black</Color>
        <ProductName Shelf="V" Bin="7" Quantity="476" />
      </Product>
    </Subcategory>
  </Category>
</Categories>
```

Figure 2-6. XML result with all XPath node test functions

50

Summary

This chapter discusses the four FOR XML modes: RAW, AUTO, EXPLICIT, and PATH. Each mode is thoroughly explained and suggestions for the best mode to use in particular situations, with tips on how to implement each mode. I also discussed directives, their functions, and how each directive interacts with the various XML modes. If you need to build a custom XML result, this chapter provided direction on how to build a robust custom XML data.

The FOR XML clause provides the user with great and powerful options for efficiently building XML results from relational data. The chart in Figure 2-7 illustrates the directives supported by each of the FOR XML modes.

FOR XML Clause Directives Chart							
FOR XML	('ElementName')	BINARY BASE64	ELEMENTS ABSENT	ELEMENTS XSINIL	ROOT	TYPE	XMLSCHEMA
AUTO		■	■	■	■	■	■
EXPLICIT		■			■	■	
PATH	■	■	■	■	■	■	
RAW	■	■	■	■	■	■	■

Figure 2-7. FOR XML *directives available by mode*

The next chapter demonstrates how to store the XML result on the storage (disk, SSD drive, SAN, etc) and how to upload an XML file into a table.

CHAPTER 3

Manipulating XML Files

In Chapter 2, we discussed how to build XML from an SQL query result set. Before we begin reviewing the options on how to shred XML data, we first need to know how to store the XML result on the storage (disk, SSD drive, SAN, etc.) and how to upload an XML file into a table. This chapter will demonstrate the various options to manipulate the XML files.

3-1. Storing XML Result in a File from SQL
Problem

You want to store the XML result you generate in SQL as an .xml file.

Solution

The *BCP* (bulk copy program) utility allows the export of data into an XML file. When the file path is eligible and the SQL Server account has enough privileges to store the file, then the process can be executed from the stored procedure. Listing 3-1 demonstrates how the stored procedure creates an XML file using the provided file path in the @FilePath parameter.

Listing 3-1. Using the stored procedure to write an XML file by destination file path

```
CREATE PROCEDURE dbo.usp_WriteXMLFile
        @XML XML,
        @FilePath nvarchar(200)
AS
BEGIN
        SET NOCOUNT ON;
        IF (OBJECT_ID('tempdb..##XML') IS NOT NULL)
                DROP TABLE ##XML;

        CREATE TABLE ##XML (XMLHolder XML);

        INSERT INTO ##XML
```

© Alex Grinberg 2018
A. Grinberg, *XML and JSON Recipes for SQL Server*,
https://doi.org/10.1007/978-1-4842-3117-3_3

```
(
        XMLHolder
)
SELECT @XML;

-- Prepare log table
DECLARE @cmd TABLE
(
        name NVARCHAR(35),
        minimum INT,
        maximum INT,
        config_value INT,
        run_value INT
);

DECLARE @run_value        INT;

-- Save original configuration set
EXECUTE master.dbo.sp_configure 'show advanced options', 1;
RECONFIGURE;

INSERT INTO @cmd
(
        name,
        minimum,
        maximum,
        config_value,
        run_value
)
EXECUTE sp_configure 'xp_cmdshell';

SELECT @run_value = run_value
FROM @cmd;

IF @run_value = 0
BEGIN
        -- Enable xp_cmdshell
        EXEC sp_configure 'xp_cmdshell', 1;
        RECONFIGURE;
END;

DECLARE @SQL nvarchar(300) = '';

SET @SQL = 'bcp ##XML out "' + @FilePath + '\Categories_'
        + FORMAT(GETDATE(), N'yyyyMMdd_hhmmss')
        + '.xml" -S "' + @@SERVERNAME + '" -T -c';
        -- REPLACE(REPLACE(REPLACE(CONVERT(varchar(20), GETDATE(),
        120), '-', ''), ' ', '_'), ':', '')
```

```
-- for those who still using SQL Server 2008 R2 or below, use REPLACE
instead of FORMAT. FORMAT function introduced in SQL 2012.
        EXECUTE master..xp_cmdshell @SQL;

        IF @run_value = 0
        BEGIN
                -- Disable xp_cmdshell
                EXECUTE sp_configure 'xp_cmdshell', 0;
                RECONFIGURE;
        END;

        IF (OBJECT_ID('tempdb..##XML') IS NOT NULL)
                DROP TABLE ##XML;

        SET NOCOUNT OFF;
END;
GO
```

How It Works

The stored procedure usp_WriteXMLFile, shown in Listing 3-1, has several important components to successfully create an XML file from within SQL Server. Let's break down this stored procedure to follow how the XML file-writing process works:

1. The parameter @FilePath is the XML file destination path. This parameter makes the stored procedure flexible, especially when running it in different environments, such as development, staging, and production.

2. CREATE a global temporary table (##XML), then DROP it in the end. Use a column name XMLHolder with the XML data type to get XML data. It is a rare case to need to create a global temporary table; however, the BCP command will raise an error if a session-level temporary table is referenced. Therefore, we can use either a permanent table or a global temporary table. There is always a risk in implementing a global temporary table, if the process part of the concurrent process. The global temporary table is seen throughout the entire server and if somebody else happens to use the stored procedure at the same time, one of the user's tables could be overwritten and therefore receive inaccurate results. Please reference the code samples for Chapter 3 where the stored procedure usp_WriteXMLFileDynamicTable demonstrates how to solve this problem.

3. INSERT the XML data into a global temporary table (##XML).

4. To run the BCP command from a stored procedure or SSMS, the server instance needs to be configured for "xp_cmdshell" option at value 1. This means that the instance allows the xp_cmdshell extended stored procedure to run. There are cases where due to security reasons, you may be required to maintain the configuration for the server instance at value 0 (disabled status). In this case, you would still need to incorporate code that switches the server instance from value 0 to 1, then back to 0 while creating the XML file. Since the BCP command is able to create the XML file in milliseconds, there is virtually no security risk during the milliseconds that the server is set to value 0 to enable the xp_cmdshell stored procedure to create the XML file.

    -   To preserve the original settings, the table variable @cmd is created.

    -   The system stored procedure sp_configure uses the parameter value 'xp_cmdshell.' This result is inserted into the table variable @cmd, which reflects the current status of the 'xp_cmdshell' option.

    -   The following statement *SELECT @run_value = run_value FROM @cmd* populates the local variable *@run_value* to preserve the xp_cmdshell option run_value for further analysis.

    -   The conditional statement IF @run_value = 0 detects whether or not the option value needs to be changed from 0 to 1.

5. The variable @SQL is created to compose the statement for the BCP utility.

6. The final command depends on the instance and database name and could be the following:

    ```
    BCP ##XML out "C:\TEMP\Categories_20170310_164701.xml"
    -S "APRESS\SQL2016" -T -c
    ```

7. Let's take a closer look at all of the arguments and switches that are required by BCP to create the XML file:

    -   BCP – the bulk copy utility executable name.

    -   ##XML – name of table with XML data.

    -   out – indicator that copies the data from the table and sends it to the destination.

    -   "C:\TEMP\Categories_20170310_164701.xml" – the file path.

    -   -S "APRESS\SQL2016" – server name.

- -T – specifies that the BCP command runs under a trusted connection. To run the BCP with SQL Server credentials then instead of -T, please use -U login_Name -P password options.

- -c – specifies that the output content is in the character data type.

Caution The BCP arguments leading with a dash are case sensitive. For example, -T is an option for a trusted connection; however, -t is the field terminator.

---

8. The statement *exec master..xp_cmdshell @SQL* runs the BCP command

9. The statement IF @run_value = 0 conditionally detects whether the option value needs to be changed from 1 back to 0.

10. To finalize the process, the ##XML table should be destroyed.

```
IF (OBJECT_ID('tempdb..##XML') IS NOT NULL)
        DROP TABLE ##XML;
```

To test the stored procedure, run following code:

```
DECLARE @x XML

SET @x = (
      SELECT ProductCategory.Name AS "Category/CategoryName",
                (
                      SELECT DISTINCT Location.Name "text()", ',
                      cost rate $',
                                  Location.CostRate "text()"
                      FROM Production.ProductInventory Inventory
                            INNER JOIN Production.Location Location
                                  ON Inventory.LocationID = Location.
                                  LocationID
                      WHERE Product.ProductID = Inventory.ProductID
                            FOR XML PATH('LocationName'), TYPE
                ) AS "Locations/node()",
                Subcategory.Name AS "Category/Subcategory/SubcategoryName",
                Product.Name AS "Category/Subcategory/Product/ProductName",
                Product.Color AS "Category/Subcategory/Product/Color",
                Inventory.Shelf AS "Category/Subcategory/Product/
                ProductName/@Shelf",
                Inventory.Bin AS "Category/Subcategory/Product/ProductName/
                @Bin",
```

```
                Inventory.Quantity AS "Category/Subcategory/Product/
                ProductName/@Quantity"
                FROM Production.Product Product
                        INNER JOIN Production.ProductInventory Inventory
                        ON Product.ProductID = Inventory.ProductID
                        INNER JOIN Production.ProductSubcategory Subcategory
                        ON Product.ProductSubcategoryID = Subcategory.
                        ProductSubcategoryID
                        INNER JOIN Production.ProductCategory
                        ON Subcategory.ProductCategoryID = ProductCategory.
                        ProductCategoryID
                ORDER BY ProductCategory.Name, Subcategory.Name, Product.Name
                FOR XML PATH('Categories'), ELEMENTS XSINIL, ROOT
                ('Products')
)

EXECUTE usp_WriteXMLFile @x, 'C:\TEMP'
```

When the stored procedure usp_WriteXMLFile execution is completed, the BCP
utility returns the completion status with the runtime in milliseconds. As shown in
Figure 3-1, my runtime to create the XML file was 15 milliseconds. The XML file is created
in the C:\TEMP directory. Figure 3-1 illustrates the BCP utility output.

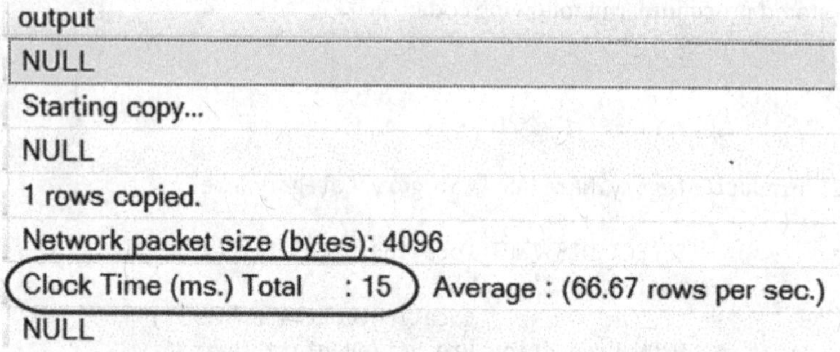

Figure 3-1. Showing the BCP utility completion status

If you need to hide the completion output status, then add the following code to the
stored procedure before executing the xp_cmdshell extended stored procedure:

```
DECLARE @stat TABLE
(
        BCPStat VARCHAR(500)
);
INSERT INTO @stat
```

```
(
       BCPStat
)
```

```
EXECUTE master..xp_cmdshell @SQL;
```

The @stat table variable absorbs the BCP completion output; therefore the stored procedure does not return any messages.

■ **Note**   Both Recipes "3-1 Storing XML Result in a File from SQL" and "3-3 Loading XML from a Stored Procedure" implement the xp_cmdshell extended stored procedure. The xp_cmdshell stored procedure is associated with security risk, which is why it's a disabled SQL Server by default. Both recipes implement xp_cmdshell, which is self-detected to turn the logic on and off to minimize the security risk. However, if for any reason you have a problem utilizing xp_cmdshell in your environment, consider Recipe "3-5 Implementing a CLR Solution" as an alternative to xp_cmdshell.

3-2. Creating XML from an SSIS Package
Problem
You want to develop an alternative to using the BCP utility to create an XML file from a result set?

Solution
The BCP utility is a handy legacy command-line utility, but SSIS is Microsoft's standard ETL solution.The SSIS package can provide a comprehensive solution for the data transformation processes. SSIS provides at least three options to perform the task of creating an XML file:

1.   Script task

2.   Flat File Destination

3.   Export Column transform

Each of those options is relatively easy to complete; however, my preference is Script Task. I have several arguments to defend my preference:

- Script Task is an easy and fast solution for file manipulation.

- In a few lines of code (either C# or VB.NET), you can provide the task solution (even if you don't have any .NET knowledge, simply copy provided code).

- Easy and productive debugging process.

- With the Script Task, you have full control over the process.

For a complete SSIS solution, we need to create three Control Flow tasks:

1. An Execute SQL Task called "Get XML Content," to obtain the XML result from the database.

2. Set an expression for the TimeStamp variable to get date and time for the XML file name.

3. A Script Task named "Create XML File," to write the XML file to the destination.

Figure 3-2 Illustrates a simple SSIS package control flow.

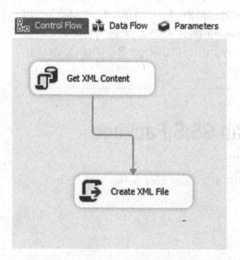

Figure 3-2. *Showing SSIS package*

To create the SSIS package, create a New Integration Services Project. Name the package CreateXMLFile, and save the project. Then from the Tool Box drag and drop the Execute SQL Task onto the package designer pane. If the Tool Box does not show up for your new project, press the button in the upper-right corner, as shown in Figure 3-3.

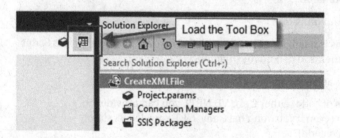

Figure 3-3. *Showing Tool Box button location*

1. We need to create three package-level variables. To create a variable, right-mouse click on an empty area of the designer pane. On the pop-up menu select "Variables" to load the Variables dialog, as shown in Figure 3-4.

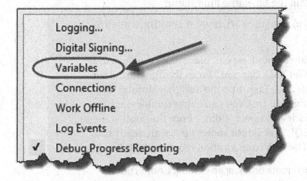

Figure 3-4. Variables option of the pop-up context menu

In the Variables dialog:

- Click the "Add Variable" button.

- Type the variable name.

- Choose the appropriate data type (in our case, choose the String data type).

- Provide the variable default when needed.

- Also, make sure that the variable has SSIS Package Scope.

Figure 3-5 Illustrates the Variables Form entries.

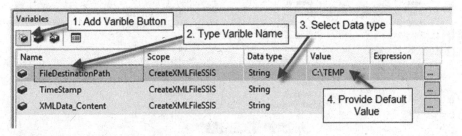

Figure 3-5. Showing the Variables Form entries

■ **Tip** It's good practice to utilize variables in place of hard-coded values so you can have more flexibility when executing a package.

The variables above are created, and below is a description of their purpose:

- *FileDestinationPath* – to specify the destination folder. This variable can be modified outside of the package, practically providing the parameter functionality.

- *TimeStamp* – to obtain the file name time stamp.

- *XMLData_Content* – to store the XML result that will be written to the file.

- Once the variables are created, we can place and configure the Execute SQL Task "Get XML Content." From the Tool Box, drag and drop the Execute SQL Task onto the designer surface. To configure the Execute SQL Task you can either double-click on the task or right-click it and select "Edit..." from the context menu. When the Execute SQL Task Editor shows up, we are ready to configure the task. The task configuration requires the following:

  a) First, we need to create or select an existing Connection to SQL Server. On the Execute SQL Task Editor, select General from the Editor options list located on the left side.

  b) Click Connection.

  c) On the right side select the drop-down arrow.

  d) Click on <New connection> to open the Connection dialog, or select an existing connection. Figure 3-6 illustrates the steps to select an existing connection, or call the Configure OLE DB Connection Form.

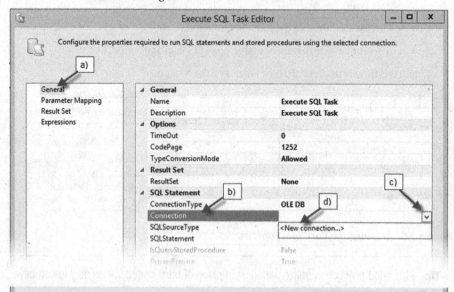

Figure 3-6. Showing steps to Configure OLE DB Connection Form

Configure the OLE DB Connection Form by clicking the "New..." button. In the Connection Manager dialog:

a) Select or enter the source server name from the Server name drop-down list.

b) From the "Log on to the server" option, select the type of authentication.

c) From the "Connect to a database" option, select the database name

d) Optionally, but recommended, click the Test Connection button to confirm your configuration. Figure 3-7 illustrates the Connection Manager dialog configuration steps.

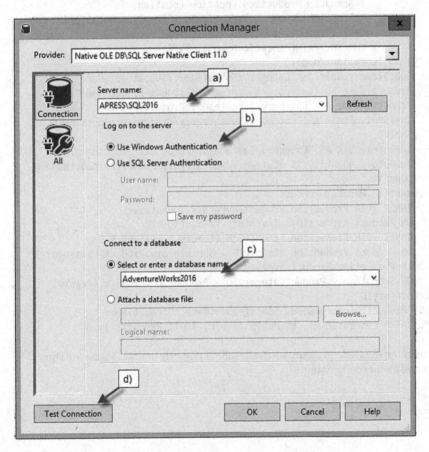

Figure 3-7. Showing the Connection Manager Form configuration steps

Once the connection is ready, the next step is to add the SQL query. Under the Connection property, check the SQLSourceType property. By default, the value is Direct input, but double-check that Direct input is selected. One of the most important properties is SQLStatement. We will take the query that was demonstrated in Chapter 2 for this example. To configure the SQLStatement property, simply add the query from the Listing 3-2 SQL query for SSIS package.

Listing 3-2. Listing Categories query for SSIS package

```
SELECT ProductCategory.Name AS "Category/CategoryName",
       (
                SELECT DISTINCT Location.Name "text()", ', cost rate $',
                       Location.CostRate "text()"
                FROM Production.ProductInventory Inventory
                INNER JOIN Production.Location Location
                       ON Inventory.LocationID = Location.LocationID
                WHERE Product.ProductID = Inventory.ProductID
                FOR XML PATH('LocationName'), TYPE
       ) AS "Locations/node()",
       Subcategory.Name AS "Category/Subcategory/SubcategoryName",
       Product.Name AS "Category/Subcategory/Product/ProductName",
       Product.Color AS "Category/Subcategory/Product/Color",
       Inventory.Shelf AS "Category/Subcategory/Product/ProductName/@
       Shelf",
       Inventory.Bin AS "Category/Subcategory/Product/ProductName/@Bin",
       Inventory.Quantity AS "Category/Subcategory/Product/ProductName/@
       Quantity"
FROM Production.Product Product
       INNER JOIN Production.ProductInventory Inventory
       ON Product.ProductID = Inventory.ProductID
       INNER JOIN Production.ProductSubcategory Subcategory
       ON Product.ProductSubcategoryID = Subcategory.ProductSubcategoryID
INNER JOIN Production.ProductCategory
       ON Subcategory.ProductCategoryID = Production.ProductCategory.
ProductCategoryID
ORDER BY ProductCategory.Name, Subcategory.Name, Product.Name
FOR XML PATH('Categories'), ELEMENTS XSINIL, ROOT('Products');
```

Finally, on the General menu, set the ResultSet property to XML. Figure 3-8 shows the General menu configurations.

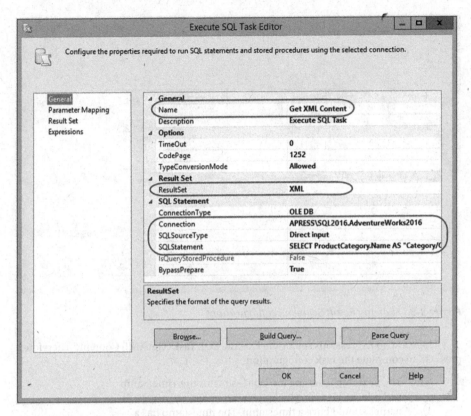

Figure 3-8. *Showing configurations for General menu*

The query for the "Get XML Content" task does not have any parameters. To set the proper parameters, click on the Result Set menu. The query that we set in the General menu returns the XML as a scalar CLOB (Character Large Object) value. Therefore, the returned result we will bind to one of the variables that were previously created. From the Variable Name drop-down list, select the XMLData_Content variable. Set the Result Name property to 0. Since we do not have a name for the result set, setting it to 0 will choose the first column from the result set. Figure 3-9 illustrates the Result Set menu configurations.

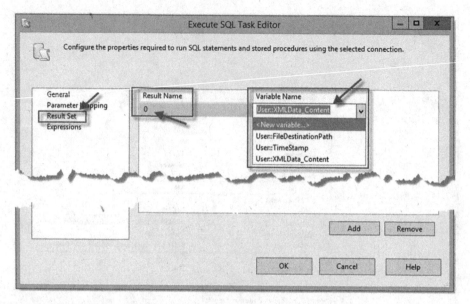

Figure 3-9. *Showing Result Set menu configurations*

There are no Expressions set for the Execute SQL Task "Get XML Content." Therefore, press OK to complete the task configuration.

1. The next step is setting the expression for the TimeStamp variable. In a real production environment, most XML file names should have a timestamp. The timestamp has a variety of format options, and the most appropriate should be chosen based on client or business needs. For example, the most often implemented format I've seen is yyyyMMdd_HHmmss. To this value, SSIS packages must have a syntax that is different from T-SQL, or even .NET applications. For example, Listing 3-3 demonstrates SSIS syntax to get the date timestamp.

Listing 3-3. Showing SSIS syntax

```
(DT_STR, 4, 1252) DATEPART("yyyy", GETDATE()) +
RIGHT("0" + (DT_STR, 2, 1252) DATEPART("mm", GETDATE()),2) +
RIGHT("0" + (DT_STR, 2, 1252) DATEPART("dd", GETDATE()),2)  + "_" +
RIGHT("0" + (DT_STR, 2, 1252) DATEPART("hh", GETDATE()),2)  +
RIGHT("0" + (DT_STR, 2, 1252) DATEPART("mi", GETDATE()),2)  +
RIGHT("0" + (DT_STR, 2, 1252) DATEPART("ss", GETDATE()),2)
```

To set the variable expression:

- Right-mouse click on the package field. Select Variables from the pop-up menu.

- Click the variable's button in the Expression section to load the Expression Builder Form.

- Place the code from Listing 3-3 into the Expression text box.

- Click the "Evaluate Expression" button to verify the expression's code.

- Click the OK button to finalize the setting. Figure 3-10 Illustrates the setup of the expressions to the variable.

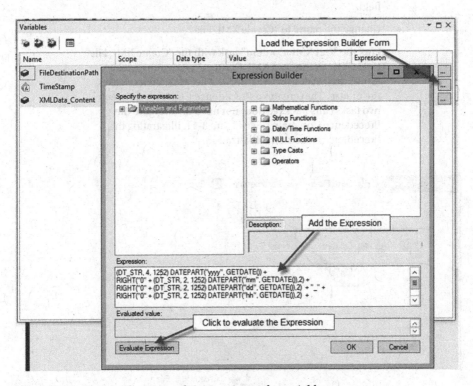

Figure 3-10. *Showing how to set the expression to the variable*

2.   The Script Task "Create XML File," as stated in its name, writes the XML file to the destination file path, which is assigned to the SSIS package via the *FileDestinationPath* variable that has a public interface and is visible outside of the package. The Script Task is a programming module where a developer can write the functionality implementing C# and VB.NET languages, which makes the Script Task very popular for SQL Server developers. However, the Script Task could simplify and extend SSIS packages functionalities. For the Script Task "Create XML File," several lines of code will need to be used to complete the process. To configure the task:

- From the Tool Box, drag the Script Task to the development field.

- Change the name to "Create XML File."

- Link the "Get XML Content" task with the "Create XML File" task. Click on the "Get XML Content" task, grab a green arrow, drag over the "Create XML File" task, then release the mouse. That creates a Precedence Constrain between two tasks (this package does not need to configure the Precedence Constrain). See Figure 3-11, illustrating the Precedence Constrain initialization.

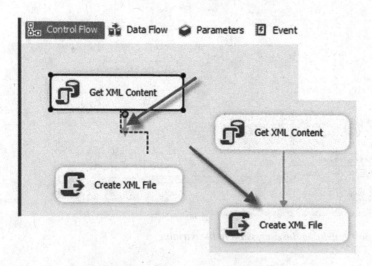

Figure 3-11. *Creating Precedence Constrain between the tasks*

- To load the Script Task Manager, double-click on the "Create XML File" task.

- The Script Task Manager, by default, has the ScriptLanguage set to Microsoft Visual C# 2015 (Microsoft Visual Basic 2015 is another option; however, this example will use C#), and the EntryPoint property is set to "Main" under the Script Task Editor (the function name that the script executes first).

- There are no changes for the variables in this task. Therefore, click on the ReadOnlyVariables property to bind the variables to the task. On the right side of the property, click the button to load the package variable list. Place a check mark next to the variables *User::FileDestinationPath, User::TimeStamp, User::XMLData_Content,* then Click OK.

- Click on the Edit Script... button to load the programming module. Figure 3-12 illustrates the Script Task Manager properties.

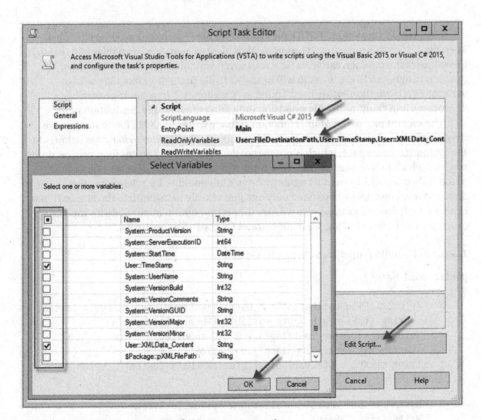

Figure 3-12. Showing Script Task Manager properties

■ **Tip**   Before you click the Edit Script... button, highlight and then copy all variables that were selected. You will need those later in the code module. Also, keep in mind that variable names are case sensitive when referenced in the code.

When the script editor window loads up, go to the Main() function. By default, Main() contains the code shown in Listing 3-4.

Listing 3-4. Showing default code for the Main() function

```
public void Main()
{
        // TODO: Add your code here

        Dts.TaskResult = (int)ScriptResults.Success;
}
```

First, replace the value "TODO: Add your code here" with the saved variables list. Keep the "//" as this indicates a comment. Next, declare two string variables and reassign the values of the package variables (use your saved variables reference). The *Main()* function variable *strFilePath* result will be the XML file path; therefore the package variable *FileDestinationPath* is hard-coded as "Categories_" plus package variable *TimeStamp* and ".xml" as the file extension indicating the XML file destination path.

The second part of the *Main()* function actually writes the XML file to storage. We need to create an instance of the *StreamWriter* object. The *StreamWriter* class belongs to the *System.IO* namespace, which is not part of the default namespaces for a programming module, which means that we have two options: add a "using System.IO;" statement to the code or use the System.IO namespace as a full qualifier for referencing the *StreamWriter* class. Hence, we need only one line of code to instantiate the *StreamWriter* class. In the following example, we will use the second option in our code for the *Main()* function. The code in Listing 3-5 demonstrates C# code to write the file.

Listing 3-5. Coding function to write the XML file

```
public void Main()
{
        // User::FileDestinationPath,User::TimeStamp,User::XMLData_Content
          string strFilePath = Dts.Variables["User::FileDestina
          tionPath"].Value.ToString() + @"\\Categories_" + Dts.
          Variables["User::TimeStamp"].Value.ToString() + ".xml";
        string strXML = Dts.Variables["User::XMLData_Content"].Value.To
        String();

          System.IO.StreamWriter file = new System.IO.Stream
          Writer(strFilePath);
          file.Write(strXML);
          file.Close();

          Dts.TaskResult = (int)ScriptResults.Success;
}
```

70

To finalize the Script Task, save and close the script editor window. Click the OK button for the Script Task. Your SSIS package is now ready to test.

To test the SSIS package, press the Start button. When SSIS completes successfully, green circles with check marks will show up on each task. Figure 3-13 illustrates a successful SSIS package completion.

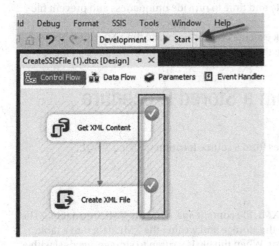

Figure 3-13. Testing the SSIS package

To stop the SSIS package, press the red square button or click on the "Package execution completed with success" URL at the bottom of the package. Figure 3-14 illustrates options to stop the package.

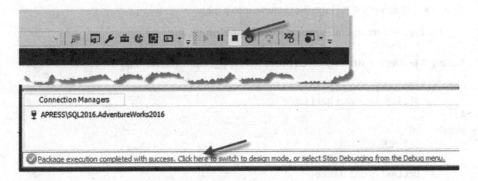

Figure 3-14. Showing the package switch to design mode options

Now the SSIS package development is completed and the XML file was created in the specified destination, "C:\TEMP" folder.

How It Works

The SSIS package "Get XML Content" Execute SQL Task submits a query to the SQL Server. The Connection Manager provides a reference to the SQL Server instance and the database name, as well as connection credentials, if necessary. The query result is assigned to the package-level variable XMLData_*Content*. The expression for the *TimeStamp* variable computes the date and time to provide uniqueness and prevent file collision.

The "Create XML File" Script Task executes C# code to write the XML result out to the file. The package variables provide the file content and the XML file path.

3-3. Loading XML from a Stored Procedure

Problem

You want to read one or more XML files from a source location utilizing T-SQL.

Solution

SQL Server has the ability to read the XML file content and write the XML into a table. The mechanics between writing the file to the storage and writing the XML data into a table from storage (load the XML) is different. When the file is written to storage, we deal with a single XML output per file. However, when we load files, one or more files could be in the source location. For this reason, the T-SQL code needs to solve the following issues:

- Obtain the file names with particular criteria; for example, all files with the extension ".xml".

- Access each file and read the file content.

- Load (INSERT) the file content into a table.

Listing 3-6 demonstrates the solution for this problem.

Listing 3-6. Demonstrating stored procedure usp_LoadXMLFromFile

```
CREATE PROCEDURE dbo.usp_LoadXMLFromFile
        @FilePath nvarchar(100)
AS
BEGIN
        SET NOCOUNT ON;
        -- Prepare log table
        DECLARE @cmd TABLE
        (
                name NVARCHAR(35),
                minimum INT,
                maximum INT,
                config_value INT,
                run_value INT
```

```
);
DECLARE @run_value        INT;

-- Save original configuration set
INSERT @cmd
(
        name,
        minimum,
        maximum,
        config_value,
        run_value
)
EXEC sp_configure 'xp_cmdshell';

SELECT @run_value = run_value
FROM @cmd;

IF @run_value = 0
BEGIN
        -- Enable xp_cmdshell
        EXEC sp_configure 'xp_cmdshell', 1;
        RECONFIGURE;
END;

IF NOT EXISTS
(
        SELECT *
        FROM sys.objects
        WHERE object_id = OBJECT_ID(N'[dbo].[_XML]') AND type in (N'U')
)
CREATE TABLE dbo._XML
(
        ID INT NOT NULL IDENTITY(1,1) PRIMARY KEY,
        XMLFileName NVARCHAR(300),
        XML_LOAD XML,
        Created DATETIME
)
ELSE
        TRUNCATE TABLE dbo._XML;

DECLARE @DOS NVARCHAR(300) = N'',
        @DirBaseLocation NVARCHAR(500),
        @FileName NVARCHAR(300),
        @SQL NVARCHAR(1000) = N'';

DECLARE @files TABLE
(
```

```
            tID INT IDENTITY(1,1) NOT NULL PRIMARY KEY,
            XMLFile NVARCHAR(300)
);

-- Verify that last character is \
SET @DirBaseLocation = IIF(RIGHT(@FilePath, 1) = '\', @FilePath,
@FilePath + '\');

SET @DOS = 'dir /B /O:-D ' + @DirBaseLocation;
INSERT @files
(
        XMLFile
)
EXEC master..xp_cmdshell @DOS;

IF @run_value = 0
BEGIN
        -- Disable xp_cmdshell
        EXECUTE sp_configure 'xp_cmdshell', 0;
        RECONFIGURE;
END;

DECLARE cur CURSOR
FOR         SELECT XMLFile
        FROM @files
        WHERE XMLFile like '%.xml';
OPEN cur;

FETCH NEXT
FROM cur
INTO @FileName;

WHILE @@FETCH_STATUS = 0
BEGIN

        BEGIN TRY
                SET @SQL = 'INSERT INTO _XML SELECT ''' +
                @DirBaseLocation + @FileName
                        + ''', X, GETDATE()  FROM OPENROWSET
                        (BULK N''' + @DirBaseLocation + @FileName
                        + ''', SINGLE_BLOB) as tempXML(X)';

                EXECUTE sp_executesql @SQL;

                FETCH NEXT
                FROM cur
                INTO @FileName;
        END TRY
```

```
            BEGIN CATCH
                    SELECT @SQL, ERROR_MESSAGE();
            END CATCH
        END;

        CLOSE cur;

        DEALLOCATE cur;
        SET NOCOUNT OFF;
END;
GO
```

How It Works

The stored procedure usp_LoadXMLFromFile, shown in Listing 3-6, provides a solution for loading XML data from one or more files. The stored procedure has one input parameter, @FilePath, of nvarchar(100) data type. The parameter provides the location of your XML source files.

1. The mechanism to enable/disable an extended stored procedure xp_cmdshell is described in Recipe 3-1. This process is the same for the stored procedure usp_ LoadXMLFromFile.

2. We need to make sure that the destination table (_XML) exists. If the table is not in a database, then the table needs to be created. When the table exists, depending on the business requirements, the data can be truncated or the table can retain historical data. The following example shows a truncated the table:

```
IF NOT EXISTS (SELECT * FROM sys.objects
    WHERE object_id = OBJECT_ID(N'[dbo].[_XML]') AND
    type in (N'U'))
    CREATE TABLE _XML
    (
        ID int IDENTITY(1,1) PRIMARY KEY
        ,XMLFileName nvarchar(300)
        ,XML_LOAD XML, Created datetime
    )
ELSE
    TRUNCATE TABLE _XML
```

3. Declare several variables for processing needs:

```
@DOS nvarchar(300) = '' - prepare DOS command.
@DirBaseLocation nvarchar(500) - verify and format
source path.
@FileName nvarchar(300) - to obtain the file name.
@SQL nvarchar(1000) = '' - prepare SQL for INSERT
process.
@files TABLE - to obtain all file name from source
location.
```

4. Verify that last character is a backslash (\). We need to make sure that the stored procedure receives a valid path with \ as the last character. If the last backslash is missing, then we need to add a backslash to the provided path. For example:

```
IIF(RIGHT(@FilePath, 1) = '\', @FilePath, @FilePath + '\');
```

The IIF function was introduced by SQL Server version 2012. The function has three parameters:

I. Condition - *RIGHT(@FilePath, 1)* = '\' to check if the last character is a \.

II. True result – when the character is found, then do nothing.

III. False result – when not found, then add a \ to the parameter.

5. Prepare the Windows Command Shell command to obtain a list of all files from the source location. The Windows Command Shell command *dir* returns all files and subdirectories for a specified path. However, the *dir* command returns other information along with the file name. "/B" indicates the use of bare format (file name only), and "/O:-D" - specifies the sort order by date created, descending.

```
SET @DOS = 'dir /B /O:-D ' + @DirBaseLocation  ;
```

6. The extended stored procedure xp_cmdshell executes the Windows Command Shell command and inserts all available files from the source location.

```
INSERT @files
EXEC master..xp_cmdshell @DOS;
```

7. Next, we need to iterate through each file with the extension ".xml". This can be accomplished by declaring a cursor for the table variable and establishing a loop over the cursor.

```
DECLARE cur CURSOR
FOR     SELECT XMLFile
        FROM @files
        WHERE XMLFile like '%.xml';
OPEN cur;

FETCH NEXT
FROM cur
INTO @FileName;

WHILE @@FETCH_STATUS = 0
```

8. Inside the WHILE loop, we need to compose the INSERT
    statement for each file that reads the file content and inserts
    the XML into the _XML table. For example:

```
INSERT INTO _XML
SELECT 'C:\TEMP\Categories.xml', X, GETDATE()
FROM OPENROWSET(BULK N'C:\TEMP\Categories.xml',
SINGLE_BLOB) AS tempXML(X);
```

    The key to the SQL code above is the OPENROWSET() function.
    The BULK option specifies that we will be reading all of the
    contents from the source file in bulk. Then there is a space
    after BULK, followed by the file location. The SINGLE_BLOB
    option specifies that the file content is returned as a single
    column with the data type VARBINARY(MAX), which is a good
    fit for XML data. The alias syntax AS tempXML(X) must be in
    table(column) format:

    • tempXML – table alias

    • X – column alias

    Other OPENROWSET options SINGLE_CLOB (returns
    varchar(max)) and SINGLE_NCLOB (returns nvarchar(max))
    are not a good fit for XML import data, because only SINGLE_
    BLOB supports all Windows encoding conversions.

9. The system stored procedure sp_executesql executes the
    composed SQL.

```
EXECUTE sp_executesql @SQL;
```

10. The error handler allows the process to run and returns error
    details with problematic SQL. Optionally, you can create a
    table to log the errors.

    Code sample to run the stored procedure:

```
EXEC dbo.usp_LoadXMLFromFile 'C:\Temp'
```

However, the disadvantage is that you will lose the error handler logging, and if one of the files that is being loaded fails, then the file will not be loaded.

3-4. Loading XML from SSIS Package

Problem

You want to load one or more XML files into the database using an SSIS ETL package.

Solution

SSIS provides a comprehensive set of tools to load XML files from a specified directory.

An SSIS package to load multiple XML files is more complex than the SSIS package that writes an XML file, shown in Recipe 3-2, "Creating XML from an SSIS Package." The SSIS package LoadXMLFromFile is created based on the following business rules:

1. Check whether.xml files exist in the source directory.

2. If no files are found in the source location, stop package execution.

3. If matching files are found, truncate the destination table.

4. Load XML content from all available files with the .xml extension.

5. Move all processed files into an Archive folder.

The LoadXMLFromFile SSIS package is composed of:

1. A "Check If File Exists" Script Task, which uses C# code to verify whether any XML files exist in the source location.

2. The Precedence Constraint (green arrow between "Check If File Exists" and "Truncate Table") formula conditionally verifies the *FlagIsFileExist* variable and plays the "STOP" or "GO" role.

3. An Execute SQL Task "Truncate Table" conditionally executes T-SQL code to CREATE or TRUNCATE the table.

4. The "Load XML Content" Foreach Loop Container iterates through the XML files.

5. The "Insert XML Data" Execute SQL Task executes a T-SQL statement that inserts the XML file content into the _XML table.

6. The "Archive File" File System Task moves the XML file into the Archive folder. Figure 3-15 illustrates the SSIS package.

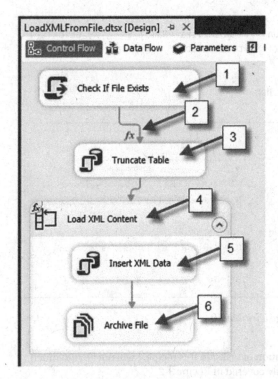

Figure 3-15. *Showing "LoadXMLFromFile" SSIS package in design mode*

The following SSIS package variables were created to provide package flexibility and functionality:

1. ArchiveFile – Supplies the File System Task "Archive File," DestinationVariable property. Created with the expression @[User::ArchiveLocation] + @[User::FileName].

2. ArchiveLocation – Provides the destination path to the archive folder.

3. FileName – Mapped to the Foreach Loop Container "Load XML Content." Takes the XML file name from each iteration.

4. FlagIsFileExist – Is assigned a "true" or "false" value and controls the Precedence Constraint expression.

5. SourceFile – Supplies the File System Task "Archive File," SourceVariable. Creates the expression @[User::SourceLocation] + @[User::FileName].

6. SourceLocation – Provides the source path to source folder.

7. SQLScript – Composes T-SQL to insert the XML content into the _XML table using the expression:

```
"INSERT INTO _XML
SELECT '" + @[User::SourceLocation] + @[User::FileName] + "', X, GETDATE()
FROM OPENROWSET(BULK N'" + @[User::SourceLocation] + @[User::FileName] +
"', SINGLE_BLOB) as tempXML(X)"
```

Figure 3-16 illustrates the variable list.

Name	Scope	Data type	Value	Expression
ArchiveFile	LoadXMLFromFile	String	C:\TEMP\Archive\Catego...	@[User::ArchiveLocation...
ArchiveLocation	LoadXMLFromFile	String	C:\TEMP\Archive\	
FileName	LoadXMLFromFile	String	Categories.xml	
FlagIsFileExist	LoadXMLFromFile	Boolean	False	
SourceFile	LoadXMLFromFile	String	C:\TEMP\Categories.xml	@[User::SourceLocation]...
SourceLocation	LoadXMLFromFile	String	C:\TEMP\	
SQLScript	LoadXMLFromFile	String	INSERT INTO _XML SELEC...	"INSERT INTO _XML SEL...

Figure 3-16. *Showing the SSIS package variable list*

Now we will discuss the configuration of tasks. In this recipe, I will not go into much detail because this topic was thoroughly covered in Recipe 3-2.

1. Script Task "Check If File Exists." This time the Script Task checks whether the source location has files with extension .xml. No other task can provide this functionality. Two variables are mapped to the task:

   - SourceLocation – ReadOnlyVariable.

   - FlagIsFileExist – ReadWriteVariable. The code could modify the variable value. Figure 3-17 illustrates the variables.

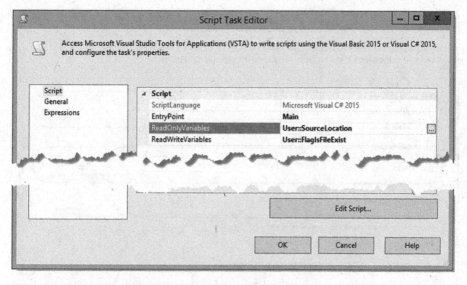

Figure 3-17. *Demonstrating the Script Task variables mapping*

Click on the Edit Script command button. Add the following code into the Main() function:

```
Dts.Variables["User::FlagIsFileExist"].Value
=            (System.IO.Directory.GetFiles(Dts.Variab
les["User::SourceLocation"].Value.ToString(), "*.xml").
Length != 0);
```

Save and then Close the code window. Click the OK command button to complete the settings.

2. Precedence Constraint (green arrow between "Check If File Exists" and "Truncate Table"). To load the Precedence Constraint Editor, double-click on the arrow. On the Precedence Constraint Editor:

- Select the Evaluation operation: Expression

- For the Expression property type the expression: @[User::FlagIsFileExist] == true

Click OK to save the settings. Figure 3-18 illustrates the Precedence Constraint Editor.

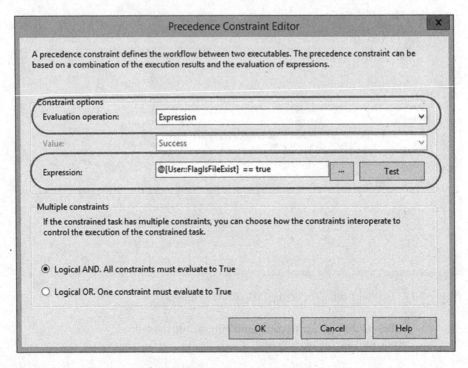

Figure 3-18. *Showing Precedence Constraint Editor settings*

3. Execute the SQL Task "Truncate Table." Open the Execute SQL Task Editor on the General menu:

- For the Connection property, add a new connection. Specify the destination server and database.

- Add the following code to the SQLStatement property:

```
IF NOT EXISTS (SELECT * FROM sys.objects
        WHERE object_id = OBJECT_ID(N'[dbo].[_XML]')
        AND type in (N'U'))
        CREATE TABLE _XML
        (
                ID int IDENTITY(1,1) PRIMARY KEY
                ,XMLFileName nvarchar(300)
                ,XML_LOAD XML, Created datetime
        )
ELSE
        TRUNCATE TABLE _XML
```

Click OK to complete the settings. Figure 3-19 illustrates the Execute SQL Task Editor.

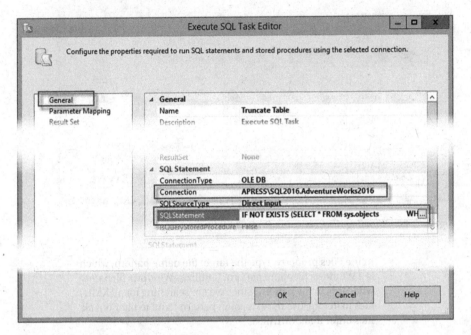

Figure 3-19. *Showing Execute SQL Task settings*

4. The "Load XML Content" Foreach Loop Container. Open the Foreach Loop Editor and click on the Collect menu:

    - Select an Expression then load the Expression Property Editor.

    - Select the Directory property and add the expression: @[User::SourceLocation].

    - Click OK to complete the settings. Figure 3-20 illustrates the Expression Property Editor. The expression value is reflected in the Folder property.

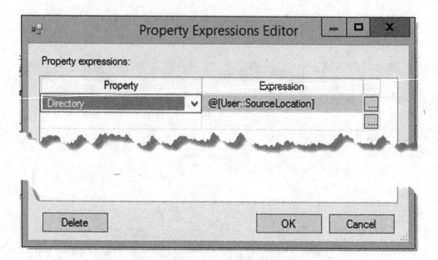

Figure 3-20. *Showing the Expression Property Editor*

- In the Files property, type the target file name pattern, which is a Windows filename pattern. It utilizes Windows filename wildcards in the pattern. Since we are searching for all XML files to iterate, use the extension pattern *.xml to filter out all files other than XML files.

- To Retrieve the file name property, select the Name and extension. Figure 3-21 illustrates the Collection menu.

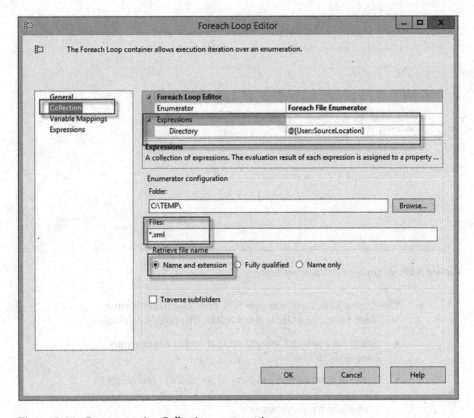

Figure 3-21. *Demonstrating Collection menu settings*

5. Click the Variable Mapping menu. Select the FileName
    variable from the drop-down list. Figure 3-22 illustrates the
    Variable Mapping menu. Click OK to complete the settings.

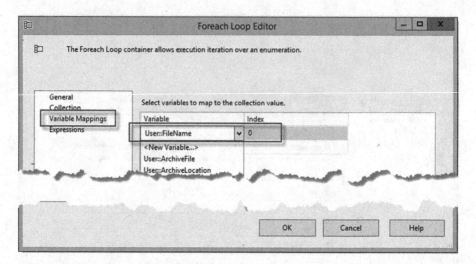

Figure 3-22. *Mapping FileName variable*

6. The "Insert XML Data" Execute SQL Task. Open the Execute SQL Task Editor. The General tab will be displayed by default.

- Select the existing Connection that was in the previous Execute SQL Task.

- In the SQLStatement property, type "*exec sp_executesql ?*". The question mark specifies that the task will have an input variable as a parameter.

Figure 3-23 illustrates the General menu.

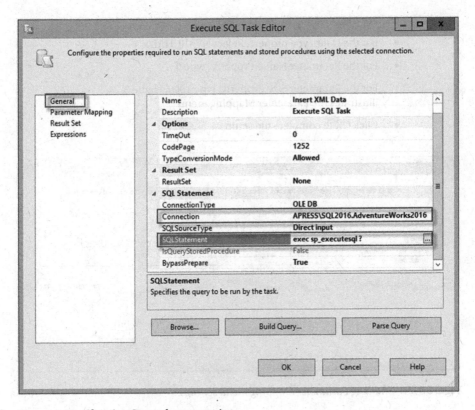

Figure 3-23. *Showing General menu settings*

Click on the Parameter Mapping menu.

- Select the *User::SQLScript* variable from the drop-down list. The *SQLScript* variable composes the INSERT T-SQL statement through an expression formula. When the Foreach Loop Container "Load XML Content" assigns the file name to the *FileName* variable, then the *SQLScript* expression formula constantly recomposes the new T-SQL code as it loops through all the files in the specified directory, as demonstrated in the following example:

```
INSERT INTO _XML
SELECT 'C:\TEMP\Categories.xml', X, GETDATE()
FROM OPENROWSET(BULK N'C:\TEMP\Categories.xml', SINGLE_BLOB)
as tempXML(X)
```

- For the Direction property select Input
- For the Data Type property select NVARCHAR
- For the Parameter Name Property, type 0
- For the Parameter Size Property, type 1000. Figure 3-24 illustrates the Parameter Mapping menu.
- Click OK to complete the settings.

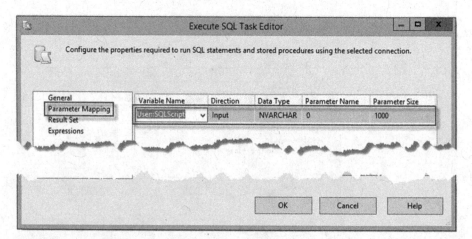

Figure 3-24. Showing Parameter Mapping menu settings

7. File System Task "Archive File": open the File System Task Editor. On General menu:

- Set the Operation property to "Rename file."
- IsSourcePathVariable property set to "True."
- For the SourceVariable property select the "*User::SourceFile*" variable.
- Set the IsDestinationPathVariable property to "True."
- For the DestinationVariable property select "*User::ArchiveFile*" variable.
- Set the OverwriteDestination property to "True."
- Click OK to complete the settings. Figure 3-25 illustrates the File System Task Editor.

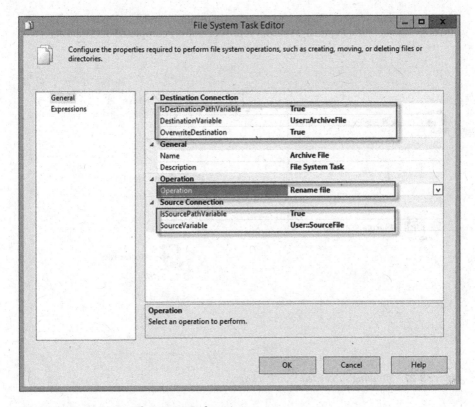

Figure 3-25. *Showing File System Task settings*

I recommend setting the File System Task property (located on the right side of SSIS IDE) DelayValidation to *True* in order to prevent an error in case the package loads and the default file name does not exist in the source location. Figure 3-26 illustrates the property.

Figure 3-26. *Showing settings for the property DelayValidation*

Congratulations, the SSIS package LoadXMLFromFile configuration is completed! Be sure to save your work. Figure 3-27 shows your successfully completed SSIS Package.

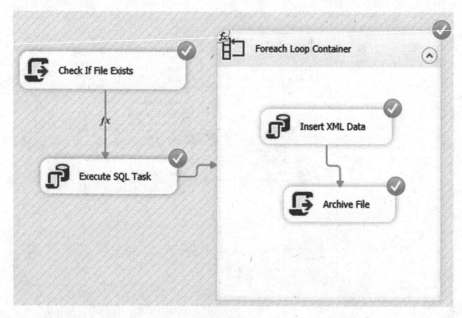

Figure 3-27. *Showing succeeded SSIS Package*

How It Works

The SSIS package starts the process by inspecting the files with an .xml extension in the source location indicated by the *SourceLocation* variable. The default value can be modified outside the package. The code is as follows:

```
Dts.Variables["User::FlagIsFileExist"].Value = (System.IO.Directory.
GetFiles(Dts.Variables["User::SourceLocation"].Value.ToString(), "*.xml").
Length != 0);
```
returns count of the files (if any). Comparison condition *!=0* returns boolean values; *true* - when count greater than 0 or *false* - when count equal 0. The result value assignes to *FlagIsFileExist* variable.

The expression *@[User::FlagIsFileExist] == true* in the Precedence Constraint conditionally inspects the *User::FlagIsFileExist* variable value. When the expression returns true then the package goes to the next task. When the expression returns a negative result (false), the package execution is terminated.

The "Truncate Table" Execute SQL Task removes the old value and prepares the table _XML for a new set of rows.

As the package progresses, the Foreach Loop Container is configured to inspect the source location and retrieve all available files with .xml extension. The Foreach Loop Container iterates the list of filenames and assigns each filename to the *User::FileName* variable on each iteration.

The expression formula for the variable *SQLScript* changes the INSERT T-SQL statement each time the *FileName* variable receives a new value. The "Insert XML Data" Execute SQL Task sends the INSERT T-SQL statement to the SQL Server instance.

The File System Task sends the processed files from the source location to the archive location.

An alternative to the File System Task is the Script Task, which is my personal preference for those DBAs who feel uncomfortable with the C# programing language used in the Script Task. Therefore, the File System Task is a set task, and there is no code involved with the configuration of the task. For those who prefer more control over the process of moving the files, I would suggest implementing the Script Task instead of the File System Task. To configure the Script task, please complete the following steps:

- Drag and drop the Script Task inside the Foreach Loop Container "Load XML Content."

- Double-click on the Script Task to open the Script Task Editor.

- For the ScriptLanguage property, select *Microsoft Visual C#*.

- For the ReadOnlyVariable property, add the variable *User::ArchiveFile* and *User::SourceFile* (highlight and copy the variable's name).

- Click the *Edit Script...* button.

- Go to Main() function and add following code:

```
string from = Dts.Variables["User::SourceFile"].Value.
ToString();
string to = Dts.Variables["User::ArchiveFile"].Value.
ToString();
System.IO.File.Move(from, to); // move a file
```

- Save and close the C# Visual Studio

- Click the OK button to complete the configuration.

As you can see from this example, with a little bit of minor coding, you now have full control over moving the files from the source location to the archive directory.

The SSIS package can be deployed through the SQL Server Agent job, which will run automatically on a customized schedule. The package can also be executed from the stored procedure. Listing 3-7 demonstrates how to execute the SSIS package from the stored procedure.

Listing 3-7. Showing the code to execute the SSIS package from a stored procedure

```
DECLARE @SourceLocation VARCHAR(200) = 'C:\\TEMP\\';
DECLARE @ArchiveLocation VARCHAR(200) = 'C:\\TEMP\\Archive\\';

SET @SQLQuery = 'DTEXEC /FILE ^"C:\SQL2016\Chapter3\CreateXMLFile\
CreateXMLFile\LoadXMLFromFile.dtsx^" '
SET @SQLQuery = @SQLQuery + ' /SET \Package.Variables[SourceLocation].
Value;^"'+ @SourceLocation + '^"
/SET \Package.Variables[ArchiveLocation].Value;^"'+ @ArchiveLocation + '^"';
EXEC master..xp_cmdshell @SQLQuery;
```

3-5. Implementing a CLR Solution
Problem

You want to create SQL Server objects to write and read XML files that that do not implement extended stored procedures and provide more secure functionalities.

Solution

The CLR (Common Language Runtime) functions could extend T-SQL functionality and operate the same way as a SQL Server user-defined object (user-defined functions, for this recipe solution). However, CRL objects require a dll (dynamic link library) file format (extension .dll) that is used for Windows program codes and procedures. For this recipe, the code demonstrates using Visual Studio C#. Listing 3-8 demonstrates the code for the C# file.

Listing 3-8. Creating WriteXMLFile and ReadXMLFile SQL Server CLR functions

```csharp
using System;
using System.Data;
using System.Data.SqlClient;
using System.Data.SqlTypes;
using Microsoft.SqlServer.Server;
using System.IO;

public partial class XMLFileETL
{
    [SqlFunction]
    public static SqlString WriteXMLFile(SqlString XMLContent,
        SqlString DirPath,
        SqlString FileName,
        SqlBoolean DateStamp)
    {
        /* Parameters:
         XMLContent: Contains XML document.
```

```
    DirPath: The directory path to write to.
    FileName: The file name.
    DateStamp: Determines add datetime stamp to the file or not.
    */

    try
    {
        string strXMLFile = "";
        // Check input parameters for NULL.
        if (!XMLContent.IsNull &&
            !DirPath.IsNull &&
            !FileName.IsNull)
        {
            // Build File Path string
            string strStamp = (DateStamp) ? "_" + DateTime.Now.To
            String("yyyyMMdd_HHmmss") : "";
            strXMLFile = DirPath.Value + "\\" + FileName.Value +
            strStamp + ".xml";

            // Initialize a new instance of the StreamWriter class
            using (var newFile = new StreamWriter(strXMLFile.Value))
            {
                // Write the file.
                newFile.WriteLine(XMLContent);
            }
            // Return the file path on success.
            return strXMLFile;
        }
        else
            // Return warning when any of input value is NULL.
            return "Input parameters with NULL detected";
    }
    catch (Exception ex)
    {
        // Return null on error.
        return ex.Message.ToString();
    }
}
[SqlFunction]
public static SqlString ReadXMLFile(SqlString FilePath)
{
    // Parameters:
    // FilePath: The file path to the XML file.
    try
    {
        // Declare local variable
        string fileContent = "";
```

```
            // Check paremeter for null.
            if (!FilePath.IsNull)
            {
                // Initialize a new instance of the StreamReader class for
                the specified path.
                var fileStream = new FileStream(FilePath.Value, FileMode.
                Open, FileAccess.Read);
                using (var streamReader = new StreamReader(fileStream))
                {
                    fileContent = streamReader.ReadToEnd();
                }
            }
            // Return XML document
            return fileContent;
        }
        catch (Exception ex)
        {
            // Send exception message on error.
            return ex.Message.ToString();
        }
    }
};
```

To register the C# code file:

- Create folder "Chapter3."

- Save the XML_ETL.cs file (the file available in the book code samples) the in "Chapter3" folder.

- Open Windows Command Line (cmd.exe) and then run the command line that is shown in Listing 3-9. The cmd.exe output is shown in Figure 3-28.

Listing 3-9. Eemonstrating the Command Line to register the dll.

```
C:\Windows\Microsoft.NET\Framework\v3.5\csc.exe /target:library /out:C:\
Chapter3\ReadWriteXML.dll C:\Chapter3\XML_ETL.cs
```

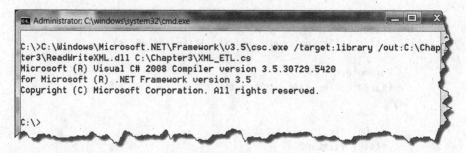

Figure 3-28. Showing the command-line result

Listing 3-10 demonstrates the T-SQL solution to configure the server and database. Created scalar functions are shown in Figure 3-29.

Listing 3-10. Creating CLR functions

```
-- Enable CLR
USE master
GO
        sp_configure 'clr enabled', 1;
GO
RECONFIGURE
GO
-- Configure
USE AdventureWorks
GO

ALTER DATABASE AdventureWorks SET TRUSTWORTHY ON;

GO
-- Create Assembly
CREATE ASSEMBLY ReadWriteXML
        FROM 'C:\Chapter3\ReadWriteXML.dll'
WITH PERMISSION_SET = EXTERNAL_ACCESS;
GO

-- Create functions
CREATE FUNCTION dbo.WriteXMLFile(
        @Content nvarchar(MAX),
        @DirPath nvarchar(500),
        @FileName nvarchar(100),
        @DateStamp bit)
RETURNS nvarchar(MAX) WITH EXECUTE AS CALLER
AS
EXTERNAL NAME ReadWriteXML.XMLFileETL.WriteXMLFile;
GO

CREATE FUNCTION dbo.ReadXMLFile(@FilePath nvarchar(500))
RETURNS nvarchar(MAX) WITH EXECUTE AS CALLER
AS
EXTERNAL NAME ReadWriteXML.XMLFileETL.ReadXMLFile;
GO
```

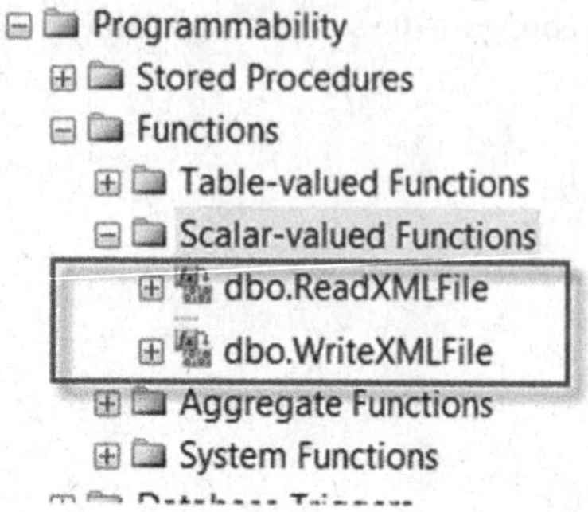

☐ 🗀 Programmability
  ⊞ 🗀 Stored Procedures
  ☐ 🗀 Functions
    ⊞ 🗀 Table-valued Functions
    ☐ 🗀 Scalar-valued Functions
      ⊞ 🔧 dbo.ReadXMLFile
      ⊞ 🔧 dbo.WriteXMLFile
    ⊞ 🗀 Aggregate Functions
    ⊞ 🗀 System Functions
  ⊞ 🗀 Database Triggers

Figure 3-29. Showing created CLR functions

How It Works

The CLR project combines reading and writing XML files. It is more practical to have several C# functions in one class rather creating one class per function. Therefore, both read and write functionality is wrapped into one C# class object. To create a C# file, MS Visual Studio C# or VB is the tool to use. Covering how to create Visual Studio project is beyond the scope of this this book. There are many resources available that explain how to create CRL projects in great detail.

The top part of the C# code lists namespaces or libraries that are necessary to recognize code functions and methods. The *using* method adds a namespace to a class. When a new project starts, a class lists default namespaces. The System.IO namespace that contains reading and writing as part of the file's functionality is not part of the default list. Therefore, you must add the System.IO namespace manually. A CLR class must have a *partial* type. The procedure attribute specifies a SQL Server target object. For example: a user-defined function is the *[SQLFunction]* attribute, a stored procedure is *[SQLProcedure]*, etc. A CLR procedure type must be *public static*.

The WriteXMLFile function returns a created file full path on success and an error message on failure or when a NULL parameter value is detected.

The function has four input parameters:

- XMLContent – required, data type SQLString, Contains XML document.

- DirPath – required, data type SQLString, the directory path to write to.

- FileName – required, data type SQLString, the file name.

- DateStamp – required, data type SQLBoolean, determines whether to add a datetime stamp to the file or not.

After validating the input parameters, the next step is to build up a file path. First, the parameter *DateStamp* needs to check whether a datetime stamp will be part of the file name, then concatenate the parameters and the variable:

```
string strStamp = (DateStamp) ? "_"
                + DateTime.Now.ToString("yyyyMMdd_HHmmss") : "";
  strXMLFile = DirPath.Value + "\\" + FileName.Value + strStamp + ".xml";
```

As a final point – write an XML file with the provided path:

```
using (var newFile = new StreamWriter(strXMLFile.Value))
{
        newFile.WriteLine(XMLContent);
}
```

The ReadXMLFile function returns XML file content on success and an error message on failure. The function has one parameter:

- FilePath - required, data type SQLString, the file path to the XML file.

When the FileStream function establishes a connection to the XML file, then the StreamReader function reads the entire file and the ReadXMLFile function returns the XML document:

```
var fileStream = new FileStream(FilePath.Value, FileMode.Open,
FileAccess.Read);
using (var streamReader = new StreamReader(fileStream))
{
fileContent = streamReader.ReadToEnd();
}
return fileContent;
```

If you develop a CRL procedure with Visual Studio, then you could build the solution to create a dll file or run a Command Line to build and register a dll file:

```
C:\Windows\Microsoft.NET\Framework\v3.5\csc.exe /target:library /out:C:\
Chapter3\ReadWriteXML.dll C:\Chapter3\XML_ETL.cs
```

When the dll file is ready then we are moving to the SSMS to:

1. Make sure that the 'clr enabled' option is enabled:

   ```
   sp_configure 'clr enabled', 1
   ```

2. Swith to user database and SET TRUSTWORTHY ON.

3. Create an assembly that sets the reference to dll:

```
CREATE ASSEMBLY ReadWriteXML FROM
'C:\Chapter3\ReadWriteXML.dll'
WITH PERMISSION_SET = EXTERNAL_ACCESS
```

For the assembly, after the name and dll file path are specified, you need to set the PERMISSION_SET argument that has three options:

- SAFE – preferred, used when a dll cannot access external system resources, for example, the registry, files, environment variables, or the network.

- EXTERNAL_ACCESS – the dll can access to the registry, files, and environment variables. However, these cannot be accessed outside an instance of SQL Server.

- UNSAFE – unrestricted access.

The ReadWriteXML.dll accesses to files; therefore, the EXTERNAL_ACCESS option is set to the PERMISSION_SET for the assembly of ReadWriteXML. Once the ASSEMBLY is created, the functions can now be created. For example:

```
CREATE FUNCTION dbo.ReadXMLFile(@FilePath nvarchar(500))
RETURNS nvarchar(MAX) WITH EXECUTE AS CALLER
AS
EXTERNAL NAME ReadWriteXML.XMLFileETL.ReadXMLFile
```

In the *CREATE FUNCTION* section after the schema and name, you need to list all of the parameters to match to the function in the C# dll. Make sure that the positions and the data types are the same. The *RETURNS* section must match the data type as well. The EXTERNAL NAME has three references, for example:

```
EXTERNAL NAME ReadWriteXML.XMLFileETL.ReadXMLFile
```

1. The ASSEMBLY name

2. CLR class name

3. CLR function name

Listing 3-11 demonstrates the execution of T_SQL for the WriteXMLFile functions. The result is shown in Figure 3-30.

Listing 3-11. Executing the WriteXMLFile functions

```
SELECT  dbo.WriteXMLFile(N'<Category>
  <CategoryName>Accessories</CategoryName>
  <Subcategory>
    <SubcategoryName>Bike Racks</SubcategoryName>
    <Product>
      <Name>Hitch Rack - 4-Bike</Name>
```

```
        <Number>RA-H123</Number>
        <Price>120.0000</Price>
      </Product>
    </Subcategory>
    <Subcategory>
      <SubcategoryName>Bike Stands</SubcategoryName>
      <Product>
        <Name>All-Purpose Bike Stand</Name>
        <Number>ST-1401</Number>
        <Price>159.0000</Price>
      </Product>
    </Subcategory>
  </Category>', 'C:\Chapter3', 'CategoriesXML', 0) NewFilePath
```

NewFilePath
C:\Chapter3\CategoriesXML.xml

Figure 3-30. *Showing the function result*

Listing 3-12 demonstrates the execution of T_SQL for the ReadXMLFile functions. The result is shown in Figure 3-31.

Listing 3-12. Executing the ReadXMLFile functions

```
SELECT cast(dbo.ReadXMLFile('C:\Chapter3\CategoriesXML.xml') as xml) XMLFile
```

Figure 3-31. *Showing the function result*

The CRL procedures provide a secure way to extend SQL Server functionality. However, programming skills are preferred when dealing with CLR procedures.

Summary

This chapter demonstrates a variety of solutions detailing how to write the XML result into a file, and how to load the XML file (or files) from the source location. Please be aware that this is not the only solution, since in today's world, such tasks could be completed using other technologies, such as PowerShell, .NET applications (either C# or VB.NET), among others. However, these are excellent solutions to compiling SSIS packaged using SQL Server the T-SQL code.

In the next chapter the recipes will cover how to convert an XML document into rows and columns, also known as "XML Shredding."

CHAPTER 4

■ ■ ■

Shredding XML

Converting XML data into relational columns and rows is not an easy process. The OPEXML function was introduced to shred XML data in SQL Server 2000, and then XML shredding was improved by the XPath language (also known as XQuery) in SQL Server 2005. Since then, the process of querying XML data became a solid solution to deliver results. This chapter will demonstrate how to query XML data as a single unit and return the retrieved data across a table's column.

4-1. Shredding XML with Internal ENTITY Declarations

Problem

You want to return a rowset result out of the XML data that is passing to a stored procedure as a parameter or retrieved out of the table as the single XML value.

Solution

The OPEXML function provides a comprehensive solution to query XML data assigned to VARCHAR, NVARCHAR, and XML data typed variable and parameters. The T-SQL code in Listing 4-1 demonstrates the solution. A sample set of data can be found in the AdventureWorks database.

Listing 4-1. Shredding the XML with the OPENXML function

```
DECLARE @xml nvarchar(max),
        @idoc int,
        @ns varchar(200) =
N'<root xmlns:df="http://schemas.microsoft.com/sqlserver/2004/07/
adventure-works/ProductModelManuInstructions" />';

SELECT @xml = cast(Instructions as nvarchar(max))
FROM [Production].[ProductModel]
WHERE ProductModelID = 7;
```

```
EXECUTE sp_xml:preparedocument @idoc OUTPUT, @xml, @ns;

SELECT StepInstruction,
       LaborStation,
       LaborHours,
       LotSize,
       MachineHours,
       SetupHours,
       Material,
       Tool
FROM OPENXML(@idoc, 'df:root/df:Location/df:step', 2)
WITH (
              LaborStation INT '../@LocationID',
              LaborHours REAL '../@LaborHours',
              LotSize INT '../@LotSize ',
              MachineHours REAL '../@MachineHours ',
              SetupHours REAL '../@SetupHours ',
              Material VARCHAR(100) 'df:material',
              Tool VARCHAR(100) 'df:tool',
              StepInstruction VARCHAR(2000) '.'
       );

EXECUTE sp_xml:removedocument @idoc;
```

The query output is shown in Figure 4-1.

Step Instruction	LaborStati...	LaborHo...	LotSi...	MachineHo...	SetupHours	Material	Tool
Insert aluminum sheet MS-2341 into the T-85A fr...	10	2.5	100	3	0.5	aluminum sheet M...	T-85A framing tool
Attach Trim Jig TJ-26 to the upper and lower rig...	10	2.5	100	3	0.5	NULL	Trim Jig TJ-26
Using a router with a carbide tip 15, route the al...	10	2.5	100	3	0.5	NULL	router with a carbide t...
Insert the frame into Forming Tool FT-15 and pre...	10	2.5	100	3	0.5	NULL	Forming Tool FT-15
When finished, inspect the forms for defects per ...	10	2.5	100	3	0.5	NULL	NULL
Remove the frames from the tool and place the...	10	2.5	100	3	0.5	NULL	NULL
Assemble all frame components following blueprint...	20	1.75			0.15	NULL	NULL
Add W... ...l ...	50						
Inspect Front Derailleur.	50	3	1	NULL	0.25	NULL	NULL
Inspect Rear Derailleur.	50	3	1	NULL	0.25	NULL	NULL
Perform final inspection per engineering specific...	60	4	1	NULL	NULL	NULL	NULL
Complete all required certification forms.	60	4	1	NULL	NULL	NULL	NULL
Move to shipping.	60	4	1	NULL	NULL	NULL	NULL

Figure 4-1. Showing the process output

How It Works

Before we shred the XML, the first step is to determine the XML structure and which elements and attributes will be a part of the result set. This can be done on the AdventureWorks database executing SQL to analyze the XML data as shown in Listing 4-2.

Listing 4-2. Query to retrieve sample XML instructions for one product model

```
SELECT Instructions
FROM Production.ProductModel
WHERE ProductModelID = 7;
```

The XML result is too large to display in a book page. For this reason, the XML snippet in Listing 4-3 has been formatted for demonstration purposes.

Listing 4-3. XML Snippet demonstrating the result data

```
<root xmlns="http://schemas.microsoft.com/sqlserver/2004/07/adventure-works/
ProductModelManuInstructions">
                Adventure Works CyclesFR-210B Instructions....
    <Location LaborHours="2.5"
        LotSize="100" MachineHours="3" SetupHours="0.5" LocationID="10">
            Work Center 10 - Frame Forming...
            <step>Insert
                    <material>aluminum sheet MS-2341</material> into the
                    <tool>T-85A framing tool</tool>.
            </step>
...
    </Location>
</root>
```

The <root> element has a namespace that must be part of the XML initialization of the OPENXML function. Therefore, several variables were declared. The purpose for these variables is the following:

1. *@xml* XML – Retrieve the XML data as a single unit from the table.

2. *@idoc* INT – Store the returned document handle from the *sp_xml:preparedocument* system stored procedure to allow OPENXML to access the XML data.

3. *@ns* VARCHAR(200) – Store the XML namespace to supply to the *sp_xml:preparedocument* system stored procedure, and the parameter *xpath_namespaces* to specify the namespace declaration.

■ **Note**   When XML has a namespace, the namespace cannot be avoided. The OPENXML function will not return the result set when the namespace is not declared and specified in the *sp_xml:preparedocument* system stored procedure. The namespaces help to avoid name conflict and uniquely identify the elements and attributes in the XML data.

The value assigned to the @ns variable needs more clarification. In Listing 4-1, the namespace declaration in the <root> element is a little different from the one assigned to the @ns variable. The root element namespace looks like Listing 4-4.

Listing 4-4. Namespace declaration in the <root> element

```
<root xmlns="http://schemas.microsoft.com/sqlserver/2004/07/adventure-works/
ProductModelManuInstructions">
```

The @ns variable namespace declaration in the sample code looks slightly different, as shown in Listing 4-5.

Listing 4-5. @ns variable namespace declaration

```
<root xmlns:df="http://schemas.microsoft.com/sqlserver/2004/07/adventure-
works/ProductModelManuInstructions" />
```

The value of the variable @ns has an extra part *xmlns:df=...*, where the *df* (short for "default") can specify any alias. The most commonly used alias is *ns*. The namespace is used as a reference to the elements of the OPENXML function. In simple terms, it's the same reference as if the ProductModel table were referenced without the schema "Production." We must use Production.ProductModel to provide a reference to the table; otherwise SSMS will throw an error: "object not found." The main difference is that the XML parser will not raise an error and will simply ignore the elements and the element's attributes. Therefore, no results will be returned.

The code in Listing 4-6 builds on Listing 4-2 by assigning the result to an XML variable:

Listing 4-6. Assigning XML sample data to an XML variable

```
SELECT @xml = Instructions
FROM Production.ProductModel
WHERE ProductModelID = 7;
```

The system stored procedure *sp_xml:preparedocument* uses the MSXML parser (Msxmlsql.dll) to parse the XML data, and returns a numeric (INT data type) value that provides a pointer (variable *@doc*) to access the XML.

The stored procedure sp_xml:preparedocument has three parameters:

1. @hdoc INT OUTPUT – required, integer data type.

2. @xmltext NTEXT – required, can be any texual data type (VARCHAR, NVARCHAR, XML, TEXT, or NTEXT). The data type used must be implicitly convertible to the legacy NTEXT data type; so VARBINARY is not allowed.

3. @xpath_namespaces NTEXT – optional, can be any texual data type (VARCHAR, NVARCHAR, XML, TEXT, NTEXT, or XML). Note the type conversion restrictions on this parameter are the same as for the @xmltext parameter.

When the XML document is loaded into the memory after the stored procedure sp_xml:preparedocument is executed and retuned, the XML document handler (memory pointer) returns the value by outputting value into an @doc variable, as demonstrated in Listing 4-7.

Listing 4-7. Calling the sp_xml:preparedocument procedure

```
EXECUTE sp_xml:preparedocument @doc OUTPUT, @xml, @ns;
```

Now the process is ready to convert the XML document into a relational result set. The query that returns the result set has three parts:

- *SELECT* clause – delivers the result to the user.

- *OPENXML* function – provides access to the XML document and sets the XPath to the startup element.

- *WITH* construct – defines the table that describes each element and attribute that form the XML data.

The XML shredding process starts with the *OPENXML* function. The *OPENXML* function has three input parameters:

1. *@idoc* INT – [required] is an internal representation of an XML document that is created by executing the sp_xml:preparedocument stored procedure.

2. *@rowpattern* NVARCHAR – [required] is the XPath pattern that identifies the startup element

3. *@flags* BYTE – [optional] indicates the mapping for the XML document. The flag values are listed in Table 4-1.

Table 4-1. *Listing values for the @flags parameter*

Flag	Description
0	Defaults to attribute-centric mapping.
1	Specifies attribute-centric mapping of the data.
2	Specifies element-centric mapping of the data.
8	Can be combined with flag 1 or flag 2, with the bitwise OR operator. This flag indicates that the consumed data should not be copied to the overflow property @mp:xmltext.

The OPENXML function is part of the FROM clause because the XML data is the data source. Listing 4-1 demonstrated the OPENXML function set with the values in the FROM clause: FROM OPENXML(@idoc, 'df:root/df:Location/df:step', 2).

The first parameter is straightforward output from the stored procedure sp_ xml:preparedocument, where we provide the function with output that is stored in the variable. The XPath pattern is not intuitive, and requires detailed XML structure analysis. Let's remove the data from the XML that is shown in Sample 4-1, to isolate and analyze the structure, as shown in Listing 4-8.

Listing 4-8. Showing snippet of bare XML structure

```
<root>
        <Location>
                <step>
                        <material></material>
                        <tool></tool>
                </step>
                <step>
                        <material></material>
                        <tool></tool>
                </step>
...
        </Location>
...
</root>
```

The rule that I am using to properly define XPath and shred the XML is this:

- When the same child element is listed more than once, the XPath pattern must point to that element.

- The hierarchy for the <step> element is: root/Location/step.

- This analysis is very important to specify an efficient XPath for the OPENXML function. The query from Listing 4-1 returns the result where the LaborStation attribute (property of the Location element) with value "10" has 6 steps in this particular example, however the number of steps can vary. The element hierarchy from Listing 4-8 is *root/Location/step/*, so both <material> and <tool> are the child step elements, and they each contain a single text node. Therefore, XPath *root/Location/step* will satisfy the @rowpattern parameter for an OPENXML function. Later, we will provide a precise path for each element and attribute data cell in the WITH construct.

For the optional parameter @flags we have provided a value of 2, because the XPath final point <step> is an element, and the <Location> element has several attributes that will be part of the result set. This combination of element-centric and attribute-centric properties is the best scenario for @flags = 2.

The WITH construct provides the specification for the resulting output. The XML is hierarchical data, so in order to retrieve a specific element and attribute, we need to provide a precise source data location. In most cases the source data is located outside of the location that is specified for the *@rowpattern* parameter.

The hierarchical structure of XML data can be compared to the Windows folder/file structure. Imagine navigating the folder structure. In simple terms, if you need to copy several files from different folders into a new folder, then you are navigating from one folder to another to collect all needed files. Therefore, the WITH construct builds the table that will return the collected data from elements and attributes. Unlike the tables, the WITH construct has a column name, datatype, and the XML item location path. The WITH construct from Listing 4-1, reproduced in Listing 4-9, defines the shape.

Listing 4-9. WITH clause defining XML structure

```
WITH (
        LaborStation INT '../@LocationID',
        LaborHours REAL '../@LaborHours',
        LotSize INT '../@LotSize ',
        MachineHours REAL '../@MachineHours ',
        SetupHours REAL '../@SetupHours ',
        Material VARCHAR(100) 'df:material',
        Tool VARCHAR(100) 'df:tool',
        StepInstruction VARCHAR(2000) '.'
)
```

The LocationID, LaborHours, LotSize, and MachineHours are attributes of the <Location> element (see Listing 4-3), which is the parent of the <step> element. To retrieve the data from these attributes, we need to move one level up from the <step> element, because the OPENXML function is set to the <step> element, which is one step below. In order to have XML read the proper step and account for it reading one step below, you must move one step above. The "LaborStation" is an alias for the LocationID attribute, and the data type is INT because LocationID is a whole number. The path structure for '../@LocationID' value means:

- "../" - move one level up from current location.

- "@" - specifies that this is an attribute.

- LocationID – is the original attribute name.

The same mechanism applies to other LaborHours, LotSize, and MachineHours attributes.

The <material> and <tool> elements are both children of the <step> element. Therefore, we need to move down to access the elements' data, for example:

- Material - element alias.

- VARCHAR(100) - presented data type.

- 'df:material' – df: namespace reference, and material is the element name.

The last column is StepInstruction, where the data type is VARCHAR(2000), and '.' means that the current context node is the final element from the XPath *rowpattern* parameter.

The SELECT clause returns the following columns, which are aliased in the WITH construct:

- StepInstruction – alias for the <step> element.

- LaborStation – alias for the LocationID attribute.

- LaborHours – alias for the LaborHours attribute.

- LotSize – alias for the LotSize attribute.

- MachineHours – alias for the MachineHours attribute.

- SetupHours – alias for the SetupHours attribute.

- Material – alias for the <material> element.

- Tool – alias for the <tool> element.

Finally, we need to deallocate the XML document from the memory. The stored procedure sp_xml:removedocument removes the XML document when we set the XML handler to the required parameter:

```
EXECUTE sp_xml:removedocument @idoc;
```

■ **Caution**   SQL Server does not provide garbage collection for XML documents processed by the sp_xml:*preparedocument* stored procedure. The XML document is stored in the internal cache of SQL Server, and the MSXML parser uses one-eighth of the total memory available for SQL Server. Therefore, memory deallocation must be set explicitly by the *sp_xml:removedocument* stored procedure. Otherwise, the server will have a memory leak problem and will periodically restart the procedure, which requires server memory.

4-2. Migrating OPENXML into XQuery
Problem

You need to find an alternative to OPENXML function to shred the XML documents.

Solution

SQL Server 2005 introduced the XML data type and XQuery language support via five XML data type methods: *nodes(), value(), query(),exist(), and modify()*. These methods allow comprehensive manipulation of XML data. For the XML data type, the legacy stored procedures *sp_xml:preparedocument* and *sp_xml:removedocument* are obsolete (see Solution 4-1 for details), and are unused. Listing 4-10 shows how to migrate the OPENXML() function process to XQuery code using the *nodes()* and *value()* methods.

Listing 4-10. Migrating OPENXML into XQuery

```
DECLARE @xml XML;

SELECT @xml = Instructions
FROM [Production].[ProductModel]
WHERE ProductModelID = 7;

WITH XMLNAMESPACES('http://schemas.microsoft.com/sqlserver/2004/07/
adventure-works/ProductModelManuInstructions' as df)
SELECT RTRIM(LTRIM(REPLACE(instruct.value('.', 'VARCHAR(2000)'), CHAR(10),
''))) AS StepInstruction,
        instruct.value('../@LocationID', 'INT') AS LaborStation,
        instruct.value('../@LaborHours', 'REAL') AS LaborHours,
        instruct.value('../@LotSize', 'INT') AS LotSize,
        instruct.value('../@MachineHours', 'REAL') AS MachineHours,
        instruct.value('../@SetupHours', 'REAL') AS SetupHours,
        instruct.value('df:material[1]', 'VARCHAR(100) ') AS Material,
        instruct.value('df:tool[1]', 'VARCHAR(100) ') AS Tool
FROM @xml.nodes('df:root/df:Location/df:step') prod(instruct);
```

> ■ **Caution** All XQuery methods are case sensitive; therefore, to avoid an error, the methods *nodes()*, *value()*, *query()*, *exist()*, and *modify()* must be used in lowercase only.

How It Works

The OPENXML function was introduced in SQL Server 2000 where the XML data type was nonexistent at the time. Therefore, each XML document needed to be converted from data types such as VARCHAR, NVARCHAR, BINARY, IMAGE, TEXT, and NTEXT, into an internal format that could be manipulated by MSXML. This was accomplished with the sp_xml:preparedocument stored procedure.

Since SQL Server 2005, when the XML data type was implemented, the XML shredding and the building process were dramatically simplified. The XQuery language works with the XML data type directly. Therefore, extra steps to prepare XML data are no longer necessary when the shredding process is based on the XML data type, or the XML data can be explicitly converted to the XML data type using the CAST() and CONVERT() functions.

The difference between the CONVERT and CAST functions is that the CONVERT function is not part of an ANSI-SQL specification, whereas CAST is. However, most importantly, CONVERT has a third optional parameter that provides additional functionality to the conversion process, such a controlling whitespace handling or applying an inline Document Type Definition (DTD). The following is a description of XML Style Parameter Values for the CONVERT function:

- 0 – (default) Discard insignificant whitespace in the XML and does not allow the use of an internal DTD.

- 1 - Preserve insignificant whitespace in the XML. However, does not allow the use of an internal DTD.

- 2 - Discards insignificant whitespace and enable limited internal DTD

- 3 - Preserve insignificant whitespace and enable limited internal DTD.

Listing 4-2 demonstrates the solution to migrate the OPENXML function into the XQuery language. The first line declares the XML variable, as shown in Listing 4-11.

Listing 4-11. Declaring an XML variable

```
DECLARE @xml XML;
```

Next, we assign the XML data value to the variable, as shown in Listing 4-12.

Listing 4-12. Populating the XML variable

```
SELECT @xml = Instructions
FROM Production.ProductModel
WHERE ProductModelID = 7;
```

To shred an XML document that has an xml namespace (as in Listing 4-2), we need to declare the instance of the XML namespace. The SQL Server WITH XMLNAMESPACES clause allows us to list and instantiate the XML namespaces. The declaration syntax for the WITH XMLNAMESPACES clause combines the WITH and XMLNAMESPACES keywords. Always make sure that a semicolon (;) precedes the WITH construct when writing this T-SQL code.

■ **Tip** It's a good practice to have all SQL statements terminated with a semicolon (;). The WITH XMLNAMESPACES clause, like the WITH CTE clause, must always be separated from preceding statements by a semicolon. Otherwise, SQL Server will throw an error.

To match the legacy syntax from Listing 4-1, this example creates the same xml namespace name, with "*df*", as shown in Listing 4-13.

Listing 4-13. Declaring the XML namespace with prefix "df"

```
WITH XMLNAMESPACES('http://schemas.microsoft.com/sqlserver/2004/07/
adventure-works/ProductModelManuInstructions' as df)
```

However, when the XML document has only a single XML namespace, the namespace can be declared as DEFAULT with no explicit namespace prefix requirements for the XML namespace. Listing 4-14 demonstrates shredding of the XML document with the default xml namespace.

Listing 4-14. Shredding the XML document with DEFAULT xml namespace and again with "df" prefix

```
WITH XMLNAMESPACES(DEFAULT 'http://schemas.microsoft.com/sqlserver/2004/
07/adventure-works/ProductModelManuInstructions')
SELECT RTRIM(LTRIM(REPLACE(instruct.value('.', 'varchar(2000)'),
CHAR(10), ''))) AS StepInstruction
        instruct.value('../@LocationID', 'int') AS LaborStation,
        instruct.value('../@LaborHours', 'real') AS LaborHours,
        instruct.value('../@LotSize', 'int') AS LotSize,
        instruct.value('../@MachineHours', 'real') AS MachineHours,
        instruct.value('../@SetupHours', 'real') AS SetupHours,
        instruct.value('material[1]', 'varchar(100) ') AS Material,
        instruct.value('tool[1]', 'varchar(100) ') AS Tool
FROM @xml.nodes('root/Location/step') prod(instruct);

WITH XMLNAMESPACES('http://schemas.microsoft.com/sqlserver/2004/07/
adventure-works/ProductModelManuInstructions' as df)
SELECT RTRIM(LTRIM(REPLACE(instruct.value('.', 'varchar(2000)'), CHAR(10),
''))) AS StepInstruction,
        instruct.value('../@LocationID', 'int') AS LaborStation,
        instruct.value('../@LaborHours', 'real') AS LaborHours,
        instruct.value('../@LotSize', 'int') AS LotSize,
        instruct.value('../@MachineHours', 'real') AS MachineHours,
        instruct.value('../@SetupHours', 'real') AS SetupHours,
        instruct.value('df:material[1]', 'varchar(100) ') AS Material,
        instruct.value('df:tool[1]', 'varchar(100) ') AS Tool
FROM @xml.nodes('df:root/df:Location/df:step') prod(instruct);
```

To return the table structured result set from the XML document, we need to provide an element path and then denote the element and attribute values. The nodes() method is similar to the OPENXML function for providing the element reference; however the differences are the following:

Set access to XML document from the variable using OPENXML

```
FROM OPENXML(@doc, 'df:root/df:Location/df:step', 2)
```

Compare to set access to the XML variable using nodes() method

```
FROM @xml.nodes('df:root/df:Location/df:step') prod(instruct)
```

1. The main differences between the XML data type nodes() method and the OPENXML function that XQuery is expecting the XML data type; therefore, the XML handler (@doc variable) is not needed.

2. The mapping @flags parameter is not used by the *nodes()* method.

111

The element location path is the same for both the OPENXML function and *nodes* methods. It is important to note that the *nodes()* method requires a fully qualified alias, such as *table(column)*. In Listing 4-14 the alias is *prod(instruct)*. Within my personal SQL scripts, I use the T(C) alias, which is short and simple, but in a production environment I would recommend being more specific than T(C).

To construct XML output the OPENXML function must use the WITH() construct while, when using XQuery, the *value()* method denotes the element and attribute values and the WITH() construct is not used. The major difference between the WITH() construct and the *value()* method is that the WITH() construct syntax sequence is *ALIAS + DATATYPE + ITEM*, while the value() method all is the reverse: *ITEM + DATATYPE + ALIAS*; for example:

```
Part of OPENXML out put specification
WITH (
                LaborStation INT '../@LocationID',
                LaborHours REAL '../@LaborHours',
                LotSize INT '../@LotSize ',
                MachineHours REAL '../@MachineHours ',
                SetupHours REAL '../@SetupHours ',
                Material VARCHAR(100) 'df:material',
                Tool VARCHAR(100) 'df:tool',
                StepInstruction VARCHAR(2000) '.'
        )
Compare to XQuery out put specificationSELECT  instruct.value('.',
'varchar(2000)') AS StepInstruction,
        instruct.value('../@LocationID', 'int') AS LaborStation,
        instruct.value('../@LaborHours', 'real') AS LaborHours,
        instruct.value('../@LotSize', 'int') AS LotSize,
        instruct.value('../@MachineHours', 'real') AS MachineHours,
        instruct.value('../@SetupHours', 'real') AS SetupHours,
        instruct.value('df:material[1]', 'varchar(100) ') AS Material,
        instruct.value('df:tool[1]', 'varchar(100) ') AS Tool
```

The value() method has two parameters:

1. The XPath path indicating the element or attribute.

2. The target data type from conversion.

Both parameters are NVARCHAR; therefore, the values must be surrounded by single quotes, and value() method must be based on the column alias that is specified in the nodes() method. If references are not specified, the error *"Msg 195, Level 15, State 10, Line # 'value' is not a recognized built-in function name"* will be thrown.

Another important difference between the OPENXML() WITH clause and the *value()* method is that the value() method requires a singleton atomic value, indicated by a one-based index reference ("[1]") for element references. For example:

```
instruct.value('df:material[1]', VARCHAR(100)') AS Material
```

The singleton atomic value indicated has a one-based array index (most modern programming languages implement a zero-based array index). That provides the ability for the XML data to list the same element name multiple times. For example, the XML has the element *Address* listed several times:

```
<Address>Line 1</Address>
<Address>Line 2</Address>
<Address>Line 3</Address>
```

In this case, in order to display all three Address lines, the *value()* method code would look like the following:

```
c.value('Address[1]', 'VARCHAR(100)') AS Line1
c.value('Address[2]', 'VARCHAR(100)') AS Line2
c.value('Address[3]', 'VARCHAR(100)') AS Line3
```

When the singleton is missing then the compiler will throw the error: "*Msg 2389, Level 16, State 1, Line # XQuery [value()]: 'value()' requires a singleton (or empty sequence).*" Therefore, make sure the singleton atomic value always provides for an element when using the *value()* method.

4-3. Shredding XML from a Column
Problem

Shredding the XML documents that is shown in previous recipes (4-1 and 4-2) is a cursor process required to navigate from one XML value to another. You need to shred the XML across the table's column without opening the cursor.

Solution

Recipes 4-1 and 4-2 are based on shredding the XML content of a single XML variable one at a time. However, in many situations we need to shred the XML across an entire table or at least multiple rows, as demonstrated in Listing 4-15.

Listing 4-15. Showing the XML from table Sales.Store column Demographics

```
<StoreSurvey xmlns="http://schemas.microsoft.com/sqlserver/2004/07/
adventure-works/StoreSurvey">
  <AnnualSales>800000</AnnualSales>
  <AnnualRevenue>80000</AnnualRevenue>
  <BankName>United Security</BankName>
  <BusinessType>BM</BusinessType>
  <YearOpened>1996</YearOpened>
  <Specialty>Mountain</Specialty>
  <SquareFeet>21000</SquareFeet>
```

```
<Brands>2</Brands>
<Internet>ISDN</Internet>
<NumberEmployees>13</NumberEmployees>
</StoreSurvey>
```

The XML data type allows you to shred the XML data from not only an XML variable, but also directly from an XML type column in a table. Listing 4-16 demonstrates how to query the XML column.

Listing 4-16. Showing the XQuery code to return the result set from the XML column

```
WITH XMLNAMESPACES(default 'http://schemas.microsoft.com/sqlserver/2004/07/
adventure-works/StoreSurvey')
SELECT details.value('AnnualSales[1]', 'MONEY') AS AnnualSales,
        details.value('AnnualRevenue[1]', 'MONEY') AS AnnualRevenue,
        details.value('BankName[1]', 'VARCHAR(50)') AS BankName,
        details.value('BusinessType[1]', 'VARCHAR(10)') AS BusinessType,
        details.value('YearOpened[1]', 'INT') AS YearOpened,
        details.value('Specialty[1]', 'VARCHAR(50)') AS Specialty,
        details.value('SquareFeet[1]', 'INT') AS SquareFeet,
        details.value('Brands[1]', 'VARCHAR(10)') AS Brands,
        details.value('Internet[1]', 'VARCHAR(10)') AS Internet,
        details.value('NumberEmployees[1]', 'SMALLINT') AS NumberEmployees
FROM Sales.Store
CROSS APPLY Demographics.nodes('StoreSurvey') survey(details);
```

The results are shown in Figure 4-2.

AnnualSales	AnnualRevenue	BankName	BusinessType	YearOpened	Specialty	SquareFeet	Brands	Internet	NumberEmp
800000.00	80000.00	United Security	BM	1996	Mountain	21000	2	ISDN	13
800000.00	80000.00	International Bank	BM	1991	Touring	18000	4+	T1	14
800000.00	80000.00	Primary Bank & Reserve	BM	1999	Road	21000	2	DSL	15
800000.00	80000.00	International Security	BM	1994	Mountain	18000	2	DSL	16
800000.00	80000.00	Guardian Bank	BM	1987	Touring	21000	4+	DSL	17
300000.00	30000.00	International Bank	BM	1982	Road	9000	AW	T2	8
300000.00	30000.00	Primary Bank & Reserve	BM	1990	Mountain	7000	AW	T1	9
800000.00	80000.00	International Security	BM	1985	Mountain	17000	4+	DSL	10
3000000.00	300000.00	Primary Bank & Reserve	OS	1979	Mountain	72000	4+	DSL	66
1500000.00	150000.00	International Security	OS	1974	Road	39000	4+	T1	40
1500000.00	150000.00	Primary Bank & Reserve	OS	1980	Mountain	41000	4+	DSL	43

Figure 4-2. *Resulting from XQuery process*

How It Works

The XML document from the table Sales.Store, column Demographics demonstrated in Listing 4-17 is relatively simple. The XML has the root element <StoreSurvey>, and all subsequent elements are children of this XML root. This is a one-level deep XML structure. Such a structure is common in production environments, because database designers prefer to keep a simple XML structure within a column, when possible for performance reasons. Therefore, to convert XML data into rows, we need to provide a reference to the root element in the *nodes()* method. After that, the *value()* method displays each element in a separate column, as shown previously in Figure 4-2.

To navigate over the table's column, SQL Server 2005 introduced two operators:

1. CROSS APPLY - allows a table-valued function to be invoked on each row returned by an outer-table expression of a query. The XML nodes() method is treated as a table-valued functionin terms of CROSS APPLY.

2. OUTER APPLY - equivalent to LEFT OUTER JOIN, when the result set returns all rows from the outer-table expression of a query.

The solution is in Listing 4-16, implementing CROSS APPLY operator for the query. However, the OUTER APPLY operator returns the same result set, because the Demographics column does not have any rows containing NULL values.

Let's compare the differences between shredding the XML value based on the XML variable in Listing 4-17, and the table's column demonstrated in Listing 4-15.

Listing 4-17. Shredding XML variable

```
DECLARE @x XML;

SELECT @x = Demographics  FROM Sales.Store  WHERE BusinessEntityID = 292;

WITH XMLNAMESPACES(default 'http://schemas.microsoft.com/sqlserver/2004/07/
adventure-works/StoreSurvey')
SELECT details.value('AnnualSales[1]', 'MONEY') AS AnnualSales,
       details.value('AnnualRevenue[1]', 'MONEY') AS AnnualRevenue,
       details.value('BankName[1]', 'VARCHAR(50)') AS BankName,
       details.value('BusinessType[1]', 'VARCHAR(10)') AS BusinessType,
       details.value('YearOpened[1]', 'INT') AS YearOpened,
       details.value('Specialty[1]', 'VARCHAR(50)') AS Specialty,
       details.value('SquareFeet[1]', 'INT') AS SquareFeet,
       details.value('Brands[1]', 'VARCHAR(10)') AS Brands,
       details.value('Internet[1]', 'VARCHAR(10)') AS Internet,
       details.value('NumberEmployees[1]', 'SMALLINT') AS NumberEmployees
FROM @x.nodes('StoreSurvey') survey(details);
```

The major SQL code differences are seen in Listing 4-18. When we reference the variable in the FROM clause the nodes() method applied to a variable returns a rowset that represents the result of shredding a single document. This is as opposed to CROSS APPLY against a table, which shreds the XML from each row of the table and generates a single rowset. Listing 4-17 shows the code difference between shredding an XML variable and column.

```
FROM @x.nodes('StoreSurvey') survey(details);
```

115

Shredding XML from a variable, and compare to:

```
FROM Sales.Store CROSS APPLY Demographics.nodes('StoreSurvey')
survey(details);
```

        Shredding XML from a column

The SELECT clause is identical for both the variable and column shredding processes. To retrieve an element value, the *value()* method needs to be given the XPath path indicating the element name with a singleton index indicator and the data type. For example: details.value('SquareFeet[1]', 'INT') AS SquareFeet.

It is always good practice to list the column alias in the SELECT clause. We do not receive an error when the alias is missing, and personally, I prefer not to receive a result with the default column name "(No column name)."

■ **Caution**   The XML *elements* and *attributes* are case sensitive; therefore, when the *elements* and *attributes are* referenced in the *value()* method then the case must be identical to the XML document. Otherwise, for XML type columns, the parser will throw an error. For example, when the element AnnualSales is specified as details. value('annualsales[1]', 'money') then you will receive the error: Msg 2263, Level 16, State 1, Line 2 XQuery [Sales.Store.Demographics.value()]: There is no element named "{http://schemas.microsoft.com/sqlserver/2004/07/adventure-works/StoreSurvey}:annualsales" in the type element "({http://schemas.microsoft.com/sqlserver/2004/07/adventure-works/StoreSurvey}:StoreSurvey,#anonymous)". If the XML value stores the columns as untyped XML then the shredding result of the incorrectly specified item will be *NULL*. The same applies to the XML variable. I keep warning my readers about XML case sensitivity because it is the most common mistake for those who are new to XQuery. SQL Server T-SQL does not raise any errors when we type the function *CASE*, for instance, in lower, upper, or mixed case. However, XQuery does not provide us with such a convenient luxury and we must follow the case rules. However, when an SQL Server instance or a database is installed in any type of binary collation, then object name metadata (tables, columns, etc.) is case sensitive.

4-4. Dealing with Legacy XML Storage
Problem

You want to process XML data that has been stored in a table column as a data type other than XML.

Solution

Over the last two decades SQL Server has changed dramatically. One of the biggest modifications was delivered in SQL Server 2005. Microsoft introduced a revolutionary RDBMS product to the IT market. The NTEXT, TEXT, and IMAGE data types were deprecated. However, in legacy databases, XML documents could be stored in columns of VARCHAR, NVARCHAR, VARBINARY, IMAGE, TEXT, and NTEXT data types. In this case the column has to be converted to the XML data type.

■ **Note** There are several cases when you would store data in a column type other than XML, for example: XML data contains internal DTDs or ENTITY declarations and Business requirement to store XML data exactly as it was received, including insignificant whitespace. However, NTEXT, TEXT, and IMAGE data types should not be considered. Use VARCHAR, NVARCHAR, VARBINARY instead.

As an example, SQL Server continues to use the IMAGE data type to store SSIS packages in the *msdb.dbo.syssispackages* table, shown in Figure 4-3. All SSIS packages are XML documents.

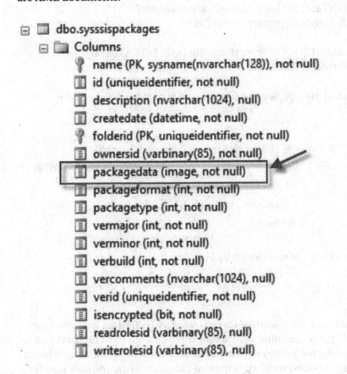

Figure 4-3. Showing msdb.dbo.syssispackages structure

Let's set this scenario: you have an assignment to find all servers where backup databases were run by the SQL Server Maintenance Plan, and list all databases that were used in the plan. This task is easy to do for a few servers. You also need to inspect several hundred SQL Server instances. Instead of logging in to each instance and opening each individual Maintenance Plan, you can shred the *packagedata* column from the *sysssispackages* table, as shown in Listing 4-18, as this is a much more efficient process.

Listing 4-18. Shredding SSIS package code

```
WITH XMLNAMESPACES ('www.microsoft.com/SqlServer/Dts' AS DTS,
         'www.microsoft.com/sqlserver/dts/tasks/sqltask' AS SQLTask),
Package
AS
(
      SELECT name,
              CAST(CAST(packagedata AS VARBINARY(MAX)) AS XML) AS package
      FROM msdb.dbo.sysssispackages
      WHERE packagetype = 6
)
SELECT Package.name as MaintenancePlanName,
    PKG.value('@SQLTask:DatabaseName', 'NVARCHAR(128)')  AS DatabaseName,
    PKG.value('(../@SQLTask:BackupDestinationAutoFolderPath)',
'NVARCHAR(500)') AS BackupDestinationFolderPath
FROM Package
CROSS APPLY package.nodes('//DTS:ObjectData/SQLTask:SqlTaskData/
SQLTask:SelectedDatabases') SSIS(PKG);
```

The result of shredding the SQL Server Maintenance Plan SSIS package is shown in Figure 4-4.

	MaintenancePlanName	DatabaseName	BackupDestinationFolderPath
1	Full_Backup	AdventureWorks2016	C:\SQLBackup
2	Full_Backup	AdventureworksDW2016	C:\SQLBackup
3	Full_Backup	Northwind	C:\SQLBackup

Figure 4-4. Result of shredding the maintenance plan

How It Works

As I mentioned in the Solution, the *packagedata* column is an IMAGE data type and cannot be processed by the *nodes()* method directly. Therefore, the column must be converted to the XML data type. This is why the solution query has an XMLNAMESPACES declaration block and a CTE named Package to convert the *packagedata* column into the XML data type for further shredding.

These SQL Maintenance Job SSIS packages contain two namespaces, so the XMLNAMESPACES declaration has to include them both:

1. 'www.microsoft.com/SqlServer/Dts' - <DTS:Executable> top element.

2. 'www.microsoft.com/sqlserver/dts/tasks/sqltask' - <SQLTask:SqlTaskData> child element.

The Package CTE prepares the *packagedata* column for the XQuery shredding process. The CTE returns the SSIS package's name and explicitly converts the *packagedata* column to the XML data type. The IMAGE data type cannot be converted explicitly in the XML data type. The first step is to explicitly convert the IMAGE data type to VARBINARY(MAX), which is eligible to be converted into XML, for example: CAST(CAST(packagedata AS varbinary(MAX)) AS XML).

The *packagetype* column has five possible values.

- 0 - default value

- 1 - SQL Server Import and Export Wizard

- 3 - SQL Server Replication

- 5 - SSIS Designer

- 6 - Maintenance Plan Designer or Wizard

In this example, we are focusing on Maintenance Plans; therefore, we can filter the result to *packagetype = 6* in the WHERE clause.

The final part of the solution query shreds the Maintenece Plan XML and delivers the result set. Before we process the values in the SELECT clause, we need to establish an element path in the XML data. As we process the table and column, the CROSS APPLY operator helps navigate through the values. The *nodes()* method does not have a full path to the source element. The SSIS XML is large; therefore, "//" provides a shortcut path to the source element and matchs an expression pattern within the XML document. You can also use a leading wildcard "%" in a WHERE clause. The element path '*//DTS:ObjectData/SQLTask:SqlTaskData/SQLTask:SelectedDatabases*' tells you to ignore the leading elements and match the rightmost part in the XML structure. Remember that the double-part alias is required for the *nodes()* method, so SSIS(PKG) is the table(column) alias.

The SELECT clause along with Package.name column returns two values from the XML data, part of the XML demonstrated in Sample 4-6:

1. PKG.value('@SQLTask:DatabaseName', 'NVARCHAR(128)') as DatabaseName, is the *SQLTask:DatabaseName* attribute of the *SQLTask:SelectedDatabases* element. To process an attribute within the value() method the "@" character directs you to the method that the value is the attribute, and no singleton is required.

2. PKG.value('(../@SQLTask:BackupDestinationAuto FolderPath)', 'NVARCHAR(500)') can be used as the BackupDestinationFolderPath.

The *SQLTask:BackupDestinationAutoFolderPath* is an attribute as well. However, the *nodes()* method is set to the SQLTask:SelectedDatabases element that is the child of SQLTask:SqlTaskData element. Therefore, to access the *SQLTask:BackupDestinationAuto FolderPath* attribute, we need to step up one XML level to SQLTask:SqlTaskData element. The step operator "../" completes the process.

Listing 4-19. Demonstrating a formatted snippet of the source XML

```
<DTS:ObjectData>
    <SQLTask:SqlTaskData ... SQLTask:BackupDestinationAutoFolderPath=
    "C:\SQLBackup">
        <SQLTask:SelectedDatabases
        SQLTask:DatabaseName="AdventureWorks2016" />
        <SQLTask:SelectedDatabases
        SQLTask:DatabaseName="AdventureworksDW2016" />
        <SQLTask:SelectedDatabases SQLTask:DatabaseName="Northwind" />
    </SQLTask:SqlTaskData>
</DTS:ObjectData>
```

4-5. Navigating Typed XML Columns
Problem
You want to fix the "Cannot implicitly atomize or apply 'fn:data()' to complex content elements" error encountered when shredding a typed XML column.

Solution
When you attempt to shred a typed XML column, as shown in Listing 4-20, the XPath paths might generate errors.

Listing 4-20. First attempt at shredding a typed XML column

```
WITH XMLNAMESPACES('http://schemas.microsoft.com/sqlserver/2004/07/
adventure-works/ProductModelManuInstructions' as df)
SELECT ProductModelID,
        instruct.value('.', 'VARCHAR(2000)') AS StepInstruction,
        instruct.value('../@LocationID', 'INT') AS LaborStation,
        instruct.value('../@LaborHours', 'REAL') AS LaborHours,
        instruct.value('../@LotSize', 'INT') AS LotSize,
        instruct.value('../@MachineHours', 'REAL') AS MachineHours,
        instruct.value('../@SetupHours', 'REAL') AS SetupHours,
        instruct.value('df:material[1]', 'VARCHAR(100) ') AS Material,
        instruct.value('df:tool[1]', 'VARCHAR(100) ') AS Tool
FROM Production.ProductModel
CROSS APPLY Instructions.nodes('df:root/df:Location/df:step')
prod(instruct);
```

This code, however, generates an error similar to the following:

```
Msg 9314, Level 16, State 1, Line 2
XQuery [Production.ProductModel.Instructions.value()]: Cannot implicitly
atomize or apply 'fn:data()' to complex content elements, found type
'df{http://schemas.microsoft.com/sqlserver/2004/07/adventure-works/Product
ModelManuInstructions}:StepType' within inferred type 'element(df{http://
schemas.microsoft.com/sqlserver/2004/07/adventure-works/ProductModelManuInst
ructions}:step,df{http://schemas.microsoft.com/sqlserver/2004/07/adventure-
works/ProductModelManuInstructions}:StepType)'.
```

To fix this error we have to introduce the XQuery data accessor function fn:string() to prevent the error when the value() method access a singleton atomic instance using the "../" step operator, as shown in Listing 4-21.

Listing 4-21. Applying the fn:string() function to fix Msg 9314 error

```
WITH XMLNAMESPACES('http://schemas.microsoft.com/sqlserver/2004/07/
adventure-works/ProductModelManuInstructions' as df)
SELECT ProductModelID,
        instruct.value('fn:string(.)', 'varchar(2000)') AS StepInstruction,
        instruct.value('fn:string(../@LocationID)', 'int') AS LaborStation,
        instruct.value('fn:string(../@LaborHours)', 'real') AS LaborHours,
        instruct.value('fn:string(../@LotSize)', 'int') AS LotSize,
        instruct.value('fn:string(../@MachineHours)', 'real') AS
        MachineHours,
        instruct.value('fn:string(../@SetupHours)', 'real') AS SetupHours,
        instruct.value('df:material[1]', 'varchar(100) ') AS Material,
        instruct.value('df:tool[1]', 'varchar(100) ') AS Tool
FROM Production.ProductModel
CROSS APPLY Instructions.nodes('df:root/df:Location/df:step')
prod(instruct);
```

The query result is demonstrated in Figure 4-5.

ProductModelID	Step Instruction	LaborStation	LaborHours	LotSize	MachineHours	SetupHours	Material	Tool
48	Attach the grips.	50	3.5	1	0	0	grips	NULL
48	Inspect per sp...	50	3.5	1	0	0	NULL	NULL
53	Visually exami...	50	0.5	1	0	0	left and right pedals	NULL
53	Apply a small a...	50	0.5	1	0	0	grease	NULL
53	If the threads do not turn...	50	0.5	1	0	0	NULL	NULL
67	Put the Seatp...	50	1	1	0	0.25	Seatpost Lug (Pr...	NULL
67	Insert the Pinc...	50	1	1	0	0.25	Pinch Bolt (Produ...	NULL
67	Attach the HL ...	50	1	1	0	0.25	HL Seat (Product...	NULL
67	Inspect per sp...	50	1	1	0	0.25	NULL	NULL

Figure 4-5. Result of shredding typed XML column with fn:string() function

How It Works

SQL Server XQuery implements three data accessor functions:

- *fn:string()* – extracts the string values of the elements or attributes.

- *fn:data()* – extracts scalar (typed) values from the elements or attributes.

- *text()* – returns a single value from the elements or attributes.

As you can see, these three functions are very similar in functionality. To examine each function's functionality, let's analyze the result of Listing 4-22, where the XML partially simulates the XML from the column *Instructions*.

Listing 4-22. Analyzing the data accessor functions. A query() method covered in the next Recipe 4-6, "Retrieving a Subset of Your XML Data"

```
DECLARE @x XML = '<top>
            <level1>1</level1>
            <level2>2</level2>
</top>
<!-- second reference to <top> element -->
<top><level3>3</level3></top>';

SELECT @x.query('/top/level1/text()') Text_Function,
       @x.query('fn:data(/*)') Data_Function,
       @x.query('fn:string(/*[1])') String_Function;
```

The results of this query are shown in Figure 4-6.

Text Function	Data Function	String Function
1	12 3	12

Figure 4-6. *Showing data accessor function results*

The code in Listing 4-22 and its result, shown in Figure 4-6, demonstrate the data accessor functions:

- *text()* function returns single value "1" from the element <level1>.

- *fn:data()* function concatenated.

- fn:string() function requires singleton, and returns values for *level1* and *level2* elements.

For the solution in Listing 4-22 the fn:string() function is most appropriate, because of the local element reference: *instruct.value('fn:string(.)', 'varchar(2000)')*. For example, *fn:data()*,returns an error, and text() function returns a partial value for the *Instructions* column, as shown in Listing 4-23.

Listing 4-23. Demonstrating result difference between text() and fn:string() functions

```
WITH XMLNAMESPACES('http://schemas.microsoft.com/sqlserver/2004/07/
adventure-works/ProductModelManuInstructions' as df)
SELECT instruct.value('./text()[1]', 'varchar(2000)') AS Step_Instruction_
by_text,
        instruct.value('fn:string(.)', 'varchar(2000)') AS Step_Instruction_
by_string
FROM Production.ProductModel
CROSS APPLY Instructions.nodes('df:root/df:Location/df:step')
prod(instruct);
```

The result of Listing 4-23 is shown in Figure 4-7.

Step Instruction by text()	Step Instruction by string()
Insert	Insert aluminum sheet MS-2341 into the T-8...
Attach	Attach Trim Jig TJ-26 to the upper and lower ...
Using a	Using a router with a carbide tip 15, route the...
Insert the frame into	Insert the frame into Forming Tool FT-15 and...
When finished, inspect the for...	When finished, inspect the forms for defects ...
Remove the frames from the tool and place t...	Remove the frames from the tool and place them in the Co...
Assemble all frame componen...	Assemble all frame components following blu...
Weld all frame components to...	Weld all frame components together as show...
Inspect all weld joints per Adve...	Inspect all weld joints per Adventure Works C...
Using the	Using the standard debur tool, remove all exc...
Using	Using Acme Polish Cream, polish all weld are...
Attach	Attach a maximum of 20 frames to paint harn...
Mix	Mix PA-529S Test spray pattern on s...

Figure 4-7. *Difference between text() and fn:string() functions*

4-6. Retrieving a Subset of Your XML Data
Problem
You want to return a specific subset from your XML document and maintain the XML format.

Solution
The query() method allows you to retrieve a specific part of an XML instance. Listing 4-24 demonstrates how to query the execution plans from SQL Server's Dynamic Management Views (DMVs) and retrieve the Statements section out of the execution plans.

Listing 4-24. Returning SQL Statements XML from the Execution Plan

```
SELECT TOP (25)
        @@SERVERNAME as ServerName,
        qs.Execution_count as Executions,
        qs.total_worker_time as TotalCPU,
        qs.total_physical_reads as PhysicalReads,
        qs.total_logical_reads as LogicalReads,
        qs.total_logical_writes as LogicalWrites,
        qs.total_elapsed_time as Duration,
        qs.total_worker_time/qs.execution_count as [Avg CPU Time],
        DB_NAME(qt.dbid) DatabaseName,
        qt.objectid,
        OBJECT_NAME(qt.objectid, qt.dbid) ObjectName,
        qp.query_plan  as XMLPlan,
        query_plan.query('declare default element namespace
        "http://schemas.microsoft.com/sqlserver/2004/07/showplan";
                //Batch/Statements') as SQLStatements
FROM sys.dm_exec_query_stats qs
        CROSS APPLY sys.dm_exec_sql_text(qs.sql_handle) as qt
        CROSS APPLY sys.dm_exec_query_plan(plan_handle) as qp
WHERE qt.dbid IS NOT NULL
ORDER BY TotalCPU DESC;
```

How It Works

Among XQuery methods, the *query()* method is straightfordard and simple to use.
To return the subset of an XML instance, you need to specify an XML variable or column, and the path to the target element or attribute. The *query()* method returns an instance of the XML data type. For example, to return *Features* XML out of the ProductDescription XML instance assigned to the untype variable demonstarted in Listing 4-25, the result is shown in Figure 4-8.

Listing 4-25. Returning Features subset fromthe XML

```
DECLARE @x XML ='<ProductDescription>
        <Manufacturer>
                <Name>AdventureWorks</Name>
                <Copyright>2002</Copyright>
                <ProductURL>HTTP://www.Adventure-works.com</ProductURL>
        </Manufacturer>
        <Features>
                <Warranty>
                        <WarrantyPeriod>3 years</WarrantyPeriod>
                        <Description>parts and labor</Description>
                </Warranty><Maintenance>
                        <NoOfYears>10 years</NoOfYears>
```

```
                    <Description>maintenance contract available
                    through your dealer or any AdventureWorks retail
                    store.</Description>
            </Maintenance>
        </Features>
        <Picture>
                <Angle>front</Angle>
                <Size>small</Size>
                <ProductPhotoID>118</ProductPhotoID>
        </Picture>
</ProductDescription>';

SELECT @x.query('ProductDescription/Features');
```

The result is shown in Listing 4-26.

Listing 4-26. Resulting of query() method

```
<Features>
  <Warranty>
    <WarrantyPeriod>3 years</WarrantyPeriod>
    <Description>parts and labor</Description>
  </Warranty>
  <Maintenance>
    <NoOfYears>10 years</NoOfYears>
    <Description>maintenance contract available through your dealer or any
AdventureWorks retail store.</Description>
  </Maintenance>
</Features>
```

Listing 4-25 demonstrates returning results from an XML variable that does not contain any namespaces. Therefore, no XMLNAMESPACES are specified for the query() method. However, for typed XML the query() method is required to declare a namespace, as demonstrated in the Solution section of this recipe, in Listing 4-24. The solution uses the default syntax to declare a namespace, because the execution plan XML only references a single namespace:

```
query_plan.query('declare default element namespace "http://schemas.
microsoft.com/sqlserver/2004/07/showplan";
//Batch/Statements') as SQLStatements
```

Alternatively, Listing 4-27 has two namespaces defined in the XML instance. Therefore, each namespace has to be declared individually, as shown.

Listing 4-27. Declaring multiple namespaces in XQuery, in the query() method

```
SELECT name,
        CAST(CAST(packagedata AS varbinary(MAX)) AS XML) AS package,
        CAST(CAST(packagedata AS varbinary(MAX)) AS XML).query('declare
        namespace          DTS="www.microsoft.com/SqlServer/Dts";
declare namespace SQLTask="www.microsoft.com/sqlserver/dts/tasks/sqltask";
                //DTS:ObjectData//SQLTask:SqlTaskData/SQLTask:Selected
                Databases') as SQLStatements
FROM msdb.dbo.sysssispackages
WHERE packagetype = 6;
```

To declare the namespaces, you can use either the internal XQuery format of the *query()* method or the XMLNAMESPACES syntax, as shown in Listing 4-28.

Listing 4-28. Using XMLNAMESPACES instead of XQuery namespace declaration in the query() method

```
WITH XMLNAMESPACES('www.microsoft.com/SqlServer/Dts' as DTS,
'www.microsoft.com/sqlserver/dts/tasks/sqltask' as SQLTask)
SELECT name,
        CAST(CAST(packagedata AS varbinary(MAX)) AS XML) AS package,
        CAST(CAST(packagedata AS varbinary(MAX)) AS XML).query
        ('//DTS:ObjectData//SQLTask:SqlTaskData/SQLTask:SelectedDatabases')
        as SQLStatements
FROM msdb.dbo.sysssispackages
WHERE packagetype = 6;
```

To finalize this recipe, I would like to demonstrate one more example when the subset of the XML instance is returned with user-defined root element, Listing 4-29. The syntax for this is *query('<Root>{/XMLPath/}</Root>')*.

Listing 4-29. Returning query() function result with user-defined root element

```
WITH XMLNAMESPACES('www.microsoft.com/SqlServer/Dts' as DTS,
'www.microsoft.com/sqlserver/dts/tasks/sqltask' as SQLTask)
SELECT name,
        CAST(CAST(packagedata AS varbinary(MAX)) AS XML) AS package,
        CAST(CAST(packagedata AS varbinary(MAX)) AS XML).query('<Root>
        {//DTS:ObjectData//SQLTask:SqlTaskData/SQLTask:SelectedDatabases}
        </Root>') as SQLStatements
FROM msdb.dbo.sysssispackages
WHERE packagetype = 6;
```

You can pick your own preference on which syntax to use for the *query()* method.

4-7. Finding All XML Columns in a Table
Problem
You want to find XML documents that can be stored with a data type other than XML.

Solution
I have never been in the situation where I needed to detect the XML document on the client side; however, the client is not sure where XML is stored. Simply relying on the XML data type is not a good strategy. As explained in Recipe 4-4, the XML documents could store the columns with XML, VARCHAR, NVARCHAR, VARBINARY, IMAGE, TEXT, and NTEXT data types. Therefore, I developed a SQL script that dynamically "sniffs" the XML document across all columns within a database, as shown in Listing 4-30.

Listing 4-30. Detecting the XML document across the tables and columns

```
SET NOCOUNT ON;

DECLARE @SQL nvarchar(1000),
        @tblName nvarchar(200),
        @clmnName nvarchar(100),
        @DType nvarchar(100);

IF (OBJECT_ID('tempdb.dbo.#Result')) IS NOT NULL
        DROP TABLE #Result;

CREATE TABLE #Result
(
        XMLValue XML,
        TopElement NVARCHAR(100),
        tblName NVARCHAR(200),
        clmnName NVARCHAR(100),
        DateType NVARCHAR(100)
);

IF (OBJECT_ID('tempdb.dbo.#XML')) IS NOT NULL
        DROP TABLE #XML;

CREATE TABLE #XML
(
        Val XML,
        TopElmn VARCHAR(100)
);

DECLARE cur
```

```
CURSOR FOR
SELECT XMLClmn = 'WITH CTE AS
(SELECT TOP 1 '+ CASE t.name WHEN 'IMAGE' THEN ' TRY_CONVERT(XML, CAST(' +
QUOTENAME(c.name) + ' AS VARBINARY(MAX))) AS tst, '
        ELSE ' TRY_CONVERT(XML, ' + QUOTENAME(c.name) + ') as tst, ' END +
        QUOTENAME(c.name) + ' FROM '
        + QUOTENAME(s.name) +'.' + QUOTENAME(o.name) +
        '
WHERE '+ CASE t.name WHEN 'IMAGE' THEN ' TRY_CONVERT(XML, CAST(' +
QUOTENAME(c.name) + ' AS VARBINARY(MAX)))'
        ELSE ' TRY_CONVERT(XML, ' + QUOTENAME(c.name) + ') ' END +' IS NOT
        NULL
)
SELECT TOP (1) tst,
        c.value(''fn:local-name(.)[1]'', ''VARCHAR(200)'') AS TopNodeName
FROM CTE CROSS APPLY tst.nodes(''/*'') AS t(c);',
        s.name + '.' + o.name AS TableName,
        c.name AS ColumnName,
        t.name
FROM sys.columns c
INNER JOIN sys.types t
        ON c.system_type_id = t.system_type_id
INNER JOIN sys.objects o
        ON c.object_id = o.object_id
        AND o.type = 'u'
INNER JOIN sys.schemas s
        ON s.schema_id = o.schema_id
WHERE (t.name IN('xml','varchar', 'nvarchar', 'varbinary') AND
c.max_length = -1)
        OR (t.name IN ('image', 'text', 'ntext'));

OPEN cur;

FETCH NEXT
FROM cur
INTO @SQL, @tblName, @clmnName, @DType;

WHILE @@FETCH_STATUS = 0
BEGIN

        INSERT INTO #XML
        EXEC(@SQL);

        INSERT #Result
        SELECT Val, TopElmn, @tblName, @clmnName, @DType
        FROM #XML;

        TRUNCATE TABLE #XML;
```

```
        FETCH NEXT FROM cur INTO @SQL, @tblName, @clmnName, @DType;
END

DEALLOCATE cur;

SELECT XMLValue,TopElement,tblName,clmnName,DateType
FROM #Result;

DROP TABLE #Result;
DROP TABLE #XML;

SET NOCOUNT OFF;
```

To demonstrate the result, the SQL script is executed against the *msdb* database, as shown in Figure 4-8.

XMLValue	TopElement	tblName	clmnName	DateType
<xs:schema xmlns:xs="http://www...	schema	dbo.syscollector_collect...	parameter_schema	xml
<xsl:stylesheet xmlns:xsl="http://w...	stylesheet	dbo.syscollector_collect...	parameter_formatter	xml
<ns:TSQLQueryCollector xmlns:ns...	TSQLQueryCollector	dbo.syscollector_collecti...	parameters	xml
<DTAXML xmlns:xsi="http://www.w...	DTAXML	dbo.DTA_input	TuningOptions	ntext
<DTS:Executable xmlns:DTS="ww...	Executable	dbo.sysssispackages	packagedata	image
<Operator><TypeClass>Bool</Ty...	Operator	dbo.syspolicy_condition...	expression	nvarchar
<DTAXML xmlns:xsi="http://www.w...	DTAXML	dbo.DTA_output	TuningResults	ntext

Figure 4-8. Results from the msdb database

■ **Important**   This solution uses the TRY_CONVERT() function, which is only available on SQL Server 2012 and later.

How It Works

The solution is based on several logical processes:

- The FROM clause obtains from the system tables (*sys.columns, sys. types, sys.objects, and sys.schemas*) data about the columns, their tables, and schemas that have the possibility to store XML data.

- The WHERE clause filters out the data types. Hypothetically, the XML documents could be found in the columns with the XML, VARCHAR, NVARCHAR, VARBINARY, IMAGE, TEXT, and NTEXT data types. The XML documents are lengthy by nature. Therefore, the data types VARCHAR, NVARCHAR, and VARBINARY *are* expected to have a length of -1, that is MAX in the data type length specification. Other data types IMAGE, TEXT, and NTEXT do not need to have this additional length filter.

- The SELECT clause dynamically builds verification SQL. The key function is TRY_CONVERT() has been available since SQL Server 2012. We are taking advantage of the TRY_CONVERT() behavior: when a data type fails to covert to specified type, then the function returns NULL. For example, CAST() and CONVERT() functions return an error (*Msg 9420, XML parsing: line 1, character 2, illegal xml character*) when the conversion fails. Therefore, any data value that fails to convert to the XML data type is filtered out. As explained in Recipe 4-4, the IMAGE data type cannot be converted directly to XML. Therefore, the CASE expression uses two conversion verifications; first for IMAGE data type, as shown in Listing 4-31, and the second for the VARCHAR, NVARCHAR, VARBINARY, TEXT, and NTEXT *data types,* shown in Listing 4-32.

Listing 4-31. Verifying IMAGE data type

```
WITH CTE AS
(
        SELECT TOP (1) TRY_CONVERT(XML, CAST(packagedata AS VARBINARY
        (MAX))) AS tst,
                packagedata
        FROM dbo.sysssispackages
        WHERE  TRY_CONVERT(XML, CAST(packagedata AS VARBINARY(MAX)))
        IS NOT NULL
)
SELECT TOP (1) tst,
        c.value('local-name(.)[1]', 'VARCHAR(200)') AS TopNodeName
FROM CTE
CROSS APPLY tst.nodes('/*') AS t(c);
```

Listing 4-32. Verifying VARCHAR, NVARCHAR, VARBINARY, TEXT, and NTEXT data types

```
WITH CTE AS
(
        SELECT TOP (1) TRY_CONVERT(XML, expression) as tst,
                expression
        FROM dbo.syspolicy_conditions_internal
        WHERE  TRY_CONVERT(XML, expression) IS NOT NULL
)
SELECT TOP (1) tst,
        c.value('fn:local-name(.)[1]', 'VARCHAR(200)') AS TopNodeName
FROM CTE
CROSS APPLY tst.nodes('/*') AS t(c);
```

This is how the code works:

- The cursor executes each SQL script generated in SELECT clause.

- The temp table #XML gets returned rows.

- The temp table #Result gets the row from #XML table and the variables from the cursor.

- Clean up #XML table to prepare for next row verification.

- Destroying the cursor.

- Returning the collected data.

- Dropping the temp tables.

This is the description of the process. However, I would like take a closer look at the CTE external SELECT block from Listing 4-32:

```
SELECT TOP (1) tst,
        c.value('fn:local-name(.)[1]', 'VARCHAR(200)') AS TopNodeName
FROM CTE
CROSS APPLY tst.nodes('/*') AS t(c);
```

The column *tst*, which stands for *test*, returns the XML value when it is successfully converted to the XML data type. The column *TopNodeName* returns the first available element name, that is, the root element. The *fn:local-name()* function returns an element name by the provided argument. The dot (the current context node)is the argument to the *fn:local-name()* function, and *nodes()* method set to "/*" (shortcut for child::node() and /node() axis), which is a wildcard for a single element. Therefore, the XML parser of this combination means – return the first available name out of the XML document.

We can get different effects when the *node()* method is set with "//*" (shortcut for descendant-or-self axis), which means to look and visit every element in the XML data. This can be compared to the T-SQL filter, for example, *WHERE ColumnName LIKE '%text%'.* This way the parser navigates through all the elements within the XML data, as shown in Listing 4-33. The *fn:local-name()* function with a single dot as the argument returns the current element name, for example, *details.value('local-name(.) [1]', 'VARCHAR(100)')*. With a parent axis step (double dot), it returns the element that resides one level up, that is, *parent*, for example, *details.value('local-name(..)[1]', 'VARCHAR(100)')*, as shown in Figure 4-9.

Listing 4-33. Displaying all the elements from the XML data

```
WITH ALLELEMENTS
AS
(
        SELECT TOP 1 Demographics
        FROM Sales.Store
)
```

```
SELECT
        details.value('local-name(..)[1]', 'VARCHAR(100)') AS
ParentNodeName,
        details.value('local-name(.)[1]', 'VARCHAR(100)') AS NodeName
FROM ALLELEMENTS
        CROSS APPLY Demographics.nodes('//*') survey(details);
```

Results of retrieving all elements from XML data are shown in Figure 4-9.

ParentNodeName	NodeName
	StoreSurvey
StoreSurvey	AnnualSales
StoreSurvey	AnnualRevenue
StoreSurvey	BankName
StoreSurvey	BusinessType
StoreSurvey	YearOpened
StoreSurvey	Specialty
StoreSurvey	SquareFeet
StoreSurvey	Brands
StoreSurvey	Internet
StoreSurvey	NumberEmployees

Figure 4-9. *Resulting dynamically returning XML elements*

4-8. Using Multiple CROSS APPLY Operators
Problem

You want to shred a typed XML column, but you want to navigate the XML using multiple CROSS APPLY operators.

Solution

In Recipe 4-5, "Navigating Typed XML Columns," I demonstrated how to shred a typed XML column with navigation "../". Implementing multiple CROSS APPLY operators could provide an alternate to XML navigation, as shown in Listing 4-34.

Listing 4-34. Demonstrating multiple CROSS APPLY operator solution

```
WITH XMLNAMESPACES('http://schemas.microsoft.com/sqlserver/2004/07/
adventure-works/ProductModelManuInstructions' as df)
SELECT ProductModelID,
        step.value('fn:string(.)', 'varchar(2000)') AS StepInstruction,
        instruct.value('@LocationID', 'int') AS LaborStation,
        instruct.value('@LaborHours', 'real') AS LaborHours,
        instruct.value('@LotSize', 'int') AS LotSize,
        instruct.value('@MachineHours', 'real') AS MachineHours,
        instruct.value('@SetupHours', 'real') AS SetupHours,
        step.value('df:material[1]', 'varchar(100) ') AS Material,
        step.value('df:tool[1]', 'varchar(100) ') AS Tool
FROM Production.ProductModel
        CROSS APPLY Instructions.nodes('df:root/df:Location') prod(instruct)
        CROSS APPLY instruct.nodes('df:step') ins(step);
```

The query result is shown in Figure 4-10.

Prod...	Step Instruction	LaborStation	LaborHours	LotSize	MachineHo...	SetupHo...	Material	Tool
10	Inspect Front Derailleur.	50	3	1	0	0.25	NULL	NULL
10	Inspect Rear Derailleur.	50	3	1	0	0.25	NULL	NULL
10	Perform final inspe...	60	4	1	0	0	NULL	NULL
44	Inflate tube to han pressure.	50	3		0		NULL	NULL
44	Spin the wheel and ensure the b...	50	3	1	0	0	NULL	NULL
44	Inflate the tube to 35 PSI.	50	3	1	0	0	NULL	NULL
47	Insert aluminum s...	10	1	100	2	0.1	aluminum s...	T-50 Tube F...
47	Attach Trim Jig TJ-...	10	1	100	2	0.1	NULL	Trim Jig TJ-8
47	Route the aluminum sheet follow...	10	1	100	2	0.1	NULL	NULL

Figure 4-10. Result of applying multiple CROSS APPLY operators

How It Works

The key to using multiple CROSS APPLY operators is applying one CROSS APPLY to the results of the second CROSS APPLY, as in our sample code:

```
FROM Production.ProductModel
        CROSS APPLY Instructions.nodes('df:root/df:Location') prod(instruct)
        CROSS APPLY instruct.nodes('df:step') ins(step)
```

The first CROSS APPLY references the XML Instruction column of the ProductModel table to create a base result set to feed to the second CROSS APPLY:

```
CROSS APPLY Instructions.nodes('df:root/df:Location') prod(instruct)
```

The second CROSS APPLY takes the results of the first CROSS APPLY via its instruct column alias:

```
CROSS APPLY instruct.nodes('df:step') ins(step)
```

Finally, the SELECT clause uses the *instruct* alias to retrieve the parent elements, and the *step* alias to reference child elements. The solutions in Recipes 4-5 and 4-8 produce absolutely the same result set, but the syntax in the SELECT and FROM clauses is different.

Summary

The ability to shred XML data is a very important aspect of manipulating XML in SQL Server. Many of the built-in SQL Server processes use XML; for example:

- Execution Plans
- Extended Events
- DDL triggers
- SSIS and SSRS code behind

The XQuery language simplifies SQL Server and the tasks performed by DBAs and Developers by allowing dynamic and powerful programmatic XML exploration and manipulation, utilizing operational time more efficiently.

CHAPTER 5

Modifying XML

XML XQuery has the ability to modify an XML instance for the XML variable and XML columns. The XQuery *modify()* method provides the ability to add, delete, and update the XML elements, attributes, and their values. This chapter will discuss and demonstrate real case scenarios to apply the *modify()* method for XML instances.

5-1. Inserting a Child Element into Your XML
Problem

You want to insert a child element into an existing XML instance.

Solution

You may encounter a situation in which you need to insert an XML element into an existing XML instance. Consider the simple XML data shown in Listing 5-1.

Listing 5-1. Simple XML data

```
<Root>
  <ProductDescription ProductID="1" ProductName="Road Bike">
    <Features />
  </ProductDescription>
</Root>
```

SQL Server provides XML Data Modification Language (XML DML) support via the XML data type modify() method. XML DML is an extension to the W3C XQuery standard, as XQuery lacks data manipulation statements and functions. Listing 5-2 shows how to use the modify() method's XML DML insert statement to insert a new element into a specific location within your existing XML data. The result is demonstrated in Figure 5-1.

A. Grinberg, *XML and JSON Recipes for SQL Server*,
https://doi.org/10.1007/978-1-4842-3117-3_5

```
<Root>
  <ProductDescription ProductID="1" ProductName="Road Bike">
    <Features>
      <Maintenance>3 year parts and labor extended maintenance is available</Maintenance>
    </Features>
  </ProductDescription>
</Root>
```

Figure 5-1. *Result of inserting a child element into existing XML data*

Listing 5-2. Inserting the first child element for the Features element

```
DECLARE @XMLDoc xml;
SET @XMLDoc =
'<Root>
    <ProductDescription ProductID="1" ProductName="Road Bike">
        <Features>
        </Features>
    </ProductDescription>
</Root>';

SET @XMLDoc.modify('insert <Maintenance>3 year parts and labor extended
maintenance is available</Maintenance> into (/Root/ProductDescription/
Features)[1]');
SELECT @XMLDoc;
```

The result of the XML DML insert statement is shown in Figure 5-1.

How It Works

The XML modify() method's XML DML language is comparable to the T-SQL DML INSERT, UPDATE, and DELETE methods, but with many additional options. This makes sense because XML DML must take XML structure into account when modifying your XML instance. The *modify()* method alters an XML document not only by value, but also amends its elements and attributes. Therefore, the *modify()* method can be logically considered a combination of a subset of T-SQL's DML and DDL languages. We will discuss these other XML DML statements and additional options in other recipes of this chapter.

This recipe demonstrates how to add a new child element, Maintenance, to the parent element Features in the XML instance. The Features element does not have any child elements in the original XML instance, shown in Listing 5-1. We do not need to provide a specification for the child element position to the *modify()* method since the Maintenance element is the first child of the Features element. The solution to insert a new element with the values provided in Listing 5-2 follows this pattern:

1. *insert* is the keyword specifying an "insert" pattern.

2. *<Maintenance> 3 years parts and labor extended maintenance is available</Maintenance>* – is the element value pattern, indicating the element we wish to insert.

3. *into* is the keyword the target XPath path indicating where we will insert the element within the XML.

4. *(/Root/ProductDescription/Features)[1]* is the insert target XPath path. Note that a singleton instance is a required component for the target XPath. When the singleton is not provided (via the [1] index in this case), the XML DML parser will throw the following error:

```
Msg 2226, Level 16, State 1, Line 10XQuery [modify()]: The target of
'insert' must be a single node, found 'element(Features,xdt:untyped) *'
```

The *modify(@xml:dml)* method takes one argument. Therefore, all *@xml:dml* patterns sent to the method are submitted as a single string value, as shown in Listing 5-2:

```
modify('insert
<Maintenance>3 year parts and labor extended maintenance is available
</Maintenance>
into (/Root/ProductDescription/Features)[1]');
```

5-2. Inserting a Child Element into an Existing XML Instance with Namespace
Problem

You want to insert a child element into an XML instance that contains a namespace.

Solution

When an XML instance contains an XML namespace, you need to declare the XML namespace within the *modify()* method. Listing 5-3 builds on the solution in Recipe 5-1 to demonstrate.

Listing 5-3. Declaring an XML namespace within the modify() method

```
DECLARE @XMLDoc xml;
SET @XMLDoc =
'<Root xmlns="http://schemas.microsoft.com/sqlserver/2004/07/adventure-
works/ProductModelManuInstructions">
    <ProductDescription ProductID="1" ProductName="Road Bike">
        <Features>
        </Features>
    </ProductDescription>
</Root>';
```

```
SET @XMLDoc.modify('declare namespace ns="http://schemas.microsoft.com/
sqlserver/2004/07/adventure-works/ProductModelManuInstructions";
insert <ns:Maintenance>3 year parts and labor extended maintenance is
available</ns:Maintenance> into (/ns:Root/ns:ProductDescription/ns:Features)
[1]');
SELECT @XMLDoc;
```

```
Showing the XML rusult:<Root xmlns="http://schemas.microsoft.com/
sqlserver/2004/07/adventure-works/ProductModelManuInstructions">
  <ProductDescription ProductID="1" ProductName="Road Bike">
    <Features>
      <Maintenance>3 year parts and labor extended maintenance is
      available</Maintenance>
    </Features>
  </ProductDescription>
</Root>
```

How It Works

As you can see, there is a small, but significant, difference between Listing 5-1 and Listing 5-3. Listing 5-3 has an XML namespace defined within the XML instance. This small difference affects the *modify()* method syntax. If the *modify()* method ignores the XML namespace, the XQuery won't find the target XPath path, resulting in no change to the XML, as shown in Listing 5-4. The result is shown in Figure 5-2.

Listing 5-4. XML namespace causes modify() method to not update target XML

```
DECLARE @XMLDoc xml;
SET @XMLDoc =
'<Root xmlns="http://schemas.microsoft.com/sqlserver/2004/07/adventure-
works/ProductModelManuInstructions">
    <ProductDescription ProductID="1" ProductName="Road Bike">
        <Features>
        </Features>
    </ProductDescription>
</Root>';
```

```
SET @XMLDoc.modify('insert <Maintenance>3 year parts and labor extended
maintenance is available</Maintenance> into (/Root/ProductDescription/
Features)[1]');
SELECT @XMLDoc;
```

The result, shown in Figure 5-2, demonstrates that this modify() method does not update the source XML.

```
<Root
  xmlns="http://schemas.microsoft.com/sqlserver/2004/07/adventure-works/ProductModelManuInstructions">
  <ProductDescription ProductID="1" ProductName="Road Bike">
    <Features />
  </ProductDescription>
</Root>
```

Figure 5-2. *Resulting XML when the namepspaces are ignored in the modify() method*

As you can see in Figure 5-2, the XML instance returned has not changed. To correct the problem, the XML namespace needs to be declared inside the *modify()* method. Therefore, the first pattern for the XML instance with the namespace must be the namespace declaration, for example:

```
modify('declare namespace ns = "http://schemas.microsoft.com/
sqlserver/2004/07/ adventure-works/ProductModelManuInstructions"; ... )
```

The declared name *ns* is user defined, so you can choose a name to declare the namespace as long as it complies with SQL Server naming conventions, such as no spaces in the name, the first character is alpha, the following characters are alphanumeric, etc. When the namespace is declared, this name needs to be a part of each element in the modify() method, for both new and target patterns. For example:

```
insert <ns:Maintenance>3 year parts and labor extended maintenance is
available</ns:Maintenance> into (/ns:Root/ns:ProductDescription/ns:Features)[1]
```

■ **Tip** Always verify the result after using the *modify()* method. For example, the parser does not throw an error for an ignored namespace declaration, and the action appears to complete successfully. However, modify() simply does not apply the XML DML action to your XML data.

As an alternative to the *modify()* method's internal namespace declaration syntax, it is possible to complete this task with T-SQL's external WITH XMLNAMESPACES declaration. When an XML document has one namespace, the default namespace can be used, as shown in Listing 5-5.

Listing 5-5. Using WITH XMLNAMESPACES to declare a default XML namespace

```
DECLARE @XMLDoc xml;
WITH XMLNAMESPACES(default 'http://schemas.microsoft.com/sqlserver/2004/07/
adventure-works/ProductModelManuInstructions')
SELECT @XMLDoc =
'<Root>
```

```
    <ProductDescription ProductID="1" ProductName="Road Bike">
        <Features>
        </Features>
    </ProductDescription>
</Root>';

SET @XMLDoc.modify('insert <Maintenance>3 year parts and labor extended
maintenance is available</Maintenance> into (/Root/ProductDescription/
Features)[1]');
```

When you are implementing the WITH XMLNAMESPACES clause, then the SET operator will not work. You must implement the SELECT clause instead.

5-3. Inserting XML Attributes
Problem

You want to insert an attribute into an XML element of existing XML data.

Solution

An attribute is a property of an XML element. Therefore, the *modify()* method has the *attribute* option to insert an attribute to an element, as shown in Listing 5-6.

Listing 5-6. Inserting ProductModel attribute into the Maintenance element

```
DECLARE @XMLDoc xml;
SET @XMLDoc =
'<Root>
  <ProductDescription ProductID="1" ProductName="Road Bike">
    <Features>
      <Maintenance>3 year parts and labor extended maintenance is
      available</Maintenance>
    </Features>
  </ProductDescription>
</Root>';

SET @XMLDoc.modify('insert attribute ProductModel {"Mountain-100"} into
(/Root/ProductDescription/Features/Maintenance)[1]');

SELECT @XMLDoc;
```

The result is shown in Figure 5-3.

```
<Root>
  <ProductDescription ProductID="1" ProductName="Road Bike">
    <Features>
      <Maintenance ProductModel="Mountain-100">
          3 year parts and labor extended maintenance is available
      </Maintenance>
    </Features>
  </ProductDescription>
</Root>
```

Figure 5-3. XML result of inserting an attribute into an element

How It Works

Chapter 4 explained the XPath path syntaxes for elements and attributes are different. Likewise, the *modify()* method has differences as well. First of all, the *insert* statement has an additional *attribute* option that is not specified when elements are inserted. Second, the attribute is not surrounded by angle brackets. Finally, the attribute's value is placed into curly brackets with double quotes immediately following the attribute name. Therefore, the syntax to add the attribute has the following patterns:

1. The *insert attribute* keywords indicate you wish to insert an attribute into an element.

2. *ProductModel {"Mountain-100"}* is the attribute's name and value.

3. *into* indicates the XPath path of the target element is coming up.

4. *(/Root/ProductDescription/Features/Maintenance)[1]* is the attribute target XPath path. The singleton numeric positional predicate is a required component of the target XPath.

For example:

```
modify('insert attribute ProductModel {"Mountain-100"} into (/Root/
ProductDescription/Features/Maintenance)[1]');
```

Wrapping the XPath path in parentheses and then putting the numeric positional predicate on the end means that the singleton applies to every step in the path. The XPath path without parentheses expects that the singleton applies to each element. For example: */Root[1]/ProductDescription[1]/Features[1]/Maintenance[1]*.

The sample syntax adds the attribute *ProductModel* with the value *"Mountain-100"* to the first instance of the Maintenance element.

Also the *modify()* method allows you to insert several attributes for an element. To add a list of attributes to the element:

1. Open parentheses after the *insert* directive.

2. List the attributes separated by a comma.

3. Close the parentheses.

This is demonstrated in Listing 5-7.

Listing 5-7. Inserting multiple attributes into the Maintenance element

```
DECLARE @XMLDoc xml;
SET @XMLDoc =
'<Root>
  <ProductDescription ProductID="1" ProductName="Road Bike">
    <Features>
      <Maintenance>3 year parts and labor extended maintenance is
      available</Maintenance>
    </Features>
  </ProductDescription>
</Root>';

SET @XMLDoc.modify('insert
(
        attribute ProductModel {"Mountain-100"},
        attribute LaborType {"Manual"}
) into (/Root/ProductDescription/Features/Maintenance)[1]');

SELECT @XMLDoc;
```

The result is shown in Figure 5-4.

```
<Root>
  <ProductDescription ProductID="1" ProductName="Road Bike">
    <Features>
      <Maintenance ProductModel="Mountain-100" LaborType="Manual">
          3 year parts and labor extended maintenance is available</Maintenance>
    </Features>
  </ProductDescription>
</Root>
```

Figure 5-4. *Result of inserting multiple attributes to the Maintenance element*

5-4. Inserting XML Attribute Conditionally

Problem

You want to insert an XML attribute based on a comparison condition.

Solution

The *if ... else* condition can be implemented in the *modify()* method, as shown in Listing 5-8.

Listing 5-8. Wrapping the attribute insert in an if-then-else condition

```
DECLARE @XMLDoc xml;
SET @XMLDoc =
'<Root>
  <ProductDescription ProductID="1" ProductName="Road Bike">
    <Features>
      <Maintenance>3 year parts and labor extended maintenance is
      available</Maintenance>
    </Features>
  </ProductDescription>
</Root>';

SET @XMLDoc.modify('insert
if (/Root/ProductDescription[@ProductID=1])
      then attribute ProductModel {"Road-150"}
      else (attribute ProductModel {"Mountain-100"} )
into (/Root/ProductDescription/Features/Maintenance)[1]');

SELECT @XMLDoc;
```

The result is shown in Figure 5-5.

```
<Root>
  <ProductDescription ProductID="1" ProductName="Road Bike">
    <Features>
      <Maintenance ProductModel="Road-150">
          3 year parts and labor extended maintenance is available</Maintenance>
    </Features>
  </ProductDescription>
</Root>
```

Figure 5-5. *XML result of conditional attribute insert*

How It Works

To insert a new attribute conditionally, you can use the if … then … else construct within the *modify()* method. Listing 5-8 demonstrates an example of this conditional logic. If the attribute ProductID="1" then a new attribute called ProductModel is added with the value "Road-150," and for all other ProductIDs, a new attribute called ProductModel is added with the value "Mountain-100."

After the *insert* statement (Listing 5-8), we immediately check the ProductID attribute value:

```
if (/Root/ProductDescription[@ProductID=1])
```

When the check condition returns true, the ProductModel attribute with the value "Road-150" is inserted into the Maintenance element:

```
then attribute ProductModel {"Road-150"}
```

For all other values, the else block is processed:

```
else (
                attribute ProductModel {"Mountain-100"}
          )
```

No changes are necessary for the *into* keyword, which provides the functionality establishing the target XPath path:

```
into (/Root/ProductDescription/Features/Maintenance)[1]
```

5-5. Inserting a Child Element with Position Specification

Problem

You want to insert a new element into the existing element group and enforce a certain position sequence.

Solution

The *modify()* method has four keywords that can be applied to the *insert* statement to specify the child element position among a group of elements:

- as first
- as last
- after
- before

These keywords are used to specify the placement of a new element, as shown in Listing 5-9.

Listing 5-9. Demonstrating as first, as last, after, and before keywords to arrange the child elements under the parent element Features

```
DECLARE @XMLDoc xml;
SET @XMLDoc =
'<Root>
  <ProductDescription ProductID="1" ProductName="Road Bike">
    <Features>
    </Features>
  </ProductDescription>
</Root>';

SET @XMLDoc.modify('insert <Warranty>1 year parts and labor</Warranty>
        as first  into (/Root/ProductDescription/Features)[1]');

SET @XMLDoc.modify('insert <Material>Aluminium</Material>
        as last into (/Root/ProductDescription/Features)[1]');

SET @XMLDoc.modify('insert <BikeFrame>Strong long lasting</BikeFrame>
        after (/Root/ProductDescription/Features/Material)[1]')

SET @XMLDoc.modify('insert <Color>Silver</Color>
        before (/Root/ProductDescription/Features/BikeFrame)[1]')

SELECT @XMLDoc;
```

The result is shown in Figure 5-6.

```
<Root>
  <ProductDescription ProductID="1" ProductName="Road Bike">
    <Features>
      <Warranty>1 year parts and labor</Warranty>
      <Material>Aluminium</Material>
      <Color>Silver</Color>
      <BikeFrame>Strong long lasting</BikeFrame>
    </Features>
  </ProductDescription>
</Root>
```

Figure 5-6. Results for the insert directive with position specification

How It Works

The keywords *as first, as last, after,* and *before* provide the position specification for a child element. Each of the keywords is self-explanatory:

- as first – adds the child element into the first position.
- as last – adds the child element into the last position.
- after – adds the child element after provided sibling position.
- before – adds the child element before provided sibling position.

The syntax for *as first* and *as last* differs slightly from the syntax for *after* and *before*. For example, the syntax for *as first* and *as last* is as follows:

- ```
  modify('insert <ChildElement> as first into
  (/XPath/<ParentElement>)[1]')
  ```
- ```
  modify('insert <ChildElement> as last into
  (/XPath/<ParentElement>)[1]')
  ```

The *insert* directive provides the child element and value, then *as first* or *as last* specifier indicates the position the element takes among its sibling elements. In the final step, the parent's XPath provides the child element destination.

There are two differences for the keywords *before* and *after* compared to *as first* and *as last*:

- No *into* keyword implemented.
- The XPath has a reference to the *<ParentElement>/<SiblingElement>* element, beside which the new element (before or after) will be placed.
- ```
  modify('insert <ChildElement> before (/XPath/<ParentElement>
  /<SiblingElement>)[1]')
  ```
- ```
  modify('insert <ChildElement> after (/XPath/<ParentElement>
  /<SiblingElement>)[1]')
  ```

5-6. Inserting Multiple Elements
Problem

You want to insert multiple sibling elements into an XML document.

Solution

Unlike attributes, where you can add several attributes and their values by separating them with a comma, multiple elements are not supported in a direct *insert* within the *modify()* method. However, the XQuery extension function *sql:variable()* helps solve the problem, as shown in Listing 5-10.

Listing 5-10. Inserting multiple sibling elements into an XML instance

```
DECLARE @XMLDoc xml;
SET @XMLDoc =
'<Root>
  <ProductDescription ProductID="1" ProductName="Road Bike">
    <Features>
    </Features>
  </ProductDescription>
</Root>';

DECLARE @newElements xml;
SET @newElements =
'<Warranty>1 year parts and labor</Warranty>
<Material>Aluminium</Material>
<Color>Silver</Color>
<BikeFrame>Strong long lasting</BikeFrame>';

SET @XMLDoc.modify('insert
      sql:variable("@newElements")
into (/Root/ProductDescription/Features)[1]')
SELECT @XMLDoc;
```

The resulting XML is shown in Figure 5-6 (repeating the figure).

```
<Root>
  <ProductDescription ProductID="1" ProductName="Road Bike">
    <Features>
      <Warranty>1 year parts and labor</Warranty>
      <Material>Aluminium</Material>
      <Color>Silver</Color>
      <BikeFrame>Strong long lasting</BikeFrame>
    </Features>
  </ProductDescription>
</Root>
```

How It Works

As explained in the Solution section, the *modify()* method does not support a multiple
sibling element list within the *insert* directive. The XQuery *sql:variable()* extension
function provides us a reference to an XML block, which makes the *insert* directive
mechanism operate as it inserts a new element.

To insert multiple sibling elements into an XML instance, the following is required:

1. Declare a variable as an XML data type (NVARCHAR or VARCHAR data types work as well, but I would recommend remaining consistent with the XML data type).

2. Assign an XML element list to the variable.

For example:

```
DECLARE @newElements xml;
SET @newElements =
'<Warranty>1 year parts and labor</Warranty>
<Material>Aluminium</Material>
<Color>Silver</Color>
<BikeFrame>Strong long lasting</BikeFrame>';
```

The insert part is the same as explained in Recipe 5-1, "Inserting a Child Element into Your XML." However, the function sql:variable() is used instead of the specific child element. For example:

```
modify('insert
        sql:variable("@newElements")
into (/Root/ProductDescription/Features)[1]')
```

The XQuery extension function *sql:variable()* is a key part of this simple solution for inserting multiple sibling elements into an XML instance.

5-7. Updating an XML Element Value
Problem

You want to update an XML instance element value.

Solution

The *modify()* method *replace value of* statement updates an XML instance element value. Listing 5-11 demonstrates the solution to update the *Color* element value from "Silver" to "Black."

Listing 5-11. Updating the <Color> element value

```
DECLARE @XMLDoc xml;
SET @XMLDoc =
'<Root>
  <ProductDescription ProductID="1" ProductName="Road Bike">
    <Features>
      <Warranty>1 year parts and labor</Warranty>
```

```
      <Material>Aluminium</Material>
      <Color>Silver</Color>
      <BikeFrame>Strong long lasting</BikeFrame>
    </Features>
  </ProductDescription>
</Root>';
SET @XMLDoc.modify('replace value of
(/Root/ProductDescription/Features/Color/text())[1] with "Black"')
SELECT @XMLDoc;
```

The result is shown in Figure 5-7.

```
<Root>
  <ProductDescription ProductID="1" ProductName="Road Bike">
    <Features>
      <Warranty>1 year parts and labor</Warranty>
      <Material>Aluminium</Material>
      <Color>Black</Color>
      <BikeFrame>Strong long lasting</BikeFrame>
    </Features>
  </ProductDescription>
</Root>
```

Figure 5-7. Showing the result when the value of the Color element has been updated

How It Works

The *modify()* method implements the *replace value of* statement to update an XML instance element value. When the XML data type was introduced in SQL Server 2005, many DBAs and SQL Server Developers were puzzled, at least all SQL Server professionals that I know. We expected a directive name of "update" or so; however, the *replace value of* directive updates the XML instance elements and attributes. Previous recipes provided us with many "flavors" of the *insert* directive, which is practically correct. The insert process has many options for XML instances. Compared to insert, updating an XML instance element is fairly straightforward. To modify the XML instance element value, you need the following:

1.   Specify the *modify()* method *replace value of* statement.

2.   Opening parenthesis, provide the XPath path to the XML element; implement the *text()* function for the target element; and closing the parenthesis and specifying the singleton.

3.   After the *with* keyword, specify a new element value in double quotes.

For example:

```
modify('replace value of
(/Root/ProductDescription/Features/Color/text())[1]
with "Black"')
```

5-8. Updating XML Attribute Value

Problem

You want to update the value of an attribute in an XML instance.

Solution

Updating an XML instance attribute solution is relatively close to updating the element. However, updating the attribute has some specifics that are demonstrated in Listing 5-12. The attribute ProductName value is modified from "Road Bike" to "Mountain Bike."

Listing 5-12. Updating ProductName attribute

```
DECLARE @XMLDoc xml;
SET @XMLDoc =
'<Root>
  <ProductDescription ProductID="1" ProductName="Road Bike">
    <Features>
      <Warranty>1 year parts and labor</Warranty>
      <Material>Aluminium</Material>
      <Color>Silver</Color>
      <BikeFrame>Strong long lasting</BikeFrame>
    </Features>
  </ProductDescription>
</Root>';
SET @XMLDoc.modify('replace value of
        (/Root/ProductDescription/@ProductName)[1] with "Mountain Bike"');
SELECT @XMLDoc;
```

The result is shown in Figure 5-8.

```
<Root>
  <ProductDescription ProductID="1" ProductName="Mountain-500">
    <Features>
      <Warranty>1 year parts and labor</Warranty>
      <Material>Aluminium</Material>
      <Color>Silver</Color>
      <BikeFrame>Strong long lasting</BikeFrame>
    </Features>
  </ProductDescription>
</Root>
```

Figure 5-8. *Showing the results when the attribute ProductName value is updated*

How It Works

Updating an XML instance attribute is not much different from updating an element. To modify the XML instance attribute value, you need to:

1. Specify the *modify()* method *replace value of* statement.

2. The XPath path to the XML attribute you want to update with the @ symbol preceding the attribute name, wrapped in parentheses. The XPath path must be a singleton node.

3. After the *with* keyword, specify a new attribute value in double quotes.

The major difference between modifying the element and attribute is that the attribute must be prefixed with an @ symbol and the *text()* node test is not needed to update the attribute.

5-9. Deleting an XML Attribute
Problem

You want to delete an attribute from an XML attribute.

Solution

Use the *delete* statement in the *modify()* method, as shown in Listing 5-13.

Listing 5-13. Deleting the ProductName attribute from an XML instance

```
DECLARE @XMLDoc xml;
SET @XMLDoc =
'<Root>
  <ProductDescription ProductID="1" ProductName="Road Bike">
    <Features>
      <Warranty>1 year parts and labor</Warranty>
      <Material>Aluminium</Material>
      <Color>Silver</Color>
      <BikeFrame>Strong long lasting</BikeFrame>
    </Features>
  </ProductDescription>
</Root>';
SET @XMLDoc.modify('delete /Root/ProductDescription/@ProductName')
SELECT @XMLDoc;
```

The result is shown in Figure 5-9.

```
<Root>
  <ProductDescription ProductID="1">
    <Features>
      <Warranty>1 year parts and labor</Warranty>
      <Material>Aluminium</Material>
      <Color>Silver</Color>
      <BikeFrame>Strong long lasting</BikeFrame>
    </Features>
  </ProductDescription>
</Root>
```

Figure 5-9. *Result of deleting attribute from an XML instance*

How It Works

The syntax to delete an attribute is simpler than the syntax to update an attribute. To delete an attribute from an XML instance, the *modify()* method needs the *delete* statement and an XPath path to the attribute. Just remember the attribute is prefixed by the "@" symbol. Also, the ProductDescription element is unique within the XML document, therefore no singleton needed in such a case. For example:

```
modify('delete /Root/ProductDescription/@ProductName')
```

In the case when you need to remove all attributes from an element, the XPath should have the destination element path followed by "/@*", as shown in Listing 5-14.

Listing 5-14. Deleting all attributes of the ProductDescription element

```
DECLARE @XMLDoc xml;
SET @XMLDoc =
'<Root>
  <ProductDescription ProductID="1" ProductName="Road Bike">
    <Features>
      <Warranty>1 year parts and labor</Warranty>
      <Material>Aluminium</Material>
      <Color>Silver</Color>
      <BikeFrame>Strong long lasting</BikeFrame>
    </Features>
  </ProductDescription>
</Root>';
SET @XMLDoc.modify('delete /Root/ProductDescription/@*')
SELECT @XMLDoc;
```

The result is shown in Figure 5-10.

```
<Root>
  <ProductDescription>
    <Features>
      <Warranty>1 year parts and labor</Warranty>
      <Material>Aluminium</Material>
      <Color>Silver</Color>
      <BikeFrame>Strong long lasting</BikeFrame>
    </Features>
  </ProductDescription>
</Root>
```

Figure 5-10. Showing the results when all attributes are deleted from the <ProductDescription> element

5-10. Deleting an XML Element
Problem

You want to delete an element from an XML instance.

Solution

The mechanism for removing an element from an XML instance is very similar to removing an attribute. The solution to delete the Color element from our sample XML is demonstrated in Listing 5-15.

Listing 5-15. Deleting the Color element from an XML instance

```
DECLARE @XMLDoc xml;
SET @XMLDoc =
'<Root>
  <ProductDescription ProductID="1" ProductName="Road Bike">
    <Features>
      <Warranty>1 year parts and labor</Warranty>
      <Material>Aluminium</Material>
      <Color>Silver</Color>
      <BikeFrame>Strong long lasting</BikeFrame>
    </Features>
  </ProductDescription>
</Root>';
SET @XMLDoc.modify('delete /Root/ProductDescription/Features/Color)
SELECT @XMLDoc;
```

The result is shown in Figure 5-11.

```
<Root>
  <ProductDescription ProductID="1" ProductName="Road Bike">
    <Features>
      <Warranty>1 year parts and labor</Warranty>
      <Material>Aluminium</Material>
      <BikeFrame>Strong long lasting</BikeFrame>
    </Features>
  </ProductDescription>
</Root>
```

Figure 5-11. *Result of deleting the Color element from an XML instance*

How It Works

To delete an element from an XML instance, the *modify()* method specifies the *delete* statement and the XPath path to the target element. A singleton is required to delete a specific element when the XML has several elements with the same name, for example:

```
<Material>Aluminium</Material>
    <Color>Silver</Color>
    <Color>Blue</Color>
  <BikeFrame>Strong long lasting</BikeFrame>
modify('delete /Root/ProductDescription/Features/Color[1]')
```

The result after delete is that <Color>Silver</Color> gone, <Color>Blue</Color> stays.

To remove all child elements from the parent element, the XPath should point to the parent element plus "/*", as shown in Listing 5-16.

Listing 5-16. Deleting all child elements from the Features element

```
DECLARE @XMLDoc xml;
SET @XMLDoc =
'<Root>
  <ProductDescription ProductID="1" ProductName="Road Bike">
    <Features>
      <Warranty>1 year parts and labor</Warranty>
      <Material>Aluminium</Material>
      <Color>Silver</Color>
      <BikeFrame>Strong long lasting</BikeFrame>
    </Features>
  </ProductDescription>
</Root>';
SET @XMLDoc.modify('delete /Root/ProductDescription/Features/*')
SELECT @XMLDoc;
```

The result is shown in Figure 5-12.

```
<Root>
  <ProductDescription ProductID="1" ProductName="Road Bike">
    <Features />
  </ProductDescription>
</Root>
```

Figure 5-12. XML result after all child elements are deleted from the Features element

To delete items like comments and processing instructions, or even the text within an element, you could use node tests with delete as it demonstrates in Listing 5-17. The result is shown in Figure 5-13.

Listing 5-17. Deleting other types of XML nodes by using node tests

```
DECLARE @XMLDoc xml;
SET @XMLDoc =
'<Root>
  <ProductDescription ProductID="1" ProductName="Road Bike">
    <Features>
        <!-- Comment 1-->
        <!-- Comment 2-->
        <?process abcd?>
      <Warranty>1 year parts and labor</Warranty>
      <Material>Aluminium</Material>
      <Color>Silver</Color>
      <BikeFrame>Strong long lasting</BikeFrame>
    </Features>
  </ProductDescription>
</Root>';
```

155

```
SET @XMLDoc.modify('delete (/Root/ProductDescription/Features/comment())[1]');

SET @XMLDoc.modify('delete (/Root/ProductDescription/Features/Color/text())[1]');

SET @XMLDoc.modify('delete (/Root/ProductDescription/Features/processing-
instruction())[1]');

SELECT @XMLDoc;

<Root>
  <ProductDescription ProductID="1" ProductName="Road Bike">
    <Features>
      <!-- Comment 2-->
      <Warranty>1 year parts and labor</Warranty>
      <Material>Aluminium</Material>
      <Color />
      <BikeFrame>Strong long lasting</BikeFrame>
    </Features>
  </ProductDescription>
</Root>
```

Figure 5-13. *Showing delete result*

Summary

The *modify()* method provides a comprehensive solution for manipulating the nodes of an XML instance. The directives:

- insert
- replace value of
- delete

These directives are able to modify any elements and attributes within an XML instance with a relatively simple syntax.

In the next chapter the recipes will cover how to efficiently filter the XML.

CHAPTER 6

Filtering XML

The filtering mechanism for XQuery has some differences and specifications when compared to the T-SQL WHERE clause. In my experience, when DBAs and Developers implement filters for XQuery, it is mostly based on a T-SQL strategy or to create dynamic SQL that is not efficient and could be very difficult to maintain, especially when the filter is implemented as dynamic SQL. This chapter will demonstrate many examples of how to implement filters for XQuery requests.

6-1. Implementing the exist() Method
Problem

You want to determine whether a specific element or attribute exists within your XML data.

Solution

The *exist()* method allows you to determine whether an element or attribute exists within an XML instance. Listing 6-1 is a demonstration of using the *exist()* method to retrieve all XML instances containing the *YearlyIncome* element directly below the root *IndividualSurvey* element.

Listing 6-1. Retrieving the instances that contains the YearrlyIncome element

```
WITH XMLNAMESPACES
(
        DEFAULT N'http://schemas.microsoft.com/sqlserver/2004/07/adventure-
        works/IndividualSurvey'
)
SELECT BusinessEntityID,
        Demographics
FROM Person.Person
WHERE Demographics.exist('IndividualSurvey/YearlyIncome') = 1;
```

© Alex Grinberg 2018
A. Grinberg, *XML and JSON Recipes for SQL Server*,
https://doi.org/10.1007/978-1-4842-3117-3_6

The query result is demonstrated in Figure 6-1.

BusinessEntityID	Demographics
1699	<IndividualSurvey xmlns="http://schemas.microsoft.com/sqlserver/2004/07/adventure-works/IndividualSurvey"><TotalPurchaseYTD>-16.01</TotalPurch
1700	<IndividualSurvey xmlns="http://schemas.microsoft.com/sqlserver/2004/07/adventure-works/IndividualSurvey"><TotalPurchaseYTD>-4</TotalPurchaseY
1701	<IndividualSurvey xmlns="http://schemas.microsoft.com/sqlserver/2004/07/adventure-works/IndividualSurvey"><TotalPurchaseYTD>4730.04</TotalPur
1702	<IndividualSurvey xmlns="http://schemas.microsoft.com/sqlserver/2004/07/adventure-works/IndividualSurvey"><TotalPurchaseYTD>2435.4018</TotalPu
1703	<IndividualSurvey xmlns="http://schemas.microsoft.com/sqlserver/2004/07/adventure-works/IndividualSurvey"><TotalPurchaseYTD>1647</TotalPurcha
1704	<IndividualSurvey xmlns="http://schemas.microsoft.com/sqlserver/2004/07/adventure-works/IndividualSurvey"><TotalPurchaseYTD>-699.0964</TotalPu
1705	<IndividualSurvey xmlns="http://schemas.microsoft.com/sqlserver/2004/07/adventure-works/IndividualSurvey"><TotalPurchaseYTD>1651</TotalPurcha
1706	<IndividualSurvey xmlns="http://schemas.microsoft.com/sqlserver/2004/07/adventure-works/IndividualSurvey"><TotalPurchaseYTD>15.49</TotalPurcha
1707	<IndividualSurvey xmlns="http://schemas.microsoft.com/sqlserver/2004/07/adventure-works/IndividualSurvey"><TotalPurchaseYTD>37.7</TotalPurchas
1708	<IndividualSurvey xmlns="http://schemas.microsoft.com/sqlserver/2004/07/adventure-works/IndividualSurvey"><TotalPurchaseYTD>-4.99</TotalPurchas
1709	<IndividualSurvey xmlns="http://schemas.microsoft.com/sqlserver/2004/07/adventure-works/IndividualSurvey"><TotalPurchaseYTD>-39.01</TotalPurch
1710	<IndividualSurvey xmlns="http://schemas.microsoft.com/sqlserver/2004/07/adventure-works/IndividualSurvey"><TotalPurchaseYTD>0</TotalPurchaseY
1711	<IndividualSurvey xmlns="http://schemas.microsoft.com/sqlserver/2004/07/adventure-works/IndividualSurvey"><TotalPurchaseYTD>4</TotalPurchaseY
1712	<IndividualSurvey xmlns="http://schemas.microsoft.com/sqlserver/2004/07/adventure-works/IndividualSurvey"><TotalPurchaseYTD>-2443.35</TotalPu
1713	<IndividualSurvey xmlns="http://schemas.microsoft.com/sqlserver/2004/07/adventure-works/IndividualSurvey"><TotalPurchaseYTD>-21.49</TotalPurcha
1714	<IndividualSurvey xmlns="http://schemas.microsoft.com/sqlserver/2004/07/adventure-works/IndividualSurvey"><TotalPurchaseYTD>-41.01</TotalPurch

Figure 6-1. *Filtering data by the YearlyIncome element*

How It Works

The *exist()* method verifies the existence of a provided argument and then returns:

- *TRUE* (a bit value of 1), when the XQuery expression returns a nonempty result.

- *FALSE* (a bit value of 0), when the XQuery expression returns an empty result.

- *NULL* when a NULL is passed in as the XQuery expression or the XML instance is NULL.

Therefore, to detect whether the *YearlyIncome* element is contained in an XML instance, the *exist()* method accepts an XQuery expression that returns one or more YearlyIncome elements when applied to the XML instance. The XML in Listing 6-2 is a sample of the XML that the query in Listing 6-1 is run against.

Listing 6-2. Sample XML data

```
<IndividualSurvey

xmlns="http://schemas.microsoft.com/sqlserver/2004/07/adventure-works/
IndividualSurvey">
    <TotalPurchaseYTD>-16.01</TotalPurchaseYTD>
    <DateFirstPurchase>2003-09-01Z</DateFirstPurchase>
    <BirthDate>1961-02-23Z</BirthDate>
    <MaritalStatus>M</MaritalStatus>
    <YearlyIncome>25001-50000</YearlyIncome>
    <Gender>M</Gender>
    <TotalChildren>4</TotalChildren>
    <NumberChildrenAtHome>0</NumberChildrenAtHome>
    <Education>Graduate Degree</Education>
```

```
  <Occupation>Clerical</Occupation>
  <HomeOwnerFlag>1</HomeOwnerFlag>
  <NumberCarsOwned>0</NumberCarsOwned>
  <CommuteDistance>0-1 Miles</CommuteDistance>
</IndividualSurvey>
```

The XML in Listing 6-2 has a relatively simple structure. The root element is *IndividualSurvey*, and it can contain up to 13 child elements.

To query this XML and return all rows where the XML instances contain the *YearlyIncome* element, we need to refer to the XML namespace. In the provided solution, for simplicity, the XML namespace is set to DEFAULT, as shown below:

```
WITH XMLNAMESPACES(DEFAULT
'http://schemas.microsoft.com/sqlserver/2004/07/adventure-works/
IndividualSurvey')
```

In the WHERE clause, the exist() method takes an XQuery expression that targets our element. The exist() method will return TRUE when the XQuery expression returns a nonempty result:

```
WHERE Demographics.exist('IndividualSurvey/YearlyIncome') = 1
```

When the *YearlyIncome* element is present within an XML instance, the *exist()* method returns a value of 1, (numeric for TRUE), and the row provides the result set.

The same mechanism is used to detect an attribute, with some minor syntax differences required by XQuery to match attributes. The XML provided from the Demographics column does not have attributes. Sample 6-2 demonstrates when the *YearlyIncome* element has the attribute *currency*.

Sample 6-2. Showing the YearlyIncome element with currency as an attribute

```
DECLARE @survey XML = N'<?xml version = "1.0" encoding = "utf-16" ?>
<IndividualSurvey

xmlns="http://schemas.microsoft.com/sqlserver/2004/07/adventure-works/
IndividualSurvey">
  <TotalPurchaseYTD currency = "$">-16.01</TotalPurchaseYTD>
  <DateFirstPurchase>2003-09-01Z</DateFirstPurchase>
  <BirthDate>1961-02-23Z</BirthDate>
  <MaritalStatus>M</MaritalStatus>
  <YearlyIncome currency = "$">25001-50000</YearlyIncome>
  <Gender>M</Gender>
  <TotalChildren>4</TotalChildren>
  <NumberChildrenAtHome>0</NumberChildrenAtHome>
  <Education>Graduate Degree</Education>
  <Occupation>Clerical</Occupation>
  <HomeOwnerFlag>1</HomeOwnerFlag>
  <NumberCarsOwned>0</NumberCarsOwned>
  <CommuteDistance>0-1 Miles</CommuteDistance>
```

159

</IndividualSurvey>';In this particular case the solution will be as demonstrated in Listing 6-3.

Listing 6-3. Searching for an attribute @currency

```
WITH XMLNAMESPACES
(
        DEFAULT 'http://schemas.microsoft.com/sqlserver/2004/07/adventure-
        works/IndividualSurvey'
)
SELECT @survey,
        CASE WHEN @survey.exist('IndividualSurvey/YearlyIncome/@currency')
        = 1 THEN N'IndividualSurvey/YearlyIncome/@currency attribute is
        present.'
                ELSE N'currency attribute is NOT present.'
                END AS hasCurrency;
```

As demonstrated, to detect the attributes you need to provide an XPath to the attribute.

6-2. Filtering an XML Value with the exist() Method

Problem

You want to filter an XML column by value, but the query does not implement XQuery Methods, such as nodes(), value(), and query().

Solution

The exist() method can provide filtering against XML text nodes, especially when the XML instances need to be inspected for a specific searching condition. At the same time, the SELECT clause does not have any XQuery processes. Listing 6-4 retrieves all XML instances where the TotalPurchaseYTD element contains a value greater than 9,000.

Listing 6-4. Using XQuery to filtering XML instances by values

```
WITH XMLNAMESPACES
(
        DEFAULT N'http://schemas.microsoft.com/sqlserver/2004/07/
        adventure-works/IndividualSurvey'
)
SELECT BusinessEntityID,
        Demographics
FROM Person.Person
WHERE Demographics.exist('IndividualSurvey[TotalPurchaseYTD > 9000]') = 1;
```

Figure 6-2 displays the query result.

BusinessEntityID	Demographics		
2436	<IndividualSurvey xmlns	y"><TotalPurchaseYTD>9263.6618</TotalPurchaseYTD><Dat...
4987	<IndividualSurvey xmlns	ey"><TotalPurchaseYTD>9566.43</TotalPurchaseYTD><DateFi...
16617	<IndividualSurvey xmlns	y"><TotalPurchaseYTD>9650.76</TotalPurchaseYTD><DateFi...
17731	<IndividualSurvey xmlns	ey"><TotalPurchaseYTD>9547.55</TotalPurchaseYTD><DateFi...

Figure 6-2. *Returning the rows where the TotalPurchaceYTD is greater than 9000.00*

How It Works

In addition to detecting XML elements and attributes, as described in Recipe 6-1, the exist() method can efficiently filter XML based on instance values. When the query returns columns from a table and the XML instance is not a required part of the shredding processes, but at the same time the rows from the table need to be filtered based on XML value, then the exist() Method can be used as the filtering mechanism to return rows based on the search condition.

The difference, as demonstrated in Recipe 6-1, is that the exist() Method has a filter condition for the TotalPurchaseYTD element value instead of checking for the existence of an element, for example:

```
Demographics.exist('IndividualSurvey[TotalPurchaseYTD > 9000]')
```

The filters for an XML instance have some differences when we compare it to the T-SQL WHERE clause. The XML filters specify a Boolean expression for the exist() method surrounded by square brackets ("[", "]") (the filter for the nodes() method will be demonstrated later in this chapter). The solution demonstrates filtering to return rows where *TotalPurchaseYTD* value is greater than $9000.00. The filter argument for the exist() Method has the following components:

1. the parent element IndividualSurvey

2. opening bracket

3. the child element TotalPurchaseYTD with a comparison operator and value

4. closing bracket

Putting it all together, our XQuery filter has the following syntax:

```
IndividualSurvey[TotalPurchaseYTD > 9000]
```

■ **Note**   The step in the path is implied when you apply a filter. For instance, the actual
step would be: IndividualSurvey/.[TotalPurchaseYTD > 9000]. But when a filter is applied,
the step is implied: IndividualSurvey[TotalPurchaseYTD > 9000].

The XML comparison operators are listed in Table 6-1.

Table 6-1. *Demonstrating XML comparison operators*

Operator	Value	Description
=	eq	Equal
!=	ne	Not equal
>	gt	Greater than
<	lt	Less than
>=	ge	Greater than and equal to
<=	le	Less than and equal to
<<	N/A	Node order precede comparison
>>	N/A	Node order follow comparison
Is	N/A	Node identity equality

"Document order" is a central concept to XML. It is the basis for node order
comparisons. The XQuery Node Order Comparison operators "<<", ">>", and "is" might
be new to readers, because there are no equivalent operators in T-SQL. In XQuery the
"is" comparison operator checks for node identity equality; that is, it tells you whether
the two nodes on either side of the operator are the same node. The node operators "<<"
(precede) and ">>" (follow) compare XML nodes based on document order. The "<<"
operator returns true if the node on the left precedes the node on the right of the operator,
in document order. The ">>" operator returns true if the node on the left follows the node
on the right of the operator, in document order. Listing 6-5 Compares the first instance
of the <Education> to the first instance of the <Occupation> element node position,
returning true because the <Education> element appears before the <Occupation>
element in document order.

Listing 6-5. Comparing <Education> and <Occupation> elements position

```
WITH XMLNAMESPACES
(
        DEFAULT N'http://schemas.microsoft.com/sqlserver/2004/07/adventure-
        works/IndividualSurvey'
)
```

```
SELECT BusinessEntityID,

Demographics.value('(/IndividualSurvey/Education)[1] << (/IndividualSurvey/
Occupation)[1]', 'nvarchar(20)') [Node Comparison]
FROM Person.Person
WHERE BusinessEntityID = 2436;
```

XML filtering does not support the implicit conversion between data types and returns an error in attempt to compare two incompatible values. For example, TotalPurchaseYTD element expects an xs:decimal type, but the value is implemented as an xs:string type. In this case SQL Server throws an error, in which Listing 6-6 triggered the error message.

Listing 6-6. Raising type conversion error.

```
WITH XMLNAMESPACES
(
        DEFAULT N'http://schemas.microsoft.com/sqlserver/2004/07/adventure-
        works/IndividualSurvey'
)
SELECT BusinessEntityID,
        Demographics
FROM Person.Person
WHERE Demographics.exist('IndividualSurvey[TotalPurchaseYTD > "9000"]') = 1;
```

```
Msg 2234, Level 16, State 1, Line 5
XQuery [Person.Person.Demographics.exist()]:
The operator ">" cannot be applied to "xs:decimal ?"
and "xs:string" operands.
```

Figure 6-3. Showing the error message

String type values need to be surrounded by double quotes, and numeric type values do not. The exceptions are the date, time, and datetime types, where XML filters directly handle conversion, as shown in Listing 6-7.

Listing 6-7. Filtering with date types

```
WITH XMLNAMESPACES
(
        DEFAULT N'http://schemas.microsoft.com/sqlserver/2004/07/adventure-
        works/IndividualSurvey'
)
SELECT BusinessEntityID,
        Demographics
FROM Person.Person
WHERE Demographics.exist
('IndividualSurvey[DateFirstPurchase=xs:date("2002-06-28Z")]') = 1;
```

The result is demonstrated in Figure 6-4.

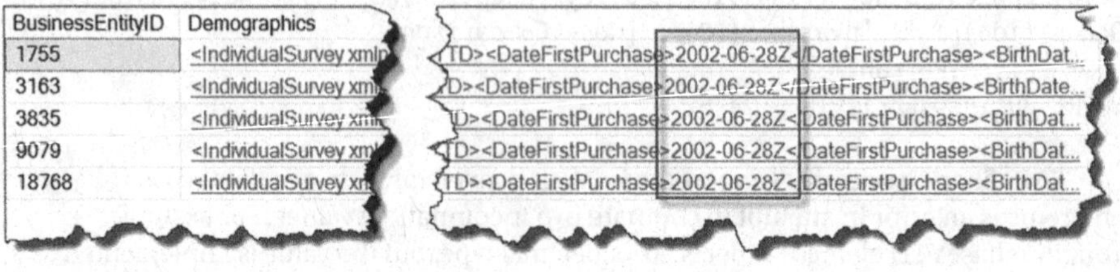

Figure 6-4. Results from the XML instance filtered by date

XQuery supports the following date and time conversion functions:

- xs:date() for date type
- xs:time() for time type
- xs:dateTime() for datetime type

The *DateFirstPurchase* element value is "2002-06-28Z," where "Z" is the *zero meridian*, that is, Z specifier ("Z" actually means UTC Offset of +00:00). For the filtered value, the "Z" is an optional, therefore, *xs:date("2002-06-28")* and *xs:date("2002-06-28Z")* will return the same result.

6-3. Finding All Occurrences of an XML Element Anywhere Within an XML Instance
Problem

You want to locate all occurrences of an XML element regardless of where it occurs within an XML instance.

Solution

Putting double forward slashes "//" (shortcut for /descendant-or-self::node()/) before step within XQuery path expression gives you a shortcut step operator to retrieve the current context node and all its descendant nodes. When it appears at the beginning of an XQuery path expression, it retrieves all nodes in the XML data. You can use this in the *node()* method to avoid explicitly specifying a full reference to the target element, as shown in Listing 6-8.

Listing 6-8. Inserting a new row via the stored procedure

```
WITH XMLNAMESPACES
(
        N'http://schemas.microsoft.com/sqlserver/2004/07/adventure-works/
        Resume' AS ns
)
SELECT

        Info.value(N'(/ns:Resume/ns:Name/ns:Name.First)[1]', 'NVARCHAR(30)')
        AS FirstName,
        Info.value(N'(/ns:Resume/ns:Name/ns:Name.Last)[1]', 'NVARCHAR(30)')
        AS LastName,

        Info.value('fn:string(../../../../ns:Address[1]/ns:Addr.Location[1]
        /ns:Location[1]/ns:Loc.CountryRegion[1])', 'NVARCHAR(100)') AS
        Country,
        Info.value('fn:string(../ns:Tel.Type[1])', 'NVARCHAR(15)') AS
        PhoneType,
        Info.value('fn:string(../ns:Tel.AreaCode[1])', 'NVARCHAR(9)')
        AS AreaCode,
        Info.value('fn:string(.)', 'NVARCHAR(20)') AS CandidatePhone FROM
HumanResources.JobCandidate
CROSS APPLY Resume.nodes('//ns:Tel.Number') AS Person(Info);
```

The query result is shown in Figure 6-5.

FirstName	LastName	Country	PhoneType	AreaCode	CandidatePhone
Christian	Kleinerman	France	Voice	5	05 02 05 02 05
Peng	Wu	US	家庭	253	555-1444
Lionel	Penuchot	France	Voice	4	04 02 03 04 05
Stephen	Jiang	US	Voice	425	555-1119
Stephen	Jiang	US	Voice	425	555-1981
สามารถ	เบญจศร	ประเทศไทย	บ้าน		555-0101
Thierry	D'Hers	France	Voice	4	04 02 04 05 04
ชาย	บางสุขศรี	ประเทศไทย	บ้าน		555-0114
Max	Benson	US	Voice	407	555-0101
Max	Benson	US	Pager	407	555-0122
Tai	Yee	US	家庭	303	555-0114
Shai	Bassli	US	Voice	276	555-0114

Figure 6-5. Showing the SQL result

How It Works

SQL Server XQuery has the ability to shorten the reference to the source element within the node() Method by adding leading double forward slashes to the source element, for example *Resume.nodes('//ns:Tel.Number')*. In this case "//" is shortcut for the XQuery "descendant-or-self::node()" path step. The XQuery engine uses this when searching for all occurrences of an element contained within the XML data that the nodes() method is acting upon.

The hierarchy for the *Tel.Number* element that is part of the HumanResources. JobCandidate table's Resume column is shown in Figure 6-6.

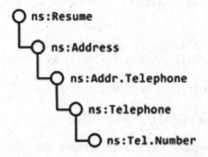

Figure 6-6. *Showing the Tel.Number element hierarchy*

The fully qualified XQuery path expression for the nodes() method to the Tel. Number element is demonstrated in Listing 6-9.

Listing 6-9. Demonstrating a fully qualified reference to the Tel.Number *element*

```
WITH XMLNAMESPACES
(
N'http://schemas.microsoft.com/sqlserver/2004/07/adventure-works/Resume' AS ns
)
SELECT
.
.
.
FROM HumanResources.JobCandidate
        CROSS APPLY Resume.nodes
('/ns:Resume/ns:Address/ns:Addr.Telephone/ns:Telephone/ns:Tel.Number')
AS Person(Info);
```

■ **Caution** It is obvious that the "//" axis operator provides a convenient way to set the reference to a deep child element. However, this technique should be tested thoroughly before coming to a final consideration because it could cause performance problems during the XML shredding process. Chapter 7 will provide more details about the nodes() method performance optimization.

6-4. Filtering by Single Value
Problem
You need to set a single value filter when shredding the XML instance.

Solution
Set the filter within the nodes() Method, Listing 6-10. The result is demonstrated in Figure 6-7.

Listing 6-10. Setting a single value filter within the nodes() Method

```
WITH XMLNAMESPACES
(
        DEFAULT N'http://schemas.microsoft.com/sqlserver/2004/07/
        adventure-works/IndividualSurvey'
)
SELECT BusinessEntityID ,
        ref.value('TotalPurchaseYTD', 'MONEY') AS TotalPurchase,
        ref.value('DateFirstPurchase', 'DATE') AS DateFirstPurchase,
        ref.value('YearlyIncome', 'NVARCHAR(20)') AS YearlyIncome,
        ref.value('Occupation', 'NVARCHAR(15)') AS Occupation,
        ref.value('CommuteDistance', 'NVARCHAR(15)') AS CommuteDistance
FROM Person.Person CROSS APPLY
        Demographics.nodes('IndividualSurvey[TotalPurchaseYTD > 9000]')
        AS dmg(ref);
```

BusinessEntityID	TotalPurchase	DateFirstPurchase	YearlyIncome	Occupation	CommuteDistance
2436	9263.6618	2003-03-14	75001-100000	Professional	5-10 Miles
4987	9566.43	2001-12-03	50001-75000	Skilled Manual	2-5 Miles
16617	9650.76	2001-11-10	75001-100000	Management	10+ Miles
17731	9547.55	2001-12-04	75001-100000	Professional	10+ Miles

Figure 6-7. Result of filtered XQuery query

How It Works

The XQuery language supports filtering from within the nodes() method. The syntax for the XQuery filter is very similar to the T-SQL WHERE clause, but it's not exactly the same. Table 6-1 lists all comparison operators for the XQuery filters (see Recipe 6-2 in the How It Works section). They are the same except for one small difference: the not equal operator, XQuery implements "!=" as the only option. On the other hand, T-SQL provides a choice for DBAs and Developers between "!=" and "<>" operators (best practice in T-SQL, however, is to use the "<>" operator).

To set a single value filter within the nodes() method you need:

1. the parent element IndividualSurvey

2. opening bracket

3. the child element TotalPurchaseYTD with comparison operator and value to compare against

4. closing bracket

Practically speaking, all steps are the same as those demonstrated in Recipe 6-2 for the exist() method. For example, the filter part for both is:

```
IndividualSurvey[TotalPurchaseYTD > 9000]
```

However, the exist() method has slightly better performance compared to the nodes() method. Because those two methods serve completely different functions, the exist() method is for filtering, and nodes() is for shredding.

6-5. Filtering XML by T-SQL Variable

Problem

You want to filter XML results based on T-SQL variable values.

Solution

The SQL Server XQuery function sql:variable() allows your XQuery query expression to access the values of T-SQL variables or parameters for inclusion in your search criteria. The best implementation and demonstration of the sql:variable() function is a stored procedure, as shown in Listing 6-11.

Listing 6-11. Creating a stored procedure with sql:variable() function

```
CREATE PROCEDURE dbo.usp_DemographicsByYearlyIncome
        @YearlyIncome NVARCHAR(20)
AS
BEGIN
        WITH XMLNAMESPACES
        (
```

```
              DEFAULT N'http://schemas.microsoft.com/sqlserver/2004/07/
              adventure-works/IndividualSurvey'
      )
      SELECT BusinessEntityID ,
              ref.value('TotalPurchaseYTD', 'MONEY') AS TotalPurchase,
              ref.value('DateFirstPurchase', 'DATE') AS DateFirstPurchase,
              ref.value('YearlyIncome', 'NVARCHAR(20)') AS YearlyIncome,
              ref.value('Occupation', 'NVARCHAR(15)') AS Occupation,
            ref.value('CommuteDistance', 'NVARCHAR(15)') AS CommuteDistance
      FROM Person.Person
              CROSS APPLY Demographics.nodes('IndividualSurvey[YearlyIncom
              e=sql:variable("@YearlyIncome")]') AS dmg(ref);
END;
GO
```

How It Works

XQuery has the function sql:variable() that allows you to filter XQuery without explicitly specify a search criteria. The sql:variable() function renders and maps a T-SQL declared variable or stored procedure parameter to the XQuery. The sql:variable() function could be a part of the nodes() and exist() Methods to provide filtering functionalities.

The syntax to implement the sql:variable() function to filter an XML element is as follows:

```
parentElement[childElement comparisonOperator sql:variable("@varible")]
```

The syntax to implement the sql:variable() function to filter an XML attribute is as follows:

```
parentElement[@attribute comparisonOperator sql:variable("@varible")]
```

Listing 6-12 demonstrates several executions of the usp_DemographicsByYearly Income stored procedure with different parameter values.

Listing 6-12. Calling the usp_DemographicsByYearlyIncome stored procedure

```
EXECUTE dbo.usp_DemographicsByYearlyIncome '0-25000';
GO

EXECUTE dbo.usp_DemographicsByYearlyIncome '25001-50000';
GO

EXECUTE dbo.usp_DemographicsByYearlyIncome '50001-75000';
GO

EXECUTE dbo.usp_DemographicsByYearlyIncome '75001-100000';
GO

EXECUTE dbo.usp_DemographicsByYearlyIncome 'greater than 100000';
GO
```

The result from the stored procedure execution with parameter value '0-25000' is demonstrated in Figure 6-8.

BusinessEntityID	TotalPurchase	DateFirstPurchase	YearlyIncome	Occupation	CommuteDistance
1706	15.49	2004-07-16	0-25000	Manual	2-5 Miles
1708	-4.99	2004-02-02	0-25000	Clerical	5-10 Miles
1713	-21.49	2003-12-30	0-25000	Clerical	0-1 Miles
1717	-539.99	2004-04-02	0-25000	Manual	0-1 Miles
1718	-1.01	2004-04-23	0-25000	Manual	0-1 Miles
1722	3499.8504	2003-05-10	0-25000	Manual	0-1 Miles
1724	-539.9882	2002-10-03	0-25000	Clerical	5-10 Miles
1726	-69.99	2004-02-07	0-25000	Manual	2-5 Miles
1727	-4.00	2003-12-25	0-25000	Manual	0-1 Miles
1731	-4.99	2004-07-01	0-25000	Manual	0-1 Miles
1732	3042.33	2002-01-21	0-25000	Manual	1-2 Miles

Figure 6-8. Showing the stored procedure result

■ **Caution** The sql:variable() function is part of XQuery; therefore the function is case sensitive and must be referenced in lowercase only. Any other case implementation will trigger the error: Msg 2395, … There is no function '{urn:schemas-microsoft-com:xml-sql}:Variable()'. However, a variable name that sends to the sql:variable() function is not case sensitive.

6-6. Comparing to a Sequence of Values
Problem

You need to filter an XML instance by list a of values, in a fashion similar to the T-SQL IN predicate for the WHERE clause.

Solution

Listing 6-13 demonstrates how to simulate the IN predicate within an XML instance using the "=" general comparison operator against a sequence of values.

Listing 6-13. Sending a list of values to filter an XML instance

```
WITH XMLNAMESPACES
(
        DEFAULT N'http://schemas.microsoft.com/sqlserver/2004/07/
        adventure-works/IndividualSurvey'
)
```

```
SELECT BusinessEntityID,
        ref.value('TotalPurchaseYTD', 'MONEY') AS TotalPurchase,
        ref.value('DateFirstPurchase', 'DATE') AS DateFirstPurchase,
        ref.value('YearlyIncome', 'NVARCHAR(20)') AS YearlyIncome,
        ref.value('Occupation', 'NVARCHAR(15)') AS Occupation,
        ref.value('CommuteDistance', 'NVARCHAR(15)') AS CommuteDistance
FROM Person.Person
        CROSS APPLY Demographics.nodes('IndividualSurvey[Occupation=
        ("Clerical","Manual", "Professional")]') AS dmg(ref);
```

The query results are demonstrated in Figure 6-9.

BusinessEntityID	TotalPurchase	DateFirstPurchase	YearlyIncome	Occupation	CommuteDistance
1699	-16.01	2003-09-01	25001-50000	Clerical	0-1 Miles
1700	-4.00	2004-06-05	50001-75000	Professional	5-10 Miles
1702	2435.4018	2001-10-27	25001-50000	Clerical	0-1 Miles
1703	1647.00	2002-04-18	50001-75000	Professional	2-5 Miles
1704	-699.0964	2002-02-14	greater than 100000	Professional	5-10 Miles
1706	15.49	2004-07-16	0-25000	Manual	2-5 Miles
1707	37.70	2003-08-12	50001-75000	Professional	5-10 Miles
1708	-4.99	2004-02-02	0-25000	Clerical	5-10 Miles
1709	-39.01	2004-05-18	75001-100000	Professional	5-10 Miles
1710	0.00	2002-08-12	50001-75000	Professional	1-2 Miles
1713	-21.49	2003-12-30	0-25000	Clerical	0-1 Miles
1714	-41.01	2004-07-19	25001-50000	Clerical	2-5 Miles
1715	2.70	2004-01-08	25001-50000	Clerical	5-10 Miles

Figure 6-9. Showing XQuery result that processed by list of values

How It Works

The mechanism for filtering an XML instance by a sequence of values is relatively simple, but it is not intuitive. The most common mistake that DBAs and Developers make is that they try to adopt the IN predicate from T-SQL to define this filter. However, the solution is much simpler. The syntax to list the values within the nodes() method is:

```
parentElement[childElement = (value1, value2, value3,...)]
```

When filtering the data by list of values, the difference between T-SQL and XQuery is that XQuery syntax uses the equal general comparison operator (=), while the IN predicate in T-SQL uses the WHERE clause.

6-7. Matching a Specified String Pattern
Problem

You want to filter an XML instance by a string pattern.

Solution

The XQuery fn:contains() function matches a string pattern within an XML element or
attribute, as shown in Listing 6-14.

Listing 6-14. Searching for the string "Manual" within the Occupation element

```
WITH XMLNAMESPACES
(
        DEFAULT N'http://schemas.microsoft.com/sqlserver/2004/07/adventure-
        works/IndividualSurvey'
)
SELECT BusinessEntityID ,
        Demographics,
        ref.value('TotalPurchaseYTD', 'MONEY') AS TotalPurchase,
        ref.value('DateFirstPurchase', 'DATE') AS DateFirstPurchase,
        ref.value('YearlyIncome', 'NVARCHAR(20)') AS YearlyIncome,
        ref.value('Occupation', 'NVARCHAR(15)') AS Occupation,
        ref.value('CommuteDistance', 'NVARCHAR(15)') AS CommuteDistance
FROM Person.Person
        CROSS APPLY Demographics.nodes('IndividualSurvey[ (
fn:contains(Occupation[1], "Manual" ) ) ]') AS dmg(ref);
```

Figure 6-10 demonstrates the result.

BusinessEntityID	TotalPurchase	DateFirstPurchase	YearlyIncome	Occupation	CommuteDistance
1701	4730.04	2002-04-07	75001-100000	Skilled Manual	1-2 Miles
1705	1651.00	2003-10-29	50001-75000	Skilled Manual	0-1 Miles
1706	15.49	2004-07-16	0-25000	Manual	2-5 Miles
1711	4.00	2004-03-12	75001-100000	Skilled Manual	10+ Miles
1717	-539.99	2004-04-02	0-25000	Manual	0-1 Miles
1718	-1.01	2004-04-23	0-25000	Manual	0-1 Miles
1719	4679.05	2002-04-16	50001-75000	Skilled Manual	1-2 Miles
1721	-30.00	2003-10-12	25001-50000	Manual	2-5 Miles
1722	3499.8504	2003-05-10	0-25000	Manual	0-1 Miles
1723	2327.70	2004-01-09	25001-50000	Skilled Manual	2-5 Miles
1726	-69.99	2004-02-07	0-25000	Manual	2-5 Miles

Figure 6-10. *Showing the XQuery result for query where IndividualSurvey element
matched a value pattern*

How It Works

The XQuery *contains()* function has two arguments:

1. an XML instance element or attribute

2. a string pattern

The *contains()* function returns an *xs:boolean* data type (true, false) depending on whether the element or the attribute value in argument 1 matches the string pattern in argument 2. The *contains()* function mechanism is similar to the T-SQL LIKE operator, when the argument is surrounded by wild cards, for example: '%ARGUMENT%', that is, matching any occurrences.

Unfortunately, SQL Server does not support the XQuery functions fn:starts-with() and fn:ends-with(). However, when your task requires you to filter values using fn:starts-with() or fn:ends-with()-type functionality, you can complete this task by using an XQuery and T-SQL hybrid solution, as shown in Listing 6-15.

Listing 6-15. Filtering an XML instance using fn:contains() XQuery and T-SQL hybrid solution

```
WITH XMLNAMESPACES
(
        DEFAULT N'http://schemas.microsoft.com/sqlserver/2004/07/adventure-
        works/IndividualSurvey'
),
Subset AS
(
        SELECT BusinessEntityID,
                ref.value('TotalPurchaseYTD', 'MONEY') AS TotalPurchase,
                ref.value('DateFirstPurchase', 'DATE') AS DateFirstPurchase,
                ref.value('YearlyIncome', 'NVARCHAR(20)') AS YearlyIncome,
                ref.value('Occupation', 'NVARCHAR(15)') AS Occupation,
                ref.value('CommuteDistance', 'NVARCHAR(15)') AS Commute
                Distance
        FROM Person.Person
                CROSS APPLY Demographics.nodes('IndividualSurvey
                [ fn:contains(Occupation[1], "Manual" ) ]') AS dmg(ref)
)
SELECT BusinessEntityID,
        TotalPurchase,
        DateFirstPurchase,
        YearlyIncome,
        Occupation,
        CommuteDistance
FROM Subset
WHERE Occupation LIKE 'Manual%';
```

Figure 6-11 demonstrates the result.

BusinessEntityID	TotalPurchase	DateFirstPurchase	YearlyIncome	Occupation	CommuteDistance
1706	15.49	2004-07-16	0-25000	Manual	2-5 Miles
1717	-539.99	2004-04-02	0-25000	Manual	0-1 Miles
1718	-1.01	2004-04-23	0-25000	Manual	0-1 Miles
1721	-30.00	2003-10-12	25001-50000	Manual	2-5 Miles
1722	3499.8504	2003-05-10	0-25000	Manual	0-1 Miles
1726	-69.99	2004-02-07	0-25000	Manual	2-5 Miles
1727	-4.00	2003-12-25	0-25000	Manual	0-1 Miles
1731	-4.99	2004-07-01	0-25000	Manual	0-1 Miles
1732	3042.33	2002-01-21	0-25000	Manual	1-2 Miles
1735	-1868.37	2002-07-17	25001-50000	Manual	1-2 Miles
1751	1085.50	2004-04-20	25001-50000	Manual	2-5 Miles

Figure 6-11. *Showing the XQuery and T-SQL hybrid solution result*

6-8. Filtering a Range of Values

Problem

You want to filter an XML instance by a range of values, similar to the T-SQL BETWEEN operator.

Solution

The XQuery logical and operator can be used to join two predicates to define a range filter for an XML instance, as shown in Listing 6-16.

Listing 6-16. Implementing the value range filter

```
WITH XMLNAMESPACES
(
        DEFAULT N'http://schemas.microsoft.com/sqlserver/2004/07/adventure-
        works/IndividualSurvey'
)
SELECT BusinessEntityID,
        ref.value('TotalPurchaseYTD', 'MONEY') TotalPurchase,
        ref.value('DateFirstPurchase', 'DATE') DateFirstPurchase,
        ref.value('YearlyIncome', 'NVARCHAR(20)') YearlyIncome,
        ref.value('Occupation', 'NVARCHAR(15)') Occupation,
        ref.value('CommuteDistance', 'NVARCHAR(15)') CommuteDistance
FROM Person.Person
        CROSS APPLY Demographics.nodes('IndividualSurvey[ TotalPurchase
        YTD >= 1000 and TotalPurchaseYTD <= 2000 ]') AS dmg(ref);
```

The result is demonstrated in Figure 6-12.

BusinessEntityID	TotalPurchase	DateFirstPurchase	YearlyIncome	Occupation	CommuteDistance
2443	1066.50	2001-12-05	25001-50000	Skilled Manual	5-10 Miles
2507	1524.7236	2003-01-20	0-25000	Manual	0-1 Miles
2650	1085.50	2003-08-26	25001-50000	Clerical	0-1 Miles
2809	1651.00	2004-04-04	50001-75000	Professional	1-2 Miles
2820	1646.9975	2002-08-07	25001-50000	Management	5-10 Miles
2852	1095.50	2004-05-25	50001-75000	Skilled Manual	2-5 Miles
2886	1679.99	2004-03-31	50001-75000	Skilled Manual	0-1 Miles
3052	1085.50	2003-07-23	25001-50000	Clerical	0-1 Miles
3077	1727.68	2004-05-07	25001-50000	Clerical	0-1 Miles
3252	1143.19	2004-05-30	50001-75000	Professional	0-1 Miles
3277	1094.4918	2002-07-14	25001-50000	Clerical	0-1 Miles
3279	1694.9818	2001-12-28	25001-50000	Clerical	0-1 Miles
3388	1543.97	2003-05-08	50001-75000	Professional	10+ Miles
3545	1685.99	2003-07-19	50001-75000	Management	10+ Miles

Figure 6-12. Showing the XQuery result with range of values filter conditions

How It Works

Setting the value range filter for XQuery uses a method of implementation similar to using the T-SQL WHERE clause. T-SQL has the BETWEEN operator as an additional option for the values range filter. However, the XQuery filter *"elementName >= value and elementName <= value"* implements the same functionality as the BEWTEEN operator. Therefore, the solution in Listing 6-16 demonstrates the value range filter for XQuery, for example: *'IndividualSurvey[TotalPurchaseYTD >= 1000 and TotalPurchaseYTD <= 2000]'*.

■ **Caution**   All operators within XQuery are case sensitive as well. To avoid errors, utilize "and" "or" operators in lowercase only.

6-9. Filtering by Multiple Conditions
Problem

You want to filter an XML instance by multiple elements, attributes, or conditions.

Solution

XQuery provides the and and or logical operators to create compound predicates, which implement multiple filtering conditions against an XML instance, as shown in Listing 6-17.

Listing 6-17. Implementing multiple filter conditions

```
WITH XMLNAMESPACES
(
        DEFAULT N'http://schemas.microsoft.com/sqlserver/2004/07/adventure-
        works/IndividualSurvey'
)
SELECT BusinessEntityID,
        ref.value('TotalPurchaseYTD', 'MONEY') AS TotalPurchase,
        ref.value('DateFirstPurchase', 'DATE') AS DateFirstPurchase,
        ref.value('YearlyIncome', 'NVARCHAR(20)') AS YearlyIncome,
        ref.value('Occupation', 'NVARCHAR(15)') AS Occupation,
        ref.value('CommuteDistance', 'NVARCHAR(15)') AS CommuteDistance
FROM Person.Person
CROSS APPLY Demographics.nodes('IndividualSurvey[ TotalPurchaseYTD >= 1001
        and TotalPurchaseYTD < 1004
        and CommuteDistance = "0-1 Miles"
        or DateFirstPurchase > xs:date("2004-07-30Z") ]'
) AS dmg(ref);
```

The result is demonstrated in Figure 6-13.

BusinessEntityID	TotalPurchase	DateFirstPurchase	YearlyIncome	Occupation	CommuteDistance
4227	1001.8936	2001-12-08	0-25000	Manual	0-1 Miles
4583	-29.51	2004-07-31	25001-50000	Skilled Manual	0-1 Miles
4820	32.69	2004-07-31	25001-50000	Skilled Manual	10+ Miles
4995	1001.8936	2001-12-15	25001-50000	Clerical	0-1 Miles
5916	-7.95	2004-07-31	25001-50000	Skilled Manual	1-2 Miles
7582	41.99	2004-07-31	25001-50000	Clerical	1-2 Miles
7808	14.98	2004-07-31	75001-100000	Professional	10+ Miles
8824	2.70	2004-07-31	50001-75000	Professional	1-2 Miles
9009	-13.01	2004-07-31	50001-75000	Professional	5-10 Miles
9888	69.02	2004-07-31	75001-100000	Skilled Manual	0-1 Miles
11004	6.49	2004-07-31	50001-75000	Professional	10+ Miles
11006	-41.52	2004-07-31	50001-75000	Skilled Manual	0-1 Miles
11861	30.99	2004-07-31	greater than 100000	Management	10+ Miles

Figure 6-13. Showing the XQuery result with multiple filter conditions

How It Works

This recipe demonstrates an XQuery filter for several elements in Listing 6-17. The logic in this recipe is to filter the XML instance where:

1. TotalPurchaseYTD values are between 1001 and 1004, AND

2. CommuteDistance is equal to "0-1 Miles," OR

3. The DateFirstPurchase > "2004-07-30Z."

The *nodes()* method implements four predicates to satisfy the filtering criteria. This recipe demonstrates the two logical operators and and or. The solution XQuery expression is written as:

```
IndividualSurvey[ TotalPurchaseYTD >= 1001
        and TotalPurchaseYTD <= 1004
        and CommuteDistance = "0-1 Miles"
        or DateFirstPurchase > xs:date("2004-07-30") ]
```

This way the recipe demonstrates multiple filtering conditions within the XML instance.

■ **Note**   For demo purposes, the table Person.Person and the column Demographics, containing 19,972 rows, has been selected for this chapter. However, the Demographics column is element-centric XML. Therefore, no filtering samples were provided for the XML attribute. There is a small difference when referencing the XML attribute. The attribute has a leading "@" when it is referenced in a predicate. Listing 6-17 demonstrates the XML portion with the TotalPurchaseYTD element currency attribute. Therefore, the syntax to filter by the attribute is: nodes('IndividualSurvey/YearlyIncome[@currency="$")').

6-10. Setting a Negative Predicate
Problem

You need to filter an XML instance by setting a negative operator. For instance, the T-SQL NOT IN predicate.

Solution

The XQuery negation function is fn:not(). When wrapped around an XQuery predicate, fn:not() returns the opposite of the Effective Boolean Value of the predicate. Listing 6-18 shows an example of using fn:not() as well as the "!=" general comparison operator, which is itself the equivalent of wrapping an "="predicate with fn:not().

Listing 6-18. Demonstrating negative operators

```
WITH XMLNAMESPACES
(
        DEFAULT N'http://schemas.microsoft.com/sqlserver/2004/07/adventure-
        works/IndividualSurvey'
)
SELECT BusinessEntityID,
        ref.value('TotalPurchaseYTD[1]', 'MONEY') AS TotalPurchase,
```

```
        ref.value('DateFirstPurchase[1]', 'DATE') AS DateFirstPurchase,
        ref.value('YearlyIncome[1]', 'NVARCHAR(15)') AS YearlyIncome,
        ref.value('Occupation[1]', 'NVARCHAR(15)') AS Occupation,
        ref.value('CommuteDistance[1]', 'NVARCHAR(15)') AS CommuteDistance
FROM Person.Person
        CROSS APPLY Demographics.nodes('IndividualSurvey[ YearlyIncome !=
        "0-25000" and fn:not( Occupation = ( "Clerical","Manual",
        "Professional" ) ) ]') AS dmg(ref);
```

The result is demonstrated in Figure 6-14.

BusinessEntityID	TotalPurchase	DateFirstPurchase	YearlyIncome	Occupation	CommuteDistance
1701	4730.04	2002-04-07	75001-100000	Skilled Manual	1-2 Miles
1705	1651.00	2003-10-29	50001-75000	Skilled Manual	0-1 Miles
1711	4.00	2004-03-12	75001-100000	Skilled Manual	10+ Miles
1712	-2443.35	2002-09-03	75001-100000	Management	0-1 Miles
1719	4679.05	2002-04-16	50001-75000	Skilled Manual	1-2 Miles
1723	2327.70	2004-01-09	25001-50000	Skilled Manual	2-5 Miles
1725	-13.01	2004-01-27	50001-75000	Management	10+ Miles
1728	26.59	2004-01-24	25001-50000	Skilled Manual	1-2 Miles
1734	-69.99	2004-03-21	75001-100000	Management	10+ Miles
1736	2196.9718	2003-06-04	greater than 10	Management	0-1 Miles
1737	27.60	2003-10-02	50001-75000	Skilled Manual	10+ Miles
1738	64.29	2003-10-08	50001-75000	Skilled Manual	5-10 Miles
1741	6.37	2004-03-03	75001-100000	Management	10+ Miles
1742	-4.99	2004-03-20	25001-50000	Skilled Manual	5-10 Miles

Figure 6-14. Showing the XQuery result with negative predicate

How It Works

XQuery has three negative operators:

- "!=" not equal operator for a general comparison
- "ne" not equal operator for a value comparison
- fn:not() function for a list and range of values

In the Solution section, Listing 6-18 demonstrates both single value criteria and a list of the values setting negative filters, for example:

IndividualSurvey[YearlyIncome ne "0-25000" and fn:not(Occupation = ("Clerical", "Manual", "Professional"))]

6-11. Filtering Empty Values
Problem

You want to filter an XML instance based on the existence of a value within an element or attribute.

178

Solution

The XQuery fn:empty() function verifies if a value exists for a given XML element or attribute, as shown in Listing 6-19.

Listing 6-19. Verifying the value existence

```
WITH XMLNAMESPACES
(
        DEFAULT N'http://schemas.microsoft.com/sqlserver/2004/07/adventure-
        works/IndividualSurvey'
)
SELECT BusinessEntityID,
        ref.value('TotalPurchaseYTD[1]', 'MONEY') AS TotalPurchase,
        ref.value('DateFirstPurchase[1]', 'DATE') AS DateFirstPurchase,
        ref.value('YearlyIncome[1]', 'NVARCHAR(15)') AS YearlyIncome,
        ref.value('Occupation[1]', 'NVARCHAR(15)') AS Occupation,
        ref.value('CommuteDistance[1]', 'NVARCHAR(15)') AS CommuteDistance
FROM person.Person
        CROSS APPLY Demographics.nodes('IndividualSurvey[fn:not(fn:empty
        (Occupation))
and fn:not( Occupation = ( "Clerical", "Manual", "Professional" ) ) ]')
AS dmg(ref);
```

The result is demonstrated in Figure 6-15.

BusinessEntityID	TotalPurchase	DateFirstPurchase	YearlyIncome	Occupation	CommuteDistance
1701	4730.04	2002-04-07	75001-100000	Skilled Manual	1-2 Miles
1705	1651.00	2003-10-29	50001-75000	Skilled Manual	0-1 Miles
1711	4.00	2004-03-12	75001-100000	Skilled Manual	10+ Miles
1712	-2443.35	2002-09-03	75001-100000	Management	0-1 Miles
1719	4679.05	2002-04-16	50001-75000	Skilled Manual	1-2 Miles
1723	2327.70	2004-01-09	25001-50000	Skilled Manual	2-5 Miles
1725	-13.01	2004-01-27	50001-75000	Management	10+ Miles
1728	26.59	2004-01-24	25001-50000	Skilled Manual	1-2 Miles
1734	-69.99	2004-03-21	75001-100000	Management	10+ Miles
1736	2196.9718	2003-06-04	greater than 10	Management	0-1 Miles
1737	27.60	2003-10-02	50001-75000	Skilled Manual	10+ Miles
1738	64.29	2003-10-08	50001-75000	Skilled Manual	5-10 Miles
1741	6.37	2004-03-03	75001-100000	Management	10+ Miles
1742	4.99	2004-03-20	25001-50000	Skilled Manual	5-10 Miles

Figure 6-15. *Showing the XQuery result with implemented fn:empty() function as a filter*

> ■ **Note** The fn:empty() XQuery function is an alternative to the exist() method within XQuery. The exist() method is not supported in the nodes() Method. Therefore, fn:empty() and fn:not() work very well within the nodes() Method, similarly to the functionality of T-SQL *IS NULL* and *IS NOT NULL* operators.

How It Works

The fn:*empty()* function checks if the XML instance elements and attribute values are empty or not. Logically, *fn:empty()* provides functionality to detect any empty values within your XML data. The Solution section demonstrates the syntax to return rows where the Occupation element has a value, that is, the element is not empty. Therefore, both fn:not() and fn:empty() are implemented in Listing 6-14:

```
IndividualSurvey[ fn:not( fn:empty( Occupation ) )
```

As mentioned in the Solution section, the *fn:empty()* function is an alternate to the *exist()* Method, Listing 6-20.

Listing 6-20. Demonstrates an alternative to the fn:empty() function

```
WITH XMLNAMESPACES
(
        DEFAULT N'http://schemas.microsoft.com/sqlserver/2004/07/
        adventure-works/IndividualSurvey'
)
SELECT BusinessEntityID,
        ref.value('TotalPurchaseYTD[1]', 'MONEY') AS TotalPurchase,
        ref.value('DateFirstPurchase[1]', 'DATE') AS DateFirstPurchase,
        ref.value('YearlyIncome[1]', 'NVARCHAR(15)') AS YearlyIncome,
        ref.value('Occupation[1]', 'NVARCHAR(15)') AS Occupation,
        ref.value('CommuteDistance[1]', 'NVARCHAR(15)') AS CommuteDistance
FROM Person.Person
        CROSS APPLY Demographics.nodes
('IndividualSurvey[fn:not( Occupation = ("Clerical", "Manual",
"Professional" ) ) ]') AS dmg(ref)
WHERE Demographics.exist('IndividualSurvey/Occupation') = 1;
```

The result is demonstrated in Figure 6-16.

BusinessEntityID	TotalPurchase	DateFirstPurchase	YearlyIncome	Occupation	CommuteDistance
20718	-2384.07	2002-05-06	greater than 10	Management	5-10 Miles
20720	1694.9775	2002-10-16	50001-75000	Skilled Manual	0-1 Miles
20723	-30.00	2004-01-02	25001-50000	Skilled Manual	5-10 Miles
20727	-1526.4392	2003-03-15	25001-50000	Management	1-2 Miles
20730	219.42	2003-08-13	25001-50000	Skilled Manual	2-5 Miles
20732	193.98	2004-01-19	50001-75000	Skilled Manual	5-10 Miles
20733	498.98	2004-03-13	50001-75000	Skilled Manual	0-1 Miles
20734	1085.5025	2002-12-10	greater than 10	Management	10+ Miles
20737	719.50	2004-04-04	25001-50000	Skilled Manual	1-2 Miles
20739	4691.05	2001-11-25	50001-75000	Skilled Manual	0-1 Miles
20742	-8.41	2004-04-08	25001-50000	Skilled Manual	1-2 Miles
20744	141.60	2003-09-22	greater than 10	Management	0-1 Miles
20747	3001.3318	2003-03-28	50001-75000	Skilled Manual	5-10 Miles
20748	1095.50	2003-12-01	50001-75000	Skilled Manual	1-2 Miles
20749	-31.00	2003-11-20	greater than 10	Management	10+ Miles
20753	-30.01	2003-12-02	50001-75000	Skilled Manual	5-10 Miles
20760	19.69	20??-04-08	75001-100000	Management	1-2 Miles

Figure 6-16. *Showing the XQuery result with implemented an alternative to the fn:empty() function*

When both Listings 6-19 and 6-20 are executed with the T-SQL SET STATISTICS TIME ON; option set, SQL Server shows that fn:empty() has a minor performance advantage over the exist() Method, as shown in Listing 6-21.

Listing 6-21. Showing the execution output for the fn:empty() function and the exist() Method

```
-- fn:empty() function
(7652 row(s) affected)
 SQL Server Execution Times:
   CPU time = 454 ms,  elapsed time = 496 ms.

-- exist() method
(7652 row(s) affected)
 SQL Server Execution Times:
   CPU time = 485 ms,  elapsed time = 577 ms.
```

■ **Note**   The output on your PC could return different performance numbers.

Summary

The "Filtering XML" chapter demonstrates the ability to implement an internal XQuery filtering mechanism for the XML instance. The T-SQL WHERE clause provides a more comprehensive filtering mechanism compared to XQuery internal filtering. However, as was demonstrated in the previous recipes, XQuery has sufficient ability to filter an XML instance.

The most common misconceptions that SQL DBAs and Developers make for filtering the XML is that they are implementing a T-SQL WHERE clause for simplicity. This is an inefficient solution to handle the filtering process for XML instances because the T-SQL WHERE clause filters the XML when the engine returns the result set, while the XQuery returns the filtered values. Listing 6-22 compares the execution CPU utilization and time for both XQuery and the WHERE clause.

Listing 6-22. Demonstrating execution differences

```
SET STATISTICS TIME ON;

WITH XMLNAMESPACES
(
        DEFAULT N'http://schemas.microsoft.com/sqlserver/2004/07/adventure-
        works/IndividualSurvey'
)
SELECT BusinessEntityID,
        ref.value('fn:string(TotalPurchaseYTD[1])', 'MONEY') AS Total
        Purchase,
        ref.value('fn:string(DateFirstPurchase[1])', 'DATE') AS Date
        FirstPurchase,
        ref.value('fn:string(YearlyIncome[1])', 'NVARCHAR (20)') AS Yearly
        Income,
        ref.value('fn:string(Occupation[1])', 'NVARCHAR(15)') AS Occupation,
        ref.value('fn:string(CommuteDistance[1])', 'NVARCHAR(15)') AS Commute
        Distance
FROM Person.Person
        CROSS APPLY Demographics.nodes('IndividualSurvey[Occupation=
        "Manual"]') AS dmg(ref);

WITH XMLNAMESPACES
(
        DEFAULT N'http://schemas.microsoft.com/sqlserver/2004/07/
        adventure-works/IndividualSurvey'
)
SELECT BusinessEntityID,
        ref.value('fn:string(TotalPurchaseYTD[1])', 'MONEY') AS
        TotalPurchase,
        ref.value('fn:string(DateFirstPurchase[1])', 'DATE') AS DateFirst
        Purchase,
```

```
        ref.value('fn:string(YearlyIncome[1])', 'NVARCHAR(20)') AS Yearly
        Income,
        ref.value('fn:string(Occupation[1])', 'NVARCHAR(15)') AS Occupation,
        ref.value('fn:string(CommuteDistance[1])', 'NVARCHAR(15)') AS Commute
        Distance
FROM Person.Person
        CROSS APPLY Demographics.nodes('IndividualSurvey') AS dmg(ref)
WHERE ref.value('fn:string(Occupation[1])', 'NVARCHAR(15)') = 'Manual';

SET STATISTICS TIME OFF;
```

The result is demonstrated in Listing 6-23.

Listing 6-23. Showing the execution output for XQuery and WHERE clause processes:

```
-- XQuery nodes() filter
(2384 row(s) affected)

 SQL Server Execution Times:
   CPU time = 235 ms,  elapsed time = 271 ms.

-- T-SQL WHERE clause
(2384 row(s) affected)

 SQL Server Execution Times:
   CPU time = 593 ms,  elapsed time = 601 ms.
```

The result in Listing 6-23 demonstrates that XQuery is more than twice as efficient as compared to the WHERE clause. Therefore, XQuery filtering should be your first choice.

■ **Note**   The output on your PC could return different performance numbers.

CHAPTER 7

■ ■ ■

Improving XML Performance

Performance efficiency is always a top concern for DBAs and developers. Indexes are a front runner to improve data delivery processes. However, the logical tree structure of XML data cannot be indexed in the same way as plain old relational data. Therefore, with the introduction of SQL Server 2005, Microsoft added an indexing mechanism for XML data type columns. XML data is not the same as scalar data in a table's column, therefore the XML indexing mechanism provides for specialized primary and secondary XML indexes. In SQL Server 2012, the XML indexes are enhanced with a Selective XML Index, which provides an improvement in search efficiency for big XML data.

7-1. Creating a Primary XML Index

Problem

You want to improve the filtering processes on an XML data type column.

Solution

Adding a primary XML index can improve the filtering processes on an XML data type column. To demonstrate, we will create a new table with an XML column, populate it with data, and then create a primary XML index on it. Listing 7-1 demonstrates how to create a primary XML index on the Demographic column of our new table. Figure 7-1 displays a created index.

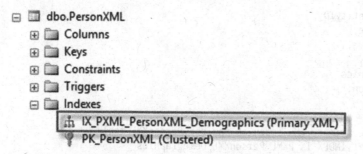

Figure 7-1. Showing the created index for a PersonXML table

© Alex Grinberg 2018
A. Grinberg, *XML and JSON Recipes for SQL Server*,
https://doi.org/10.1007/978-1-4842-3117-3_7

Listing 7-1. Creating a primary XML index

```
-- These settings are important when creating XML indexes
SET NUMERIC_ROUNDABORT OFF;
SET ARITHABORT ON;
SET ANSI_NULLS ON;
SET ANSI_PADDING ON;
SET ANSI_WARNINGS ON;
SET CONCAT_NULL_YIELDS_NULL ON;
SET QUOTED_IDENTIFIER ON;
GO
-- Drop table SQL Server 2016 syntax
DROP TABLE IF EXISTS dbo.PersonXML

-- Create and populate a table called PersonXML
CREATE TABLE dbo.PersonXML
(
        PersonID INT NOT NULL,
        FirstName NVARCHAR(30) NOT NULL,
        MiddleName NVARCHAR(20)NULL,
        LastName NVARCHAR(30) NOT NULL,
        Demographics XML NULL,
        CONSTRAINT PK_PersonXML PRIMARY KEY CLUSTERED
        (
                PersonID ASC
        )
);
GO

INSERT dbo.PersonXML
(
        PersonID,
        FirstName,
        MiddleName,
        LastName,
        Demographics
)
SELECT BusinessEntityID,
        FirstName,
        MiddleName,
        LastName,
        Demographics
FROM Person.Person;
GO

-- Now create the Primary XML index on the dbo.PersonXML table
CREATE PRIMARY XML INDEX IX_PXML_PersonXML_Demographics
ON dbo.PersonXML
```

```
(
    Demographics
);
GO
```

How It Works

In our example we created a dbo.PersonXML table to demonstrate XML index creation and performance. Listing 7-2 shows the SQL code that creates the table and loads it with data from the Person.Person table in the AdventureWorks database. Note the session-level settings shown (via the SET statements). These are important when creating XML columns in tables or adding XML indexes to XML columns.

Listing 7-2. Creating and populating a PersonXML table

```
-- These settings are important when creating XML indexes
SET NUMERIC_ROUNDABORT OFF;
SET ARITHABORT ON;
SET ANSI_NULLS ON;
SET ANSI_PADDING ON;
SET ANSI_WARNINGS ON;
SET CONCAT_NULL_YIELDS_NULL ON;
SET QUOTED_IDENTIFIER ON;
GO
-- Drop table SQL Server 2016 syntax
DROP TABLE IF EXISTS dbo.PersonXML

-- Create and populate a table called PersonXML
CREATE TABLE dbo.PersonXML
(
        PersonID INT NOT NULL,
        FirstName NVARCHAR(30) NOT NULL,
        MiddleName NVARCHAR(20)NULL,
        LastName NVARCHAR(30) NOT NULL,
        Demographics XML NULL,
        CONSTRAINT PK_PersonXML PRIMARY KEY CLUSTERED
        (
                PersonID ASC
        )
);
GO
```

Listing 7-3 demonstrates a SQL query to get a result from the XML column. Figure 7-2 shows the actual execution plan for the SQL code for this query before a primary XML index is created.

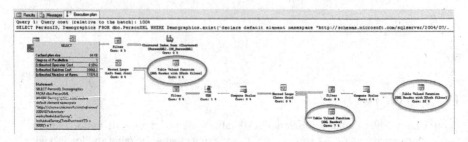

Figure 7-2. Showing the execution plan before the primary XML index is created

Listing 7-3. Sampling XQuery with a filter

```
SELECT PersonID, Demographics
FROM dbo.PersonXML
WHERE Demographics.exist('declare default element namespace "http://schemas.
microsoft.com/sqlserver/2004/07/adventure-works/IndividualSurvey";
        IndividualSurvey[TotalPurchaseYTD > 9000]') = 1;
```

Looking at the execution plan that is created for the XQuery is different by several steps that are not typical for T-SQL queries:

- *Table Valued Function [XML Reader with XPath filter]*

- *Table Valued Function [XML Reader]*

Two of these steps have the highest percentage of the total query cost, 92% and 7%, respectively. These steps specify the XML runtime shredding mechanism and is very similar to a table scan for a normal relational SQL query. That means, depending on how big your XML instance is, the XML shredding process could potentially be very costly in terms of performance. Figure 7-3 demonstrates the Table Valued Function [XML Reader] step property values.

Table Valued Function	
Table valued function.	
Physical Operation	Table Valued Function
Logical Operation	Table Valued Function
Actual Execution Mode	Row
Estimated Execution Mode	Row
Actual Number of Rows	19972
Actual Number of Batches	0
Estimated I/O Cost	0
Estimated Operator Cost	35872.9 (92%)
Estimated Subtree Cost	35872.9
Estimated CPU Cost	1.00036
Estimated Number of Executions	35860
Number of Executions	19972
Estimated Number of Rows	18
Estimated Row Size	461 B
Actual Rebinds	19972
Actual Rewinds	0
Node ID	16
Object	
[XML Reader with XPath filter]	
Output List	
[XML Reader with XPath filter].id	

Figure 7-3. Showing a Table Valued Function [XML Reader] step property

Listing 7-4. Creating the XML Primary index

```
CREATE PRIMARY XML INDEX IX_PXML_PersonXML_Demographics
ON dbo.PersonXML
(
        Demographics
);
GO
```

Once the primary XML index is created, you can re-run the query from Listing 7-5 (same as Listing 7-2) with the actual execution plan enabled on SSMS:

Listing 7-5. Querying the PersonXML table with a Primary XML index

```
SELECT PersonID, Demographics
FROM dbo.PersonXML
WHERE Demographics.exist('declare default element namespace "http://schemas.
microsoft.com/sqlserver/2004/07/adventure-works/IndividualSurvey";
        IndividualSurvey[TotalPurchaseYTD > 9000]') = 1;
```

In the resulting execution plan, the *Table Valued Function [XML Reader with XPath filter]* step and *Table Valued Function [XML Reader]* are replaced with a *Clustered Index Seek(PrimaryXML)* step. Figure 7-4 demonstrates the returned execution plan.

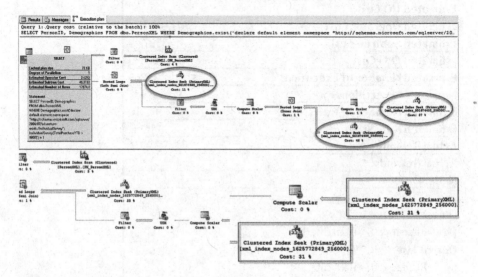

Figure 7-4. *Showing the execution plan after PRIMARY XML index created*

Figure 7-5 demonstrates a Clustered Index Seek (PrimaryXML) step property. With the primary XML index, the Estimated Operator Cost went down from 35782.9 (92%) for the Table Valued Function [XML Reader] step to 21.2796 (46%) for the Clustered Index Seek (PrimaryXML) step.

Clustered Index Seek (PrimaryXML)

Scanning a particular range of rows from a clustered index.

Physical Operation	Clustered Index Seek
Logical Operation	Clustered Index Seek
Actual Execution Mode	Row
Estimated Execution Mode	Row
Storage	RowStore
Number of Rows Read	523504
Actual Number of Rows	19972
Actual Number of Batches	0
Estimated Operator Cost	16.9354 (37%)
Estimated I/O Cost	0.003125
Estimated Subtree Cost	16.9354
Estimated CPU Cost	0.0001691
Estimated Number of Executions	32497
Number of Executions	19972
Estimated Number of Rows	2.5159
Estimated Number of Rows to be Read	11.0306
Estimated Row Size	469 B
Actual Rebinds	0
Actual Rewinds	0
Ordered	True
Node ID	10

Predicate

[AdventureWorks2016].[sys].
[xml_index_nodes_306816155_256000].[hid] as
[TotalPurchaseYTD:2].[hid]='Â€À€' AND [AdventureWorks2016].
﹍﹍﹍﹍﹍﹍﹍﹍﹍'16﹍﹍

([AdventureWorks2016].[sys].
[xml_index_nodes_306816155_256000].[id] as [IndividualSurvey:1].
[id]), End: [AdventureWorks2016].[sys].
[xml_index_nodes_306816155_256000].id < Scalar Operator
(getdescendantlimit([AdventureWorks2016].[sys].
[xml_index_nodes...

Figure 7-5. Showing the Clustered Index Seek(PrimaryXML) step property

The CREATE PRIMARY XML INDEX statement has three parts to identify the index name, the table on which to create the index, and the name of the XML column on which to create the index, as shown below:

```
CREATE PRIMARY XML INDEX <PRIMARY_XML_INDEX_NAME>
ON <TABLE_NAME>
( <XML_COLUMN_NAME> );
```

When creating a primary XML index, you need to follow several rules:

- The table that contains the XML column must have a clustered primary key.

- When a primary XML index exists, <u>the clustered primary key of the table cannot be dropped or altered with DDL statements</u>. All XML indexes must be dropped before modifying the primary key.

- A primary XML index can be created on a single XML type column.

- Each XML index must have a database-wide unique name.

- You cannot separately specify filegroup or partitioning information for the user table when creating an XML index.

- When the primary XML index is dropped, all secondary XML indexes relying on it are dropped automatically.

- Set IGNORE_DUP_KEY and ONLINE options OFF for XML indexes.

- Primary XML indexes have the same restrictions on names as views have on their names.

- Only tables with an XML type column can have an XML index. A view, table-valued variable with XML type columns, or XML type variables cannot have an XML index.

- No XML indexes should exist when changing an XML type column from untyped to typed XML. The ALTER TABLE ALTER COLUMN option could be used if an XML index exists on the table. The XML indexes must be dropped before the column type can be changed.

- The following session options must be set to ON when an XML index is created:

  ARITHABORT

  ANSI_NULLS

  ANSI_PADDING

  ANSI_WARNINGS

CONCAT_NULL_YIELDS_NULL

QUOTED_IDENTIFIER

- The option NUMERIC_ROUNDABORT must be set to OFF when an XML index is created.

A primary XML index can improve XQuery performance significantly. Therefore, XML indexing can be a very attractive solution to improving SQL Server XQuery performance. However, there are several considerations associated with XML indexing. First of all, adding a primary XML index might consume a large amount of storage space. When a PRIMARY XML index is created, SQL Server shreds the XML data in a given column into relational format, accessible only by the query execution engine. That could potentially consume more than double the storage space required to store the unindexed XML data.

Consider these recommendations when deciding whether to add a primary XML index:

- Often times, an XML index is not needed if the XML columns are not part of an XQuery process.

- Determine your query profiles. An XML index is worth considering if you are querying against a large number of rows at a time or if your XML data is large in size. If these conditions do not apply, then the storage cost could outweigh the efficiency.

- A good reason for adding a primary XML index is if you need to add a secondary XML index to increase the efficiency of a specific class of queries (discussed in the next three sections). Adding a primary XML index is mandatory if you wish to add secondary XML indexes.

7-2. Creating a Secondary PATH Type Index
Problem

You want to improve am XML column filtering with the *exist()* method.

Solution

The secondary path type XML index improves query performance for the *exist()* method of the XML data type. Listing 7-6 creates the same table from Solution 7-2 and applies a primary XML index to it, as these are both required for this solution. Listing 7-7 demonstrates how to create a secondary path XML index on the table. Figure 7-6 displays the created index.

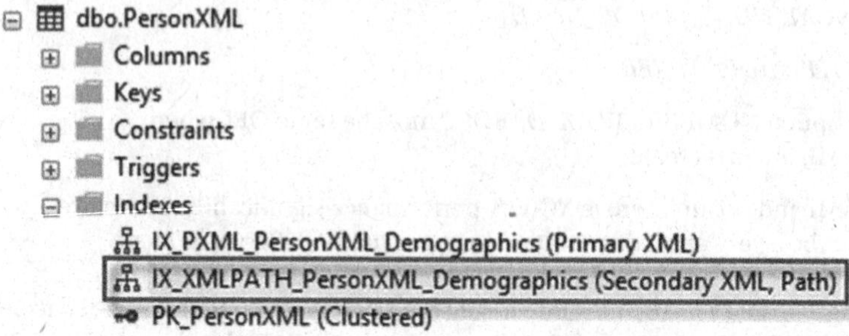

□ ⊞ dbo.PersonXML
   ⊞ ▦ Columns
   ⊞ ▦ Keys
   ⊞ ▦ Constraints
   ⊞ ▦ Triggers
   □ ▦ Indexes
        ⛁ IX_PXML_PersonXML_Demographics (Primary XML)
        ⛁ IX_XMLPATH_PersonXML_Demographics (Secondary XML, Path)
        ⊸ PK_PersonXML (Clustered)

Figure 7-6. Showing a created secondary path type XML index

Listing 7-6. Creating sample table with primary XML index

```
-- These settings are important when creating XML indexes
SET NUMERIC_ROUNDABORT OFF;
SET ARITHABORT ON;
SET ANSI_NULLS ON;
SET ANSI_PADDING ON;
SET ANSI_WARNINGS ON;
SET CONCAT_NULL_YIELDS_NULL ON;
SET QUOTED_IDENTIFIER ON;
GO
-- Drop table SQL Server 2016 syntax
DROP TABLE IF EXISTS dbo.PersonXML

-- Create and populate a table called PersonXML
CREATE TABLE dbo.PersonXML
(
        PersonID INT NOT NULL,
        FirstName NVARCHAR(30) NOT NULL,
        MiddleName NVARCHAR(20)NULL,
        LastName NVARCHAR(30) NOT NULL,
        Demographics XML NULL,
        CONSTRAINT PK_PersonXML PRIMARY KEY CLUSTERED
        (
                PersonID ASC
        )
);
GO

INSERT dbo.PersonXML
(
        PersonID,
        FirstName,
        MiddleName,
```

```
        LastName,
        Demographics
)
SELECT BusinessEntityID,
        FirstName,
        MiddleName,
        LastName,
        Demographics
FROM Person.Person;
GO

-- Now create the Primary XML index on the dbo.PersonXML table
CREATE PRIMARY XML INDEX IX_PXML_PersonXML_Demographics
ON dbo.PersonXML
(
        Demographics
);
```

GO Listing 7-7 adds a secondary path XML index to our previously-created sample table with primary XML index on it.

Listing 7-7. Creating a secondary path XML index

```
CREATE XML INDEX IX_XMLPATH_PersonXML_Demographics
ON dbo.PersonXML
(
        Demographics
)
USING XML INDEX IX_PXML_PersonXML_Demographics
FOR PATH;
```

How It Works

A primary XML index can improve the performance of queries on XML data type columns. Secondary XML indexes can increase query performance on top of the primary XML index. If your queries tend to specify the exist() method in their WHERE clauses, a SECONDARY PATH type index can potentially further improve query speed. Listing 7-8 specifies a query for the existence of an XQuery path.

Listing 7-8. Demonstrating a SECONDARY PATH type index which specifies a query path

```
SELECT PersonID, Demographics
FROM dbo.PersonXML
WHERE Demographics.exist('declare default element namespace "http://schemas.
microsoft.com/sqlserver/2004/07/adventure-works/IndividualSurvey";
/IndividualSurvey/Occupation') = 1;
```

195

Another option is demonstrated in Listing 7-9, where both the path and a predicate are specified.

Listing 7-9. Showing a secondary path type XML index specifying the path and predicate.

```
SELECT PersonID, Demographics
FROM dbo.PersonXML
WHERE Demographics.exist('declare default element namespace "http://schemas.
microsoft.com/sqlserver/2004/07/adventure-works/IndividualSurvey";
/IndividualSurvey[TotalPurchaseYTD > 9000]') = 1;
```

A secondary path type XML index, as well as value and property type secondary indexes, are each built on top of a primary XML index. The syntax of the CREATE XML INDEX to create a secondary path XML index has four parts:

```
CREATE XML INDEX <SECONDARY_PATH_XML_INDEX_Name>
ON <Table_Name>
(  <XML_data_type_Column_Name>  )
USING XML INDEX <PRIMARY_XML_INDEX_Name> FOR PATH;
```

■ **Note**   When the primary XML index is dropped, all associated secondary XML indexes are dropped automatically.

7-3. Creating a Secondary VALUE Type Index
Problem

You want to improve an XML column when a wildcard is implemented in XQuery or the path is not fully specified.

Solution

A secondary value type XML index benefits XQuery performance when the path is not fully specified or if it includes a wildcard. Listing 7-10 creates the sample table and primary XML index we previously created in Solutions 7-1 and 7-2. If you have already created this table, then you do not need to recreate it.

Listing 7-10. Creating sample table with XML column and primary XML index

```
-- These settings are important when creating XML indexes
SET NUMERIC_ROUNDABORT OFF;
SET ARITHABORT ON;
SET ANSI_NULLS ON;
SET ANSI_PADDING ON;
```

```
SET ANSI_WARNINGS ON;
SET CONCAT_NULL_YIELDS_NULL ON;
SET QUOTED_IDENTIFIER ON;
GO
-- Drop table SQL Server 2016 syntax
DROP TABLE IF EXISTS dbo.PersonXML

-- Create and populate a table called PersonXML
CREATE TABLE dbo.PersonXML
(
        PersonID INT NOT NULL,
        FirstName NVARCHAR(30) NOT NULL,
        MiddleName NVARCHAR(20)NULL,
        LastName NVARCHAR(30) NOT NULL,
        Demographics XML NULL,
        CONSTRAINT PK_PersonXML PRIMARY KEY CLUSTERED
        (
                PersonID ASC
        )
);
GO

INSERT dbo.PersonXML
(
        PersonID,
        FirstName,
        MiddleName,
        LastName,
        Demographics
)
SELECT BusinessEntityID,
        FirstName,
        MiddleName,
        LastName,
        Demographics
FROM Person.Person;
GO

-- Now create the Primary XML index on the dbo.PersonXML table
CREATE PRIMARY XML INDEX IX_PXML_PersonXML_Demographics
ON dbo.PersonXML
(
        Demographics
);
GO
```

Listing 7-11 shows how to create a secondary value XML index on the sample table, and Figure 7-7 displays the created XML index.

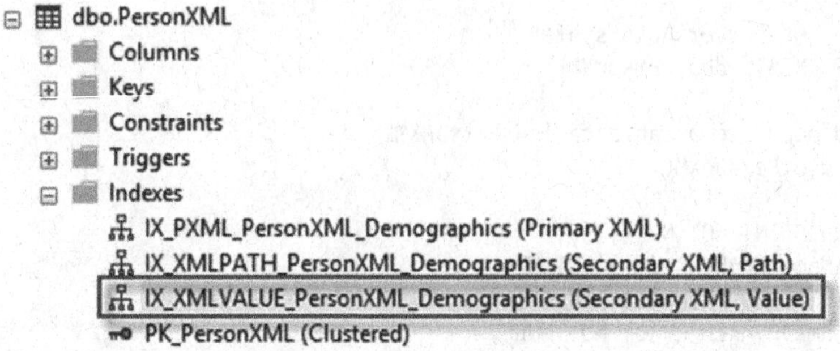

- ⊟ ▦ dbo.PersonXML
  - ⊞ ▦ Columns
  - ⊞ ▦ Keys
  - ⊞ ▦ Constraints
  - ⊞ ▦ Triggers
  - ⊟ ▦ Indexes
    - ᵃ⊞ᵃ IX_PXML_PersonXML_Demographics (Primary XML)
    - ᵃ⊞ᵃ IX_XMLPATH_PersonXML_Demographics (Secondary XML, Path)
    - ᵃ⊞ᵃ IX_XMLVALUE_PersonXML_Demographics (Secondary XML, Value)
    - ⊷ PK_PersonXML (Clustered)

Figure 7-7. *Confirming the secondary value XML index was created*

Listing 7-11. Creating a secondary value type index

```
CREATE XML INDEX IX_XMLVALUE_PersonXML_Demographics
ON dbo.PersonXML
(
        Demographics
)
USING XML INDEX IX_PXML_PersonXML_Demographics
FOR VALUE;
```

How It Works

A secondary value type index can improve the efficiency of a XQuery when the path is not fully specified, or includes wildcards, for example:

- //ELEMENT[ELEMENT = "Filter Condition"]

- /ELEMENT/@*[. = "Filter Condition"]

- //ELEMENT[@ATTRIBUTE = "Filter Condition"]

Practically speaking, the secondary value type index improves query performance where the predicate filter condition value is known. Listing 7-12 demonstrates XQuery benefits from using a value index.

Listing 7-12. Showing XQuery benefits from utilizing a secondary value XML index

```
SELECT PersonID,
        ref.value('declare default element namespace "http://schemas.
        microsoft.com/sqlserver/2004/07/adventure-works/IndividualSurvey";
                TotalPurchaseYTD[1]', 'money') TotalPurchase,
```

```
        ref.value('declare default element namespace "http://schemas.
    microsoft.com/sqlserver/2004/07/adventure-works/IndividualSurvey";
            DateFirstPurchase[1]', 'date') DateFirstPurchase,
        ref.value('declare default element namespace "http://schemas.
    microsoft.com/sqlserver/2004/07/adventure-works/IndividualSurvey";
            YearlyIncome[1]', 'varchar(20)') YearlyIncome,
        ref.value('declare default element namespace "http://schemas.
    microsoft.com/sqlserver/2004/07/adventure-works/IndividualSurvey";
            Occupation[1]', 'varchar(15)') Occupation,
        ref.value('declare default element namespace "http://schemas.
    microsoft.com/sqlserver/2004/07/adventure-works/IndividualSurvey";
            CommuteDistance[1]', 'varchar(15)') CommuteDistance
FROM PersonXML
CROSS APPLY Demographics.nodes('declare default element namespace "http://
schemas.microsoft.com/sqlserver/2004/07/adventure-works/IndividualSurvey";
        /*[YearlyIncome="50001-75000"]') dmg(ref);
```

The syntax to create a secondary value type index has four components:

```
CREATE XML INDEX <SECONDARY_VALUE_XML_INDEX_Name>
ON <Table_Name>
(  <XML_data_type_Column_Name>  )
USING XML INDEX <PRIMARY_XML_INDEX_Name> FOR VALUE;
```

■ **Caution**   An ancestor-or-self axis operator, for example *XML_Column.nodes* ('*//ELEMENT*', is a convenient way to establish the path reference in the *nodes()* method. However, this technique could slow down performance for an XML data type column where the XML instance has deeply nested elements. This is one of the most common performance issues in the XML shredding process. Therefore, I would recommend (when possible) to provide a more detailed path within the *nodes()* method. For example, *XML_Column. nodes('//ELEMENT/CHILD_ELMNT')* could improve your XML shredding performance.

7-4. Creating a Secondary PROPERTY Type Index
Problem

You want to improve performance on an XML column where XQuery retrieves one or more values from the column.

Solution

A secondary property type XML index can be beneficial if your XQuery retrieves one or more values from an XML column. Listing 7-13 creates our demonstration table we have used in Solutions 7-1, 7-2 and 7-3, and creates the primary XML index on it.

Listing 7-13. Create sample table with XML column and primary XML index

```
-- These settings are important when creating XML indexes
SET NUMERIC_ROUNDABORT OFF;
SET ARITHABORT ON;
SET ANSI_NULLS ON;
SET ANSI_PADDING ON;
SET ANSI_WARNINGS ON;
SET CONCAT_NULL_YIELDS_NULL ON;
SET QUOTED_IDENTIFIER ON;
GO
-- Drop table SQL Server 2016 syntax
DROP TABLE IF EXISTS dbo.PersonXML

-- Create and populate a table called PersonXML
CREATE TABLE dbo.PersonXML
(
        PersonID INT NOT NULL,
        FirstName NVARCHAR(30) NOT NULL,
        MiddleName NVARCHAR(20)NULL,
        LastName NVARCHAR(30) NOT NULL,
        Demographics XML NULL,
        CONSTRAINT PK_PersonXML PRIMARY KEY CLUSTERED
        (
                PersonID ASC
        )
);
GO

INSERT dbo.PersonXML
(
        PersonID,
        FirstName,
        MiddleName,
```

```
        LastName,
        Demographics
)
SELECT BusinessEntityID,
        FirstName,
        MiddleName,
        LastName,
        Demographics
FROM Person.Person;
GO

-- Now create the Primary XML index on the dbo.PersonXML table
CREATE PRIMARY XML INDEX IX_PXML_PersonXML_Demographics
ON dbo.PersonXML
(
        Demographics
);
GO
```

Listing 7-14 shows how to create a secondary property XML index. Figure 7-8 displays the created index.

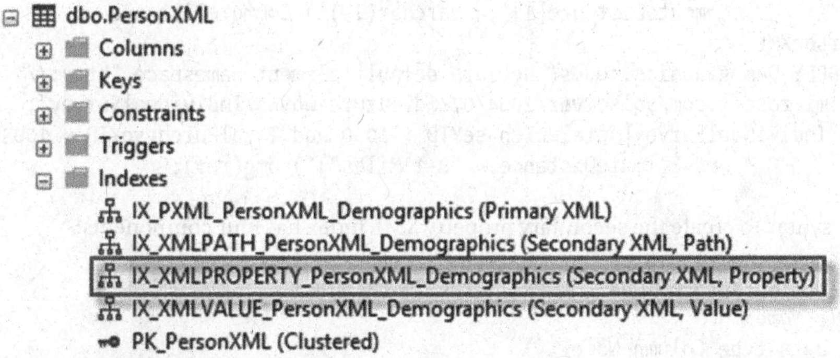

Figure 7-8. *Confirming the index was created*

Listing 7-14. Creating a secondary property XML index

```
CREATE XML INDEX IX_XMLPROPERTY_PersonXML_Demographics
ON dbo.PersonXML
(
        Demographics
)
USING XML INDEX IX_PXML_PersonXML_Demographics
FOR PROPERTY;
```

How It Works

A secondary property type index can provide performance benefits when querying an XML column that retrieves one or more values via the *value()* method. Listing 7-15 demonstrates the benefits of using XQuery when a PROPERTY index is present.

Listing 7-15. Showing the benefits of using XQuery when a PROPERTY index is present

```
SELECT PersonID,
       ref.value('declare default element namespace "http://schemas.
microsoft.com/sqlserver/2004/07/adventure-works/IndividualSurvey";
            TotalPurchaseYTD[1]', 'money') TotalPurchase,
       ref.value('declare default element namespace "http://schemas.
microsoft.com/sqlserver/2004/07/adventure-works/IndividualSurvey";
            DateFirstPurchase[1]', 'date') DateFirstPurchase,
       ref.value('declare default element namespace "http://schemas.
microsoft.com/sqlserver/2004/07/adventure-works/IndividualSurvey";
            YearlyIncome[1]', 'varchar(20)') YearlyIncome,
       ref.value('declare default element namespace "http://schemas.
microsoft.com/sqlserver/2004/07/adventure-works/IndividualSurvey";
            Occupation[1]', 'varchar(15)') Occupation,
       ref.value('declare default element namespace "http://schemas.
microsoft.com/sqlserver/2004/07/adventure-works/IndividualSurvey";
            CommuteDistance[1]', 'varchar(15)') CommuteDistance
FROM PersonXML
CROSS APPLY Demographics.nodes('declare default element namespace "http://
schemas.microsoft.com/sqlserver/2004/07/adventure-works/IndividualSurvey";
       IndividualSurvey[TotalPurchaseYTD > 1000 and TotalPurchaseYTD < 1005
            and CommuteDistance = "0-1 Miles"]') dmg(ref);
```

The syntax to create the secondary property XML index has four components:

```
CREATE XML INDEX <SECONDARY_PROPERTY_XML_INDEX_Name>
ON <Table_Name>
(  <XML_data_type_Column_Name>  )
USING XML INDEX <PRIMARY_XML_INDEX_Name> FOR PROPERTY;
```

7-5. Creating a Selective XML Index
Problem

You want to create an XML index on an XML column that stores large XML documents, but you want to minimize storage for the index.

Solution

A selective XML index is designed to improve XQuery performance and XML index storage for an XML column that stores large XML documents. Listing 7-16 creates a new sample table with an untyped XML column, populates it with sample XML data, and creates a selective XML index on it. Figure 7-9 displays the created index.

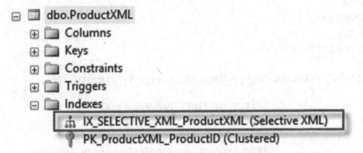

Figure 7-9. *Confirming the selective XML index was created for the ProductXML table*

Listing 7-16. Creating a selective XML index

```
-- These settings are important when creating a table with XML columns and
XML indexes
SET NUMERIC_ROUNDABORT OFF;
SET ARITHABORT ON;
SET ANSI_NULLS ON;
SET ANSI_PADDING ON;
SET ANSI_WARNINGS ON;
SET CONCAT_NULL_YIELDS_NULL ON;
SET QUOTED_IDENTIFIER ON;
GO
-- Drop table SQL Server 2016 syntax
DROP TABLE IF EXISTS dbo.ProductXML

-- Create demo table with an XML column
CREATE TABLE dbo.ProductXML
(
        ProductID INT NOT NULL,
        Name NVARCHAR(50) NOT NULL,
        ProductNumber NVARCHAR(25) NOT NULL,
        ProductDetails XML NULL
        CONSTRAINT PK_ProductXML_ProductID PRIMARY KEY CLUSTERED
        (
                ProductID ASC
        )
);
GO
```

```
-- Populate table with sample XML data
INSERT INTO dbo.ProductXML
(
        ProductID,
        Name,
        ProductNumber,
        ProductDetails
)
SELECT Product2.ProductId,
        Product2.Name,
        Product2.ProductNumber,
        (
                SELECT ProductCategory.Name AS "Category/CategoryName",
                        (
                                SELECT DISTINCT Location.Name "text()", ',
                                cost rate $',
                                        Location.CostRate "text()"
                                FROM Production.ProductInventory Inventory
                                INNER JOIN Production.Location Location
                                        ON Inventory.LocationID = Location.
                                        LocationID
                                WHERE Product.ProductID = Inventory.ProductID
                                FOR XML PATH('LocationName'), TYPE
                        ) AS "Locations/node()",
                        Subcategory.Name AS "Category/Subcategory/
                        SubcategoryName",
                        Product.Name AS "Category/Subcategory/Product/
                        ProductName",
                        Product.Color AS "Category/Subcategory/Product/Color",
                        Inventory.Shelf AS "Category/Subcategory/Product/
                        ProductLocation/Shelf",
                        Inventory.Bin AS "Category/Subcategory/Product/
                        ProductLocation/Bin",
                Inventory.Quantity AS "Category/Subcategory/Product/
                ProductLocation/Quantity"
                FROM Production.Product Product
                LEFT JOIN Production.ProductInventory Inventory
                        ON Product.ProductID = Inventory.ProductID
                LEFT JOIN Production.ProductSubcategory Subcategory
                        ON Product.ProductSubcategoryID = Subcategory.
                        ProductSubcategoryID
                LEFT JOIN Production.ProductCategory
                        ON Subcategory.ProductCategoryID = Production.
                        ProductCategory.ProductCategoryID
                WHERE Product.ProductID = Product2.ProductId
                ORDER BY ProductCategory.Name, Subcategory.Name, Product.Name
                FOR XML PATH('Categories'), ROOT('Products'), ELEMENTS, TYPE
        )
```

```
FROM Production.Product Product2;
GO

-- Create the selective XML index
CREATE SELECTIVE XML INDEX IX_SELECTIVE_XML_ProductXML
ON dbo.ProductXML
(
        ProductDetails
)
FOR
(
    Quantity = '/Products/Categories/Category/Subcategory/Product/
ProductLocation/Quantity',
    ProductName = '/Products/Categories/Category/Subcategory/Product/
ProductName'
);
GO
```

How It Works

While the primary XML index shreds all your XML data into a relational format, the selective XML index does not. A primary XML index can utilize a lot of space and consume server resources for large XML instances. The selective XML index acts against the values are specified in one or more paths. This can make the selective XML much smaller than the primary XML index in many cases. The syntax to create a selective XML index is more complex than the syntax to create a primary XML index. For example, the selective XML index, demonstrated in Listing 7-16, identifies two XQuery paths in the FOR clause, pointing to two deeply nested element nodes; namely:

- Quantity

- ProductName

A selective XML index path must be a fully qualified and complete path, i.e., no shortcuts are allowed for the path. The index contains the nodes that are identified by the paths. Listing 7-17 shows a sample XML fragment that demonstrates the XML paths to the Quantity and ProductName element nodesidentified in the selective XML index paths.

Listing 7-17. Sample XML fragment from the previous example

```
<Products>
  <Categories>
    <Locations>
      <LocationName>Tool Crib, cost rate $0.0000</LocationName>
      <LocationName>Miscellaneous Storage, cost rate $0.0000</LocationName>
      <LocationName>Subassembly, cost rate $12.2500</LocationName>
    </Locations>
    <Category>
      <Subcategory>
        <Product>
          <ProductName>Adjustable Race</ProductName>
          <ProductLocation>
            <Shelf>A</Shelf>
            <Bin>1</Bin>
            <Quantity>408</Quantity>
          </ProductLocation>
        </Product>
      </Subcategory>
    </Category>
  </Categories>
  <Categories>
</Products>
```

Products/Categories/Category/Subcategory/Product/ProductName

Products/Categories/Category/Subcategory/Product/ProductLocation/Quantity

The query from Listing 7-18 was run before the selective XML index was created. The result is demonstrated in Figure 7-10 for time statistics, with the execution plan shown in Figure 7-11.

```
(5 row(s) affected)

SQL Server Execution Times:

   CPU time = 31 ms,  elapsed time = 20 ms.
```

Figure 7-10. *Shows time statistics before the index created*

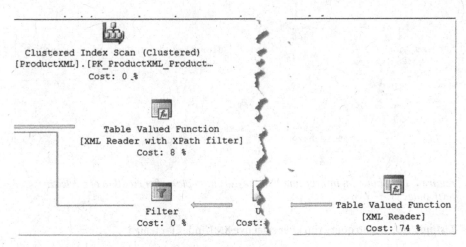

Figure 7-11. *Execution plan before the index is created*

Listing 7-18. Showing the demo query

```
SET STATISTICS TIME ON;

SELECT ProductID, Name, ProductNumber, ProductDetails
FROM dbo.ProductXML
WHERE ProductDetails.exist('Products/Categories/Category/Subcategory/
Product/ProductLocation/Quantity[.="622"]') = 1;

SET STATISTICS TIME OFF;
```

After the index IX_SELECTIVE_XML_ProductXML was created, the query from Listing 7-19 generates more efficient runtime and execution plan, as shown in Figure 7-12 and Figure 7-13.

```
(5 row(s) affected)

SQL Server Execution Times:

    CPU time = 0 ms,  elapsed time = 2 ms.
```

Figure 7-12. *Shows improved time statistics*

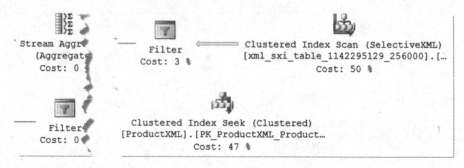

Figure 7-13. Shows an improvement in the execution plan after creation of a selective XML index

Listing 7-19. Demo query run after selective XML index is created

```
SET STATISTICS TIME ON;

SELECT ProductID, Name, ProductNumber, ProductDetails
FROM dbo.ProductXML
WHERE ProductDetails.exist('Products/Categories/Category/Subcategory/
Product/ProductLocation/Quantity[.="622"]') = 1;
```

The syntax to create the SELECTIVE XML index on an XML column without *XMLNAMESPACES* on the XML instances has following parts:

```
CREATE SELECTIVE XML INDEX <SELECTIVE_XML_Index_Name>
ON <Table_Name>
(<Column_Name>)
FOR ( Path_name1 = 'XML path',
      Path Name2 = 'XML path',
      Path Name3 = 'XML path')
```

When an XML column stores the XML instances with *XMLNAMESPACES,* the XMLNAMESPACE must be declared within the CREATE SELECTIVE INDEX statement. For example, if you want to improve search on the Resume column of the HumanResources.JobCandidate table. Listing 7-20 shows how to query an XML column with a namespace.

Listing 7-20. SQL code for searching for a job candidate

```
WITH XMLNAMESPACES('http://schemas.microsoft.com/sqlserver/2004/07/
adventure-works/Resume' as ns)
SELECT JobCandidateID, Resume
FROM HumanResources.JobCandidate
WHERE Resume.exist('/ns:Resume/ns:Name/ns:Name.First[.="Stephen"]') = 1
```

Listing 7-21 demonstrates how to create a selective XML index on the Resume column of the HumanResources.JobCandidate table. Figure 7-14 shows the SQL execution plan for the query in Listing 7-19 after the selective XML index is created.

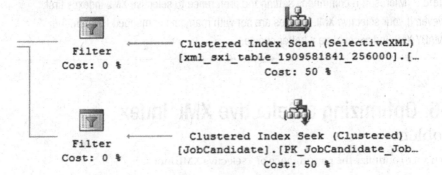

Figure 7-14. *Shows the SQL execution plan after the selective XML index is created*

Listing 7-21. The CREATE SELECTIVE XML INDEX statement on a column with XMLNAMESPACE

```
CREATE SELECTIVE XML INDEX IX_SELECTIVE_XML_HumanResources_JobCandidate
        ON [HumanResources].[JobCandidate]
(
        [Resume]
)
WITH XMLNAMESPACES
(
        DEFAULT 'http://schemas.microsoft.com/sqlserver/2004/07/adventure-
works/Resume'
)
FOR
(
        LastName = '/Resume/Name/Name.Last'
        ,FirstName = '/Resume/Name/Name.First'
);
```

The syntax to create a select XML index on an XML column with *XMLNAMESPACES* on the XML instances has the following parts:

```
CREATE SELECTIVE XML INDEX <SELECTIVE_XML_Index_Name>
ON <Table_Name>
(<Column_Name>)
WITH XMLNAMESPACES(DEFAULT 'XMLNAMESPACE URI')
FOR ( Path_Name1 = 'XML path',
        Path_Name2 = 'XML path',
        Path_Name3 = 'XML path')
```

The advantage of creating a selective XML index is that you can implement one or more XML paths to focus on the XML values that are primarily used in your search criteria.

■ **Note**　Microsoft recommends setting the preference to selective XML indexes first. However, if your selective XML indexes are set with many paths mapped to them, the PRIMARY XML index could be a better choice.

7-6. Optimizing a Selective XML Index
Problem

You want to optimize the performance of a selective XML index.

Solution

Implementing the hints can optimize a selective XML index. Listing 7-22 demonstrates different hints for the selective XML index.

Listing 7-22.　Testing different hints for the selective XML index

```
CREATE SELECTIVE XML INDEX IX_SELECTIVE_XML_ProductXML_Hint_Sample
ON dbo.ProductXML
(
        ProductDetails
)
FOR
(
        SubcategoryName = '/Products/Categories/Category/Subcategory/
        SubcategoryName' AS XQUERY 'node()',
        Shelf = '/Products/Categories/Category/Subcategory/Product/
        ProductLocation/Shelf',
        Bin = '/Products/Categories/Category/Subcategory/Product/
        ProductLocation/Bin' AS XQUERY 'xs:double' SINGLETON,
        ProductName = '/Products/Categories/Category/Subcategory/Product/
        ProductName' AS SQL nvarchar(40),
        CategoryName = '/Products/Categories/Category/CategoryName' AS
        XQUERY 'xs:string' MAXLENGTH(35)
);
```

How It Works

Selective XML index hints come in two flavors:

- SQL Server – oriented with SQL data-type mappings. For example, PathName = '/root/element' AS SQL nvarchar(40)

- XQUERY – oriented with XQuery data-type mappings. For example, PathName = '/root/element AS XQUERY 'xs:string'

Table 7-1 describes the optimization hints that could be implements to improve the selective XML index.

Table 7-1. *Descriptions of the selective XML index optimization hints*

Optimization hint	Applies to	Hint description
node()	XQuery	Reduces the amount of storage required. Check for node existence.
SINGLETON	XQuery and SQL Server	Provides assurance that there is only one instance of the group so that the index can be optimized with that in mind. Avoid adding additional instances subsequently, as this can cause issues.
DATA TYPE	XQuery	Optimizes the index with the data types. An issue could arise if something breaks the data type, then a null will show in the index.
MAXLENGTH	XQuery	It is helpful to look at the XQuery type xs:string and optimize the index with the maximum allowed value for the strings. However, this could cause an issue if the existing string is longer than the specified MAXLENGTH, since the index could fail.

Table 7-2 lists the eligible XQuery data types for selective XML index hints, created on XML typed and untyped columns.

Table 7-2. *Hint-eligible XQuery data types*

Typed XML	Untyped XML
xs:anyUri	
xs:boolean	xs:boolean
xs:date	xs:date
xs:dateTime	xs:dateTime
xs:day	
xs:decimal	
xs:double	xs:double
xs:float	
xs:int	
xs:integer	
xs:language	
xs:long	
xs:name	
xs:NCName	
xs:negativeInteger	
xs:nmtoken	
xs:nonNegativeInteger	
xs:nonPositiveInteger	
xs:positiveInteger	
xs:qname	
xs:short	
xs:string	xs:string
xs:time	xs:time
xs:token	
xs:unsignedByte	
xs:unsignedInt	
xs:unsignedLong	
xs:unsignedShort	

The selective XML index can obtain benefits when a hint applies to the index. Table 7-3 lists the benefits of the selective XML index optimization hints.

Table 7-3. *Effectiveness of selective XML index optimization hints*

Optimization hint	Storage efficiency	Performance improvement
node()	Yes	No
SINGLETON	No	Yes
DATA TYPE	Yes	Yes
MAXLENGTH	Yes	Yes

Table 7-4 lists which optimization hints are supported with each data type.

Table 7-4. *List of optimization hints and data types*

Optimization hint	XQuery data types	SQL data types
node()	Yes	No
SINGLETON	Yes	Yes
DATA TYPE	Yes	No
MAXLENGTH	Yes	No

7-7. Creating a Secondary Selective XML Index
Problem

You want to improve selective XML index performance.

Solution

A secondary selective XML index can improve the performance of a selective XML index. Listing 7-23 creates the selective XML index on the HumanResources.JobCandidate table from Solution 7-6, which is a prerequisite for this solution.

Listing 7-23. Testing different hints for the selective XML index

```
CREATE SELECTIVE XML INDEX IX_SELECTIVE_XML_ProductXML_Hint_Sample
ON dbo.ProductXML
(
        ProductDetails
)
FOR
(
        SubcategoryName = '/Products/Categories/Category/Subcategory/
        SubcategoryName' AS XQUERY 'node()',
        Shelf = '/Products/Categories/Category/Subcategory/Product/
        ProductLocation/Shelf',
```

```
        Bin = '/Products/Categories/Category/Subcategory/Product/
        ProductLocation/Bin' AS XQUERY 'xs:double' SINGLETON,
        ProductName = '/Products/Categories/Category/Subcategory/Product/
        ProductName' AS SQL nvarchar(40),
        CategoryName = '/Products/Categories/Category/CategoryName' AS
        XQUERY 'xs:string' MAXLENGTH(35)
);
```

Listing 7-24 shows how to create a secondary selective XML index on the HumanResources.JobCandidate table.

Listing 7-24. Demonstrating how to create a secondary selective XML index

```
CREATE XML INDEX IX_SELECTIVE_SECONDARY_XML_HumanResources_JobCandidate
ON HumanResources.JobCandidate
(
        Resume
)
USING XML INDEX IX_SELECTIVE_XML_HumanResources_JobCandidate
FOR (LastName);
```

How It Works

The secondary selective XML index improves the performance of a selective XML index. The syntax is similar to the syntax of a secondary XML index, the main difference being that the selective XML index is specified in the USING XML INDEX clause and the FOR clause implements one of the selective XML index paths.

The syntax to create the secondary selective XML index has following components:

```
CREATE XML INDEX <SECONDARY_SELECTIVE_XML_Index_Name>
ON <Table_Name>
(<Column_Name>)
USING XML INDEX (<SELECTIVE_XML_Index_Name>)
FOR ( <PathName> )
```

The secondary selective XML index must have a path with a promoted data type. For example:

- SQL Server type is '/Resume/Name/Name.First' AS SQL varchar(20)

- XQuery type is '/Resume/Name/Name.First' AS XQUERY 'xs:string' MAXLENGTH(20)

When a data type is not promoted, SQL Server raises an error:

```
Msg 6391, Level 16, State 0, Line 111
Path 'LastName' is promoted to a type that is invalid for use as a key
column in a secondary selective XML index.
```

214

7-8. Modifying Selective XML Indexes
Problem
You want to add or remove a path from a selective XML index.

Solution
You can add or remove a path on a selective XML index. Listing 7-25 creates the
demonstration table we previously created in Solution 7-5. It populates the table with
XML data and creates a selective XML index on the table. This is a prerequisite for this
solution.

Listing 7-25. Create demonstration table with selective XML index

```
-- These settings are important when creating a table with XML columns and
XML indexes
SET NUMERIC_ROUNDABORT OFF;
SET ARITHABORT ON;
SET ANSI_NULLS ON;
SET ANSI_PADDING ON;
SET ANSI_WARNINGS ON;
SET CONCAT_NULL_YIELDS_NULL ON;
SET QUOTED_IDENTIFIER ON;
GO
-- Drop table SQL Server 2016 syntax
DROP TABLE IF EXISTS dbo.ProductXML

-- Create demo table with an XML column
CREATE TABLE dbo.ProductXML
(
        ProductID INT NOT NULL,
        Name NVARCHAR(50) NOT NULL,
        ProductNumber NVARCHAR(25) NOT NULL,
        ProductDetails XML NULL
        CONSTRAINT PK_ProductXML_ProductID PRIMARY KEY CLUSTERED
        (
                ProductID ASC
        )
);
GO

-- Populate table with sample XML data
INSERT INTO dbo.ProductXML
(
        ProductID,
        Name,
        ProductNumber,
```

215

```
        ProductDetails
)
SELECT Product2.ProductId,
        Product2.Name,
        Product2.ProductNumber,
        (
                SELECT ProductCategory.Name AS "Category/CategoryName",
                        (
                                SELECT DISTINCT Location.Name "text()", ',
                                cost rate $',
                                        Location.CostRate "text()"
                                FROM Production.ProductInventory Inventory
                                INNER JOIN Production.Location Location
                                        ON Inventory.LocationID = Location.
                                        LocationID
                                WHERE Product.ProductID = Inventory.
                                ProductID
                                FOR XML PATH('LocationName'), TYPE
                        ) AS "Locations/node()",
                        Subcategory.Name AS "Category/Subcategory/
                        SubcategoryName",
                        Product.Name AS "Category/Subcategory/Product/
                        ProductName",
                        Product.Color AS "Category/Subcategory/Product/Color",
                        Inventory.Shelf AS "Category/Subcategory/Product/
                        ProductLocation/Shelf",
                        Inventory.Bin AS "Category/Subcategory/Product/
                        ProductLocation/Bin",
                Inventory.Quantity AS "Category/Subcategory/Product/
                ProductLocation/Quantity"
                FROM Production.Product Product
                LEFT JOIN Production.ProductInventory Inventory
                        ON Product.ProductID = Inventory.ProductID
                LEFT JOIN Production.ProductSubcategory Subcategory
                        ON Product.ProductSubcategoryID = Subcategory.
                        ProductSubcategoryID
                LEFT JOIN Production.ProductCategory
                        ON Subcategory.ProductCategoryID = Production.
                        ProductCategory.ProductCategoryID
                WHERE Product.ProductID = Product2.ProductId
                ORDER BY ProductCategory.Name, Subcategory.Name, Product.Name
                FOR XML PATH('Categories'), ROOT('Products'), ELEMENTS, TYPE
        )
FROM Production.Product Product2;
GO


-- Create the selective XML index
CREATE SELECTIVE XML INDEX IX_SELECTIVE_XML_ProductXML
ON dbo.ProductXML
```

```
(
        ProductDetails
)
FOR
(
    Quantity = '/Products/Categories/Category/Subcategory/Product/
ProductLocation/Quantity',
    ProductName = '/Products/Categories/Category/Subcategory/Product/
ProductName'
);
GO
```

Listing 7-26 demonstrates how to remove the *Quantity* path from this index and add the *CategoryName* path to it.

Listing 7-26. Altering selective XML index

```
ALTER INDEX IX_SELECTIVE_XML_ProductXML
ON dbo.ProductXML
FOR
(
    ADD CategoryName = '/Products/Categories/Category/CategoryName',
    REMOVE Quantity
);
```

How It Works

The *ALTER INDEX* statement can be used on the selective XML index to change the index contents. It is possible to drop an existing path using the *REMOVE* keyword and a new path can be added by using the *ADD* keyword within the *FOR()* clause, as demonstrated in Listing 7-26. You can combine the *ADD* and *REMOVE* keywords as we did in Listing 7-26, or they can be issued in individual *ALTER INDEX* statements, as shown in Listing 7-27.

Listing 7-27. Altering selective index with separate ALTER INDEX statements

```
ALTER INDEX IX_SELECTIVE_XML_ProductXML
ON dbo.ProductXML
FOR
(
        ADD CategoryName = '/Products/Categories/Category/CategoryName'
);
GO
```

```
ALTER INDEX IX_SELECTIVE_XML_ProductXML
ON ProductXML
FOR
(
        REMOVE Quantity
);
GO
```

Each *ALTER INDEX* statement rebuilds the entire index. Therefore, for efficiency reasons, it is more practical to implement a list of changes in a single ALTER INDEX statement instead of running the *ALTER INDEX* statement multiple times.

To drop a selective XML index, use the DROP INDEX statement, as shown in Listing Sample 7-28.

Listing 7-28. Dropping a selective XML index

```
DROP INDEX IX_SELECTIVE_XML_ProductXML
ON dbo.ProductModelXML;
```

■ **Note**   Keep in mind, similarly to the primary XML index, when the selective XML index is dropped, all associated secondary selective XML indexes are dropped automatically.

Wrapping up

This chapter completes the XML section of the book. I hope that you learned a lot from the recipes provided in the XML portion.

If you practice the solutions in the XML chapters then you should able to build XML, shred XML instances, load XML documents from different sources, utilize XML-based searches via XQuery statements, and create XML indexes.

The upcoming section will introduce JSON and demonstrate SQL Server 2016's integration with new JSON features.

JSON in SQL Server

CHAPTER 8

■ ■ ■

Constructing JSON

Welcome to Part II of this book. Part II will cover JSON for SQL Server, which was introduced in SQL Server 2016. JSON has many similarities to XML; however, they are not the same. JSON can be thought of as a "fat-free" version of XML. To run the samples for Part II, make sure that the database compatibility level in SQL Server 2016 is set to 130. The sample database for Part II is WideWorldImporters. Please use the following link to download the database: https://github.com/Microsoft/sql-server-samples/releases/tag/wide-world-importers-v1.0?utm_source=MyTechMantra.com.

JSON Introduction

JSON is an acronym for *"JavaScript Object Notation"* and is pronounced *"Jason."* It's meant to be a more easily decipherable and compact solution to represent a complex data structure and facilitate data interchange between systems.

When comparing JSON to XML, there are many benefits to choosing JSON:

- Unlike XML, JSON does not use a full markup structure, which makes it more compact.

- JSON is not a data type (at least for SQL Server 2016). SQL Server represents JSON as a string that is similar to nvarchar(max). Microsoft recommends storing JSON as an nvarchar(max).

- JSON is easy to parse and build.

- JSON data structure is easy to understand.

- JSON is the native file structure for NoSQL databases, such as CouchDB, MongoDB, and others.

The JSON model format has two blocks:

- Objects - encapsulated within opening and closing brackets {}. An empty object {} is considered valid JSON data. Listing 8-1: TopObject is an object block.

- Arrays - encapsulated within opening and closing square brackets []. An empty array [] is also considered valid JSON data. Listing 8-1: ArrayOfObjects and arrayOfValues are array blocks.

© Alex Grinberg 2018
A. Grinberg, *XML and JSON Recipes for SQL Server*,
https://doi.org/10.1007/978-1-4842-3117-3_8

Listing 8-1. Demonstrating JSON structure

```
{
    "TopObject": {
        "numericKey": 2016,
        "stringKey": "a text value",
        "nullKey": null,
        "booleanKey": true,
        "dateKey": "2017-11-14"
    },
    "arrayOfObjects": [
                        {"item": 1},
                        {"item": 2},
                        {"item": 3}
                      ] ,
    "arrayOfValues": [
                        "SQL",
                        "XML",
                        "JSON"
                      ]
}
```

A JSON member is represented by a key-value pair *{"key": "value"}*. The key of a member should be contained in double quotes. A key must be unique within the structure of an object. String type and date type values of a member are required to be contained in double quotes. Boolean and numeric values should not be contained within double quotes. However, when Boolean values use true or false literals, those values should be in lowercase. Table 8-1 demonstrates data type conversion between SQL Server data types and JSON.

Numbers with leading zeroes are considered strings. Therefore, they are required to be contained within double quotes. Each member of an object and each array value must be followed by a comma, except the last key-value pair.

Table 8-1. *Showing data type conversion from SQL Server to JSON*

Category	SQL type	JSON type
Character and string types	nvarchar, varchar, nchar, char	string
Numeric types	int, bigint, float, decimal, numeric	number
Bit type	bit	Boolean (true or false)
Date and time types	date, datetime, datetime2, time, datetimeoffset	string
CLR types	geometry, geography (except hierarchyid)	Not supported. These types return an error. Cast or convert the data to a supported JSON type, or use a CLR property or method in the SELECT list - for example, ToString() for any CLR type, or STAsText() for the geometry type. Data type hierarchyid does not require explicit conversion.
Other types	uniqueidentifier, money, varbinary, binary, timestamp, rowversion	string

A side-by-side comparison of XML and JSON data and parsing methods is demonstrated in Table 8-2.

Table 8-2. *Comparing XML and JSON*

XML Sample	JSON Sample
| ```
<employees>
  <employee>
    <firstName>Bill</firstName>
    <lastName>Adams</lastName>
  </employee>
  <employee>
    <firstName>John</firstName>
    <lastName>Smith</lastName>
  </employee>
<employee>
    <firstName>Peter</firstName>
    <lastName>White</lastName>
  </employee>
</employees>
``` | ```
{"employees":
  [
    {"firstName":"Bill",
    "lastName":"Adams"},
    {"firstName":"John",
    "lastName":"Smith"},
    {"firstName":"Peter",
    "lastName":"White"}
  ]
}
``` |

XML Parsing Method

```
Declare @x XML =
'<employees>
  <employee>
    <firstName>Bill</firstName>
    <lastName>Adams</lastName>
  </employee>
<employee>
    <firstName>John</firstName>
    <lastName>Smith</lastName>
  </employee>
<employee>
    <firstName>Peter</firstName>
    <lastName>White</lastName>
  </employee>
</employees>';
SELECT
c.value('firstName[1]',
'varchar(30)') AS firstName
,c.value('lastName[1]',
'varchar(30)') AS lastName
FROM @x.nodes('//employee') t(c);
```

JSON Parsing Method

```
declare @j nvarchar(max) =
'{"employees":
  [
    {"firstName":"Bill",
    "lastName":"Adams"},
    {"firstName":"John",
    "lastName":"Smith"},
    {"firstName":"Peter",
    "lastName":"White"}
  ]
}';
SELECT firstName, lastName
FROM OPENJSON (@j, '$.employees')
WITH
  (
    firstName varchar(30),
    lastName varchar(30)
  );
```

XML Result

firstName	lastName
Bill	Adams
John	Smith
Peter	White

JSON Result

firstName	lastName
Bill	Adams
John	Smith
Peter	White

SQL Server provides four built-in functions and the FOR JSON clause of SELECT queries to process and create JSON documents, as shown in Table 8-3.

Unlike XML methods, JSON functions are not key sensitive. However, key members remain key sensitive when referenced in JSON functions as well as the ToString() and STAsText() CLR functions.

Table 8-3. *Describing JSON built-in functions*

JSON Procedure	Procedure Type	Description
FOR JSON	Clause	Builds a JSON document.
ISJSON()	Function	Verifies whether a string has a valid JSON.
JSON_VALUE()	Function	Retrieves a scalar value from a JSON document.
JSON_QUERY()	Function	Retrieves an object or an array from a JSON document.
JSON_MODIFY()	Function	Modifies a JSON document.
OPENJSON()	Table-valued function	Converts a JSON document into a table format that contains rows and columns.

Part II of this book provides JSON recipes for SQL Server.

8-1. Building JSON with AUTO Mode
Problem
You want to build a JSON-formatted result automatically.

Solution
The *FOR JSON* clause in *AUTO* mode returns JSON-formatted rows. Listing 8-2 demonstrates a FOR JSON clause with AUTO mode from a single object. Figure 8-1 shows a JSON returned row. Listing 8-3 demonstrates a formatted JSON from the query result.

Listing 8-2. Showing

```
SELECT TOP (2) CustomerName
        ,PrimaryContact
        ,AlternateContact
        ,PhoneNumber
FROM WideWorldImporters.Website.Customers
FOR JSON AUTO;
```

Figure 8-1. *Showing JSON result in a grid*

Listing 8-3. Showing formatted JSON result

```
[
  {
    "CustomerName":"Tailspin Toys (Head Office)",
    "PrimaryContact":"Waldemar Fisar",
    "AlternateContact":"Laimonis Berzins",
    "PhoneNumber":"(308) 555-0100"
  },
  {
    "CustomerName":"Tailspin Toys (Sylvanite, MT)",
    "PrimaryContact":"Lorena Cindric",
    "AlternateContact":"Hung Van Groesen",
    "PhoneNumber":"(406) 555-0100"
  }
]
```

How It Works

The *FOR JSON* clause in *AUTO* mode formats the output into a JSON result set. AUTO mode automatically determines the JSON format based on the table (or tables) implemented in the FROM and SELECT clauses. Listing 8-3 returns simple JSON output because of the result based on the single Website.Customers table. The result, by default, is displayed in the SSMS grid as a hyperlink. When the user clicks on the result, JSON opens it in the XML Editor. However, the result will load as an unformatted single-line string. Figure 8-2 demonstrates the unformatted result in the XML Editor.

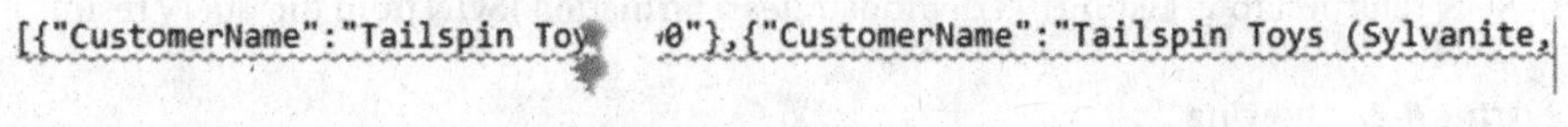

Figure 8-2. *Showing JSON result in the XML Editor*

Therefore, a small JSON result could be formatted manually, as shown in Listing 8-3. However, for a bigger JSON, manual formatting could take an enormous time to complete such a task.

There are several websites offering the capability to validate and convert a JSON unformatted value into formatted JSON data. One of my preferred JSON formatting tools is JSONFormatter, and the URL is the following: https://jsonformatter. curiousconcept.com/. This program is easy to operate:

1. JSON result from XML Editor.

2. Paste into JSONFormatter validation window, shown in Figure 8-3.

3. Click Process button.

4. Valid JSON displays in the Formatted JSON Data window, shown in Figure 8-4.

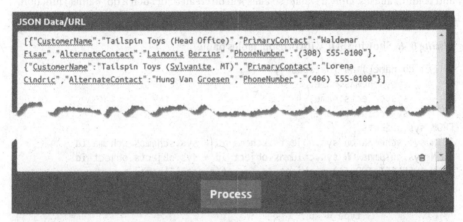

JSON Data/URL

```
[{"CustomerName":"Tailspin Toys (Head Office)","PrimaryContact":"Waldemar
Fisar","AlternateContact":"Laimonis Berzins","PhoneNumber":"(308) 555-0100"},
{"CustomerName":"Tailspin Toys (Sylvanite, MT)","PrimaryContact":"Lorena
Cindric","AlternateContact":"Hung Van Groesen","PhoneNumber":"(406) 555-0100"}]
```

Process

Figure 8-3. Showing JSONFormatter interface

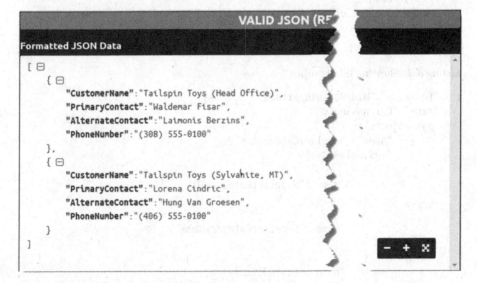

VALID JSON (RE

Formatted JSON Data

```
[
    {
        "CustomerName":"Tailspin Toys (Head Office)",
        "PrimaryContact":"Waldemar Fisar",
        "AlternateContact":"Laimonis Berzins",
        "PhoneNumber":"(308) 555-0100"
    },
    {
        "CustomerName":"Tailspin Toys (Sylvanite, MT)",
        "PrimaryContact":"Lorena Cindric",
        "AlternateContact":"Hung Van Groesen",
        "PhoneNumber":"(406) 555-0100"
    }
]
```

- + X

Figure 8-4. Showing Formatted JSON Data window

■ **Note**   As an alternative to JSONFormatter, JSON Editor Online is another formatting application; URL: http://www.jsoneditoronline.org/. I prefer JSONFormatter because this application retains all submitted JSON code. Therefore, when I need to go back to some result, I do not need to resubmit the JSON code.

When dealing with many tables in the FROM clause to return JSON data, you must keep in mind that the table and column aliases take effect on JSON output. For example, Listing 8-4 demonstrates the JSON built with a query where the query does not have table and column aliases. Only a Database alias will be created for such a db_name() function. Listing 8-5 displays the query result in JSON output.

Listing 8-4. Showing SQL with original tables name

```
SELECT db_name() as [Database],
        sys.schemas.name,
        sys.objects.name,
        sys.columns.name
FROM sys.objects
JOIN sys.schemas on sys.objects.schema_id = sys.schemas.schema_id
JOIN sys.columns ON sys.columns.object_id = sys.objects.object_id
JOIN ( SELECT TOP (1) o.object_id, count(c.name) [name]
        FROM sys.columns c
                JOIN sys.objects o ON c.object_id = o.object_id WHERE
                type = 'u'
        GROUP BY o.object_id HAVING COUNT(c.name) < 6
          ) countCol
        ON countCol.object_id = sys.objects.object_id
WHERE type = 'u'
FOR JSON AUTO;
```

Listing 8-5. Showing JSON output

```
{   "Database":"WideWorldImporters",
    "name":"Purchasing",
    "sys.objects":[
        {   "name":"SupplierCategories",
            "sys.columns":[
                {
                    "name":"SupplierCategoryID"
                },
                {
                    "name":"SupplierCategoryName"
                },
                {
                    "name":"LastEditedBy"
                },
```

```
                {
                    "name":"ValidFrom"
                },
                {

                    "name":"ValidTo"
                }
            ]
        }
    ]
}
```

Listing 8-6 demonstrates the JSON that builds with a query where the tables do have aliases. Listing 8-7 displays the query result in JSON output.

Listing 8-6. Showing SQL with the table aliases

```
SELECT db_name() as [Database],
       [Schema].name as [SchemaName],
       [Table].name  as [TableName],
       [Column].name as [ColumnName]
FROM sys.objects [Table]
JOIN sys.schemas [Schema] on [Table].schema_id = [Schema].schema_id
JOIN sys.columns [Column] ON [Column].object_id = [Table].object_id
JOIN ( SELECT TOP (1) o.object_id, COUNT(c.name) [name]
        FROM sys.columns c JOIN sys.objects o
                ON c.object_id = o.object_id where type = 'u'
        GROUP BY o.object_id HAVING COUNT(c.name) < 6)  countCol
        ON countCol.object_id = [Table].object_id
WHERE type = 'u'
FOR JSON AUTO;
```

Listing 8-7. Showing JSON output

```
{   "Database":"WideWorldImporters",
    "SchemaName":"Purchasing",
    "Table":[
        {   "TableName":"SupplierCategories",
            "Column":[
                {
                    "ColumnName":"SupplierCategoryID"
                },
                {
                    "ColumnName":"SupplierCategoryName"
                },
                {
                    "ColumnName":"LastEditedBy"
                },
                {
```

```
                 "ColumnName":"ValidFrom"
        },
        {
                 "ColumnName":"ValidTo"
        }
      ]
   }
 ]
}
```

When compared to the JSON in Listings 8-5 and 8-7, you could see that Listing 8-7 is more descriptive than Listing 8-5, for example, "sys.objects" vs "Table."

8-2. Handling NULL When JSON Build
Problem

You want to preserve key element names when a value is NULL.

Solution

The *INCLUDE_NULL_VALUES* option within the *FOR JSON* clause specifies that when a column has a *NULL* value, then a JSON key element must be presented in the JSON output. Listing 8-8 demonstrated a *FOR JSON* clause with an *INCLUDE_NULL_VALUES* option. Listing 8-9 is showing JSON output generated by the query.

Listing 8-8. FOR JSON clause with INCLUDE_NULL_VALUES option

```
USE [WideWorldImporters];
SELECT TOP (1) [CustomerName]
        ,[PrimaryContact]
        ,[AlternateContact]
        ,[PhoneNumber]
FROM [Website].[Customers] where [AlternateContact] IS NOT NULL
UNION ALL
SELECT TOP (1) [CustomerName]
        ,[PrimaryContact]
        ,[AlternateContact]
        ,[PhoneNumber]
FROM [Website].[Customers] where [AlternateContact] IS NULL
FOR JSON AUTO, INCLUDE_NULL_VALUES;
```

Listing 8-9. Showing returned JSON

```
[ {
        "CustomerName":"Tailspin Toys (Head Office)",
        "PrimaryContact":"Waldemar Fisar",
        "AlternateContact":"Laimonis Berzins",
```

```
        "PhoneNumber":"(308) 555-0100"
    },
    {

        "CustomerName":"Eric Torres",
        "PrimaryContact":"Eric Torres",
        "AlternateContact":null,
        "PhoneNumber":"(307) 555-0100"
    }

]
```

How It Works

By default, the FOR JSON clause ignores elements with default values. Therefore, key elements will be missing in the JSON output. For example, when you execute the query demonstrated in Listing 8-8 without the INCLUDE_NULL_VALUES option, then *"AlternateContact"* will be missing in the second part of the JSON output. Listing 8-10 demonstrates the query and returned JSON output.

Listing 8-10. Showing query and JSON output

```
SELECT TOP (1) [CustomerName]
        ,[PrimaryContact]
        ,[AlternateContact]
        ,[PhoneNumber]
FROM [Website].[Customers] where [AlternateContact] IS NOT NULL
UNION ALL
SELECT TOP (1) [CustomerName]
        ,[PrimaryContact]
        ,[AlternateContact]
        ,[PhoneNumber]
FROM [Website].[Customers] where [AlternateContact] IS NULL
FOR JSON AUTO;

[
    {
        "CustomerName":"Tailspin Toys (Head Office)",
        "PrimaryContact":"Waldemar Fisar",
        "AlternateContact":"Laimonis Berzins",
        "PhoneNumber":"(308) 555-0100"
    },
    {
        "CustomerName":"Eric Torres",
        "PrimaryContact":"Eric Torres",
        "PhoneNumber":"(307) 555-0100"
    }

]
```

8-3. Escaping the Brackets for JSON Output

Problem

You want to remove the square brackets that surround JSON output.

Solution

The WITHOUT_ARRAY_WRAPPER option builds JSON output without surrounding square brackets []. Listing 8-11 is demonstrating a WITHOUT_ARRAY_WRAPPER option in the FOR JSON clause. Listing 8-12 demonstrates JSON output without square brackets [].

Listing 8-11. Showing WITHOUT_ARRAY_WRAPPER option

```
SELECT TOP (2) [CustomerName]
        ,[PrimaryContact]
        ,[AlternateContact]
        ,[PhoneNumber]
FROM [WideWorldImporters].[Website].[Customers]
FOR JSON AUTO, WITHOUT_ARRAY_WRAPPER;
```

Listing 8-12. Showing JSON output

```
{
    "CustomerName":"Tailspin Toys (Head Office)",
    "PrimaryContact":"Waldemar Fisar",
    "AlternateContact":"Laimonis Berzins",
    "PhoneNumber":"(308) 555-0100"
},
{
    "CustomerName":"Tailspin Toys (Sylvanite, MT)",
    "PrimaryContact":"Lorena Cindric",
    "AlternateContact":"Hung Van Groesen",
    "PhoneNumber":"(406) 555-0100"
}
```

How It Works

By default, the FOR JSON clause returns JSON output surrounded by square brackets []. That creates a JSON output as an initial array instead of an object. However, some output does not require the surrounding brackets. In such cases, the WITHOUT_ARRAY_WRAPPER option removes square brackets that surround the JSON output.

8-4. Adding ROOT Key Element to JSON

Problem

You want to add a user-defined, single top-level key element a JSON output.

Solution

The *ROOT* option adds a single top-level key element to JSON output. Listing 8-13 demonstrates a *FOR JSON* clause with a *ROOT* option. Listing 8-14 demonstrates JSON output with the top key element "Customers."

Listing 8-13. Showing ROOT option

```
SELECT TOP (2) [CustomerName]
       ,[PrimaryContact]
       ,[AlternateContact]
       ,[PhoneNumber]
FROM [WideWorldImporters].[Website].[Customers]
FOR JSON AUTO, ROOT('Customers')
```

Listing 8-14. Showing JSON output with top key element "Customers"

```
{
"Customers":[
        {
                "CustomerName":"Tailspin Toys (Head Office)",
                "PrimaryContact":"Waldemar Fisar",
                "AlternateContact":"Laimonis Berzins",
                "PhoneNumber":"(308) 555-0100"
        },
        {
                "CustomerName":"Tailspin Toys (Sylvanite, MT)",
                "PrimaryContact":"Lorena Cindric",
                "AlternateContact":"Hung Van Groesen",
                "PhoneNumber":"(406) 555-0100"
        }
        ]
}
```

How It Works

The *ROOT* option is an optional part of a FOR JSON clause.

The ROOT option could be combined with an INCLUDE_NULL_VALUES option. However, when the *WITHOUT_ARRAY_WRAPPER* is combined with a *ROOT* option, SQL Server raises the error shown in Listing 8-15.

233

Listing 8-15. Showing the error message when ROOT combined with WITHOUT_ARRAY_WRAPPER option

```
Msg 13620, Level 16, State 1, Line 5
ROOT option and WITHOUT_ARRAY_WRAPPER option cannot be used together in FOR
JSON. Remove one of these options.
```

8-5. Gaining Control over JSON Output
Problem

You want to obtain full control over complex JSON output.

Solution

PATH mode allows you to build JSON output that is controlled by you. Listing 8-16 demonstrates a query with a FOR JSON clause with the PATH mode, which returns cascading JSON output shown in Listing 8-17.

Listing 8-16. Showing FOR JSON with PATH mode

```sql
USE WideWorldImporters;

SELECT db_name()       as 'Database',
       [Schema].name as 'Tables.SchemaName',
       [Table].name  as 'Tables.TableName',
       [Column].name as 'Tables.Columns.ColumnName'
FROM sys.objects [Table]
       JOIN sys.schemas [Schema] on [Table].schema_id = [Schema].schema_id
       JOIN sys.columns [Column] ON [Column].object_id = [Table].object_id
WHERE type = 'u' and [Table].name = 'SupplierCategories'
FOR JSON PATH;
```

Listing 8-17. Showing JSON output

```json
[{
    "Database": "WideWorldImporters",
    "Tables": {
      "SchemaName": "Purchasing",
      "TableName": "SupplierCategories",
      "Columns":          {
        "ColumnName": "SupplierCategoryID"
                 }
             }
  },
  {
    "Database": "WideWorldImporters",
    "Tables": {
```

```
          "SchemaName": "Purchasing",
          "TableName": "SupplierCategories",
          "Columns":            {
            "ColumnName": "SupplierCategoryName"
                }
                }
  },
  {
    "Database": "WideWorldImporters",
    "Tables": {
      "SchemaName": "Purchasing",
      "TableName": "SupplierCategories",
      "Columns":            {
        "ColumnName": "LastEditedBy"
                }
                }
  },
  {
    "Database": "WideWorldImporters",
    "Tables": {
      "SchemaName": "Purchasing",
      "TableName": "SupplierCategories",
      "Columns":            {
        "ColumnName": "ValidFrom"
                }
                }
  },
  {
    "Database": "WideWorldImporters",
    "Tables": {
      "SchemaName": "Purchasing",
      "TableName": "SupplierCategories",
      "Columns":            {
        "ColumnName": "ValidTo"
                }
                }
  }]
```

How It Works

PATH mode allows the specification of the structure that builds JSON output. The
difference between PATH and AUTO mode is that AUTO mode builds up a JSON output
automatically by figuring out how the FROM and SELECT clauses are structured in a
query. If a query is based on one table, then the PATH and AUTO modes return similar
JSON output. However, in most cases, JSON output is built based on multiple tables, and
in this case the AUTO mode is not the best choice because your expectation for JSON
output is not always the same as what AUTO mode returns. With the PATH mode, you
dictate how your JSON structure is going to look.

JSON structure is constructed in the SELECT clause. When alias names are separated by a comma, a parent-child level is established for the elements and value. For example, Figure 8-5 demonstrates three levels of structure:

1. Database

2. Tables {Schema and Table}

3. Columns {ColumnName}

The T-SQL results returned by the same query are demonstrated in Figure 8-5, but without the FOR JSON clause, shown in Listing 8-18.

Listing 8-18. Showing query that generated a result for Figure 8-5

```sql
SELECT db_name()      as 'Database',
       [Schema].name as 'Tables.SchemaName',
       [Table].name  as 'Tables.TableName',
       [Column].name as 'Tables.Columns.ColumnName'
FROM sys.objects [Table]
       JOIN sys.schemas [Schema] on [Table].schema_id = [Schema].schema_id
       JOIN sys.columns [Column] ON [Column].object_id = [Table].object_id
WHERE type = 'u' and [Table].name = 'SupplierCategories'
```

Database	Tables.SchemaName	Tables.TableName	Tables.Columns.ColumnName
WideWorldImporters	Purchasing	SupplierCategories	SupplierCategoryID
WideWorldImporters	Purchasing	SupplierCategories	SupplierCategoryName
WideWorldImporters	Purchasing	SupplierCategories	LastEditedBy
WideWorldImporters	Purchasing	SupplierCategories	ValidFrom
WideWorldImporters	Purchasing	SupplierCategories	ValidTo

Figure 8-5. *Showing T-SQL that will be transformed into JSON*

When we are converting the T-SQL output, we are expecting the JSON structure shown in Listing 8-19.

Listing 8-19. Showing JSON structure

```
Database : Value   -> LEVEL 1
     Tables_Collection -> LEVEL 2
     {
             SchemaName : Value
             TableName : Value
             Columns_Collection -> LEVEL 3
                 {
                         ColumnName : Value
                 }
     }
```

The aliases in the SELECT clause build the structure demonstrated in Listing 8-19. When converting the result to JSON, each period in the alias builds up an additional JSON object level. For example:

```
"Database": "WideWorldImporters", -> top LEVEL with alias 'Database'
"Tables": {   -> Database key element child LEVEL with alias 'Tables.___'
          "SchemaName": "Purchasing",              -> details 'Tables.
          SchemaName'
          "TableName": "SupplierCategories", -> details 'Tables.TableName'
                  "Columns": -> Tables child LEVEL with alias 'Tables.
                  Columns.___'
            {
    "ColumnName": "SupplierCategoryID" -> details 'Tables.Columns.
    ColumnName'
            }
         }
```

This way, the query from Listing 8-19 returns a valid JSON result set. However, there is one problem with the resulting output. The JSON object Tables{} is repeated for each column and makes the output bigger than we expected. Ideally, it would be more efficient to return the Columns section as an array instead of an object and list all columns inside the array. This way, the JSON structure will look slightly different. Listing 8-20 demonstrates JSON structure with the Columns section as an array, where the ColumnName key element and values are surrounded by square brackets [].

Listing 8-20. Showing JSON structure with Columns section as an array

```
Database : Value  -> LEVEL 1
    Tables_Collection -> LEVEL 2
    {
            SchemaName : Value
             TableName : Value
            Columns_Collection -> LEVEL 3
                 [
                       {ColumnName : Value},{ColumnName : Value}, ...
                 ]
    }
```

To accomplish such a task, we need to encapsulate the column name list into an inline subquery with the FOR JSON clause and AUTO mode as shown in Listing 8-21. However, for an inline subquery, both AUTO and PATH modes return the same result. The JSON output is demonstrated in Listing 8-22.

Listing 8-21. Encapsulating the column names within array

```
SELECT db_name() as 'Database',
       [Schema].name as 'Tables.SchemaName',
       [Table].name as 'Tables.TableName',
       (SELECT [Column].name as ColumnName FROM sys.columns [Column]
                WHERE [Column].object_id = [Table].object_id FOR JSON AUTO
       ) as 'Tables.Columns'
FROM sys.objects [Table]
       JOIN sys.schemas [Schema] on [Table].schema_id = [Schema].schema_id
WHERE type = 'u' and [Table].name = 'SupplierCategories'
FOR JSON PATH;
```

Listing 8-22. Showing JSON output with Columns array

```
[
  {
    "Database": "WideWorldImporters",
    "Tables": {
      "SchemaName": "Purchasing",
      "TableName": "SupplierCategories",
      "Columns": [
        {
          "ColumnName": "SupplierCategoryID"
        },
        {
          "ColumnName": "SupplierCategoryName"
        },
        {
          "ColumnName": "LastEditedBy"
        },
        {
          "ColumnName": "ValidFrom"
        },
        {
          "ColumnName": "ValidTo"
        }
      ]
    }
  }
]
```

As you can see, the JSON output in Listing 8-22 is much smaller than the JSON in Listing 8-17, which was provided in the Solution section. I intentionally demonstrated two ways to create a JSON output. In some cases, you need object-oriented JSON as it is demonstrated in Listings 8-16 and 8-17, and in another case you need to create compact JSON with an array of values as demonstrated in Listings 8-21 and 8-22.

8-6. Handling Escape Characters

Problem

You do not want to return an escape character "\" in the JSON output.

Solution

A JSON_QUERY() function eliminates escape characters in JSON output. Listing 8-23 demonstrates how a JSON_QUERY() function "fixes" the JSON output for the column InvoiceDate, which holds JSON data. Listing 8-24 demonstrates the JSON output. To create table CustomerInvoice, run Listing 8-25 first.

Listing 8-23. Showing JSON_QUERY() function with combination FOR JSON clause and PATH mode

```
SELECT [CustomerName]
        ,[PrimaryContact]
        ,[AlternateContact]
        ,[PhoneNumber]
        ,JSON_QUERY(InvoiceDate) InvoiceDate
FROM CustomerInvoice
FOR JSON PATH;
```

Listing 8-24. Showing fixed JSON output

```
[{
        "CustomerName":"Tailspin Toys (Head Office)",
        "PrimaryContact":"Waldemar Fisar",
        "AlternateContact":"Laimonis Berzins",
        "PhoneNumber":"(308) 555-0100",
        "InvoiceDate":{ "InvoiceDate":"03/04/2013"}
    },
    {
        "CustomerName":"Tailspin Toys (Head Office)",
        "PrimaryContact":"Waldemar Fisar",
        "AlternateContact":"Laimonis Berzins",
        "PhoneNumber":"(308) 555-0100",
        "InvoiceDate":{"InvoiceDate":"03/12/2013"}
}]
```

How It Works

To demonstrate how to implement a JSON_QUERY() function to eliminate escape characters from JSON output, we need to create a table with a JSON data column. Listing 8-8 demonstrates a query to create the table CustomerInvoice where the column InvoiceDate holds JSON data. Figure 8-6 demonstrates the result set from the table CustomerInvoice.

CustomerName	PrimaryContact	AlternateContact	PhoneNumber	InvoiceDate
Tailspin Toys (He...	Waldemar Fis...	Laimonis Berzins	(308) 555-0100	{"InvoiceDate":"03/04/2013"}
Tailspin Toys (He...	Waldemar Fis...	Laimonis Berzins	(308) 555-0100	{"InvoiceDate":"03/12/2013"}

Figure 8-6. Showing the table CustomerInvoice result set

Listing 8-25. Creating table CustomerInvoice with JSON data in column InvoiceDate

```
SELECT TOP (2)
        [CustomerName]
        ,[PrimaryContact]
        ,[AlternateContact]
        ,[PhoneNumber]
        ,CAST((QUOTENAME('"InvoiceDate":' + QUOTENAME(CONVERT(varchar(20),In
        voiceDate, 101) , '"'), '{')) AS VARCHAR(MAX)) InvoiceDate
        INTO CustomerInvoice
FROM [Website].[Customers] Customers JOIN [Sales].[Invoices]  Invoices
            ON Invoices.CustomerID = Customers.CustomerID;
```

The JSON data in the column InvoiceDate has forward slashes, for example: *{"InvoiceDate":"03/04/2013"}*, which is an invalid character for JSON. Table 8-4 lists the invalid JSON characters.

Table 8-4. The JSON invalid characters

Character	Description
"	Double quote
\	Backslash
/	Forward slash
The characters that less likely could be SQL Server data	
\r	Carriage return ASCII Code 13
\n	Line feed ASCII Code 10
\t	Horizontal Tab ASCII Code 9
\b	Backspace ASCII Code 8
\f	Form feed ASCII Code 12

If the query in Listing 8-26 executes without a JSON_QUERY() function, then JSON output will include escape character "\" in the output as shown in Listing 8-27.

Listing 8-26. Building JSON without JSON_QUERY()

```
SELECT CustomerName, PrimaryContact, AlternateContact, PhoneNumber,
InvoiceDate
FROM CustomerInvoice
FOR JSON PATH;
```

Listing 8-27. Showing JSON output built in Listing 8-26

```
[
    {
        "CustomerName":"Tailspin Toys (Head Office)",
        "PrimaryContact":"Waldemar Fisar",
        "AlternateContact":"Laimonis Berzins",
        "PhoneNumber":"(308) 555-0100",
        "InvoiceDate":"{\"InvoiceDate\":\"03\/04\/2013\"}"
    },
    {
        "CustomerName":"Tailspin Toys (Head Office)",
        "PrimaryContact":"Waldemar Fisar",
        "AlternateContact":"Laimonis Berzins",
        "PhoneNumber":"(308) 555-0100",
        "InvoiceDate":"{\"InvoiceDate\":\"03\/12\/2013\"}"
    }
]
```

Initially, the JSON_QUERY() function is very similar to the XML query() function that returns the JSON subset based on a provided path. (The Chapter 9 "Converting JSON to Row Sets" will cover the JSON_QUERY() function in greater detail.) The JSON_QUERY() function has the following two parameters:

1. JSON Expression, required.

2. JSON Path, optional.

When a column that stores JSON is sent to the JSON_QUERY(), then the FOR JSON clause trusts the JSON_QUERY(), because the function always returns a valid JSON, so the output does not require escape characters.

8-7. Dealing with CLR Data Types
Problem

You want to include a CLR data type in JSON output.

Solution

A ToString() function converts a CLR data type value into an nvarchar data type. Listing 8-28 demonstrates a query where the Customers.DeliveryLocation geography data type column is part of JSON output. Listing 8-29 shows the JSON output.

Listing 8-28. Converting CLR values into a string

```
SELECT TOP (2) Customers.CustomerName,
       People.FullName AS PrimaryContact,
       ap.FullName AS AlternateContact,
       Customers.PhoneNumber,
       Cities.CityName AS CityName,
       Customers.DeliveryLocation.ToString() AS DeliveryLocation
FROM Sales.Customers AS Customers
       JOIN [Application].People AS People
               ON Customers.PrimaryContactPersonID = People.PersonID
       JOIN [Application].People AS ap
               ON Customers.AlternateContactPersonID = ap.PersonID
       JOIN [Application].Cities AS Cities
               ON Customers.DeliveryCityID = Cities.CityID
FOR JSON PATH, ROOT('Customers');
```

Listing 8-29. Show in JSON output

```
{"Customers": [
    {
      "CustomerName": "Tailspin Toys (Head Office)",
      "PrimaryContact": "Waldemar Fisar",
      "AlternateContact": "Laimonis Berzins",
      "PhoneNumber": "(308) 555-0100",
      "CityName": "Lisco",
      "DeliveryLocation": "POINT (-102.6201979 41.4972022)"
    },
    {
      "CustomerName": "Tailspin Toys (Sylvanite, MT)",
      "PrimaryContact": "Lorena Cindric",
      "AlternateContact": "Hung Van Groesen",
      "PhoneNumber": "(406) 555-0100",
      "CityName": "Sylvanite",
      "DeliveryLocation": "POINT (-115.8743507 48.7163356)"
    }
  ]
}
```

How It Works

The ToString() function implicitly converts CLR data types geography, geometry, and hierarchyid into an nvarchar data type. The ToString() function default output is shown in Table 8-5.

Table 8-5. Showing ToString() function conversion output

Data Type	Converts to Data Type
hierarchyid	nvarchar(4000)
geography	nvarchar(max)
geometry	nvarchar(max)

■ **Note** The hierarchyid data type is an exception for this limitation. The *FOR JSON* clause does not raise an error when a column with a hierarchyid data type is part of the JSON output.

When the FOR JSON clause references unconverted geography and geometry data types, SQL Server raises the error shown in Listing 8-30.

Listing 8-30. Showing error for unconverted CLR

```
Msg 13604, Level 16, State 1, Line 1
FOR JSON cannot serialize CLR objects. Cast CLR types explicitly into one of
the supported types in FOR JSON queries.
```

The ToString() function is case sensitive, which is not typical for most SQL Server built-in functions. Therefore, any other spelling than a properly cased ToString() function will raise an error. For example, SQL Server raises an error when the function is spelled tostring(). Listing 8-31 demonstrates the error message.

Listing 8-31. Showing the error message when the ToString() function is incorrectly spelled

```
Msg 6506, Level 16, State 10, Line 5 Could not find method 'tostring' for
type 'Microsoft.SqlServer.Types.SqlGeography' in assembly 'Microsoft.
SqlServer.Types'
```

As an alternative, the *CAST()* and *CONVERT()* functions can explicitly convert geography and geometry into nvarchar and varchar data types. Listing 8-32 demonstrates a query where the column Customers.DeliveryLocation with the geography data type is explicitly converted to nvarchar(1000) using the *CAST()* function.

Listing 8-32. Using CAST() function column with geography data type

```
SELECT TOP (2) Customers.CustomerName,
       People.FullName AS PrimaryContact,
       ap.FullName AS AlternateContact,
       Customers.PhoneNumber,
       Cities.CityName AS CityName,
       CAST(Customers.DeliveryLocation as nvarchar(1000)) AS Delivery
       Location
FROM Sales.Customers AS Customers
        JOIN Application.People AS People
                ON Customers.PrimaryContactPersonID = People.PersonID
        JOIN Application.People AS ap
                ON Customers.AlternateContactPersonID = ap.PersonID
        JOIN Application.Cities AS Cities
                ON Customers.DeliveryCityID = Cities.CityID
FOR JSON PATH, ROOT('Customers');
```

Summary

SQL Server 2016 was introduced with JSON integration. This chapter covered how to build efficient and effective JSON output. This is the first chapter dedicated to JSON, and you can see that the FOR JSON clause has many similarities to the FOR XML clause. Both have AUTO and PATH modes. The ROOT option in the FOR JSON clause is the same as the FOR XML clause. As a rule of thumb, if you are familiar with XML, then JSON should be simple to learn.

The next chapter will cover the conversion of JSON values into rows and columns.

CHAPTER 9

■ ■ ■

Converting JSON
to Row Sets

In this chapter, we will discuss recipes demonstrating how to detect a JSON document, different ways to shred JSON, and how to improve performance when you want to filter a JSON document. SQL Server JSON integration provides comprehensive coverage to convert a JSON document into a scalar value and rows-columns set. You will find a variety of tested samples and possible scenarios to help you find the most appropriate solution for your task.

9-1. Detecting the Columns with JSON
Problem
You want to detect all columns with JSON data in a database.

Solution
An *ISJSON()* function detects when data is valid JSON. Listing 9-1 demonstrates the process on how to detect JSON document within a database. Figure 9-1 demonstrates the SQL script result.

Listing 9-1. Detecting JSON data

```
SET NOCOUNT ON;

DECLARE @SQL nvarchar(1000)

IF (OBJECT_ID('tempdb.dbo.#Result')) IS NOT NULL
        DROP TABLE #Result

CREATE TABLE #Result (tblName nvarchar(200),
                clmnName nvarchar(100),
                DateType nvarchar(100),
```

```
                       JSONDoc nvarchar(MAX),)

DECLARE cur CURSOR
        FOR
SELECT 'SELECT TOP (1) ''' + QUOTENAME(s.name) +'.' + QUOTENAME(o.name) +
''' as TblName, '''
+ QUOTENAME(c.name) + ''' as ClmName, '''
+ t.name + QUOTENAME(case c.max_length when -1 then 'MAX' ELSE cast
(c.max_length as varchar(5)) END , ')') + ''' as DataType, '
+ QUOTENAME(c.name)  + ' FROM '
        + QUOTENAME(s.name) +'.' + QUOTENAME(o.name) +
        ' WHERE ISJSON(' + QUOTENAME(c.name)  + ') = 1;'
FROM sys.columns c
JOIN sys.types t on c.system_type_id = t.system_type_id
        JOIN sys.objects o ON c.object_id = o.object_id AND o.type = 'u'
        JOIN sys.schemas s ON s.schema_id = o.schema_id
WHERE t.name IN('varchar', 'nvarchar')
                AND (c.max_length = -1 OR c.max_length > 100)

OPEN cur

FETCH NEXT FROM cur INTO @SQL

WHILE @@FETCH_STATUS = 0
BEGIN

        print @SQL
        INSERT #Result
        EXEC(@SQL)

        FETCH NEXT FROM cur INTO @SQL
END

DEALLOCATE cur;

SELECT JSONDoc,tblName,clmnName,DateType
FROM #Result
ORDER BY tblName, clmnName

DROP TABLE #Result

SET NOCOUNT OFF;
```

JSONDoc	tblName	clmnName	DateType
{ "OtherLanguages": ["Polish","Chinese","Japanes...	[Application].[People]	[CustomFields]	nvarchar(MAX)
["Polish","Chinese","Japanese"]	[Application].[People]	[OtherLanguages]	nvarchar(MAX)
{"theme":"blitzer","dateFormat":"yy-mm-dd","timeZ...	[Application].[People]	[UserPreferences]	nvarchar(MAX)
{ "OtherLanguages": ["Arabic"] ,"HireDate":"2009-...	[Application].[People_Archive]	[CustomFields]	nvarchar(MAX)
["Arabic"]	[Application].[People_Archive]	[OtherLanguages]	nvarchar(MAX)
{ "theme": "defaultblue", "layout": "default", "datefo...	[Application].[People_Archive]	[UserPreferences]	nvarchar(MAX)
{ "Site": { "SEO": { "Title": "WWI	Site", "De...	[Application].[SystemParameters]	[ApplicationSettings]	nvarchar(MAX)
{"Events": [{ "Event":"Ready for collection","EventT...	[Sales].[Invoices]	[ReturnedDeliveryData]	nvarchar(MAX)
{ "CountryOfManufacture": "China", "Tags": ["USB ...	[Warehouse].[StockItems]	[CustomFields]	nvarchar(MAX)
["USB Powered"]	[Warehouse].[StockItems]	[Tags]	nvarchar(MAX)
{ "CountryOfManufacture": "China", "Tags": [], "Mini...	[Warehouse].[StockItems_Archive]	[CustomFields]	nvarchar(MAX)
[]	[Warehouse].[StockItems_Archive]	[Tags]	nvarchar(MAX)

Figure 9-1. *Showing detected tables and columns with JSON data*

How It Works

An *ISJSON()* function verifies whether a string type value is valid JSON. The *ISJSON()* function returns:

- 1 when the string is valid JSON document.

- 0 when the string is invalid JSON document.

- NULL when an expression is a NULL value.

Empty curly brackets {} and empty square brackets [] are considered to be valid JSON, therefore, the *ISJSON()* function returns 1 on those values. The *ISJSON()* function will detect the JSON document, and a cursor is established to build dynamic SQL, as shown in Listing 9-2.

Listing 9-2. Building dynamic SQL to detect JSON documents

```
DECLARE cur CURSOR
        FOR
SELECT 'SELECT TOP (1) ''' + QUOTENAME(s.name) +'.' + QUOTENAME(o.name) +
''' as TblName, '''
+ QUOTENAME(c.name) + ''' as ClmName, '''
+ t.name  + QUOTENAME(case c.max_length when -1 then 'MAX'
ELSE cast(c.max_length as varchar(5)) END , ')') + ''' as DataType, '
+ QUOTENAME(c.name)  + ' FROM '
        + QUOTENAME(s.name) +'.' + QUOTENAME(o.name) +
        ' WHERE ISJSON(' + QUOTENAME(c.name)  + ') = 1;'
FROM sys.columns c
        JOIN sys.types t on c.system_type_id = t.system_type_id
        JOIN sys.objects o ON c.object_id = o.object_id AND o.type = 'u'
        JOIN sys.schemas s ON s.schema_id = o.schema_id
WHERE t.name IN('varchar', 'nvarchar')
            AND (c.max_length = -1 OR c.max_length > 100);
```

The columns that store JSON have *nvarchar* and *varchar* data types. Theoretically, the columns with nchar and char data types could store the JSON as well; however, a fixed length data type is not appropriate for JSON. The wrong design consideration could be implemented in binary data types, such as varbinary and image for JSON documents.

■ **Note**   Microsoft recommends nvarchar(max) as a standard data type to store the JSON documents, as it is implemented in the WideWorldImporters sample database (Figure 9-1). All columns that store JSON have the nvarchar(max) data type.

Therefore, the dynamic SQL (Listing 9-1) for the cursor filters the table *sys.types* and column *name* by *'varchar'*, *'nvarchar'*. In Chapter 4, Recipe 4-7 demonstrated how to detect an XML column when the data type filter is included in four more data types: varbinary, image, text, and ntext. Also, it is less likely to store JSON where the column length is less than 100. Therefore, the column *max_length* from the table *sys.columns* is filtered by -1, which is *MAX* OR greater than *100*.

The SELECT statement for a cursor produces dynamic SQL output of:

1.   Schema.TableName – defines schema and table

2.   ColumnName – defines column name

3.   DataType(data length) – defines data type

4.   Column name – defines returned JSON document

The WHERE clause implements *ISJSON()* with a column name as an argument. The output for a dynamic SQL row is demonstrated in Listing 9-3. The result from the dynamic SQL is shown in Figure 9-2.

Listing 9-3. Resulting code for dynamic SQL

```
SELECT TOP (1) '[Application].[People]' as TblName,
'[CustomFields]' as ClmName,
'nvarchar(MAX)' as DataType,
[CustomFields]
FROM [Application].[People]
WHERE ISJSON([CustomFields]) = 1;
```

TblName	ClmName	DataType	CustomFields
[Application].[People]	[CustomFields]	nvarchar(MAX)	{ "OtherLanguages": ["Polish","C

Figure 9-2. Showing the output from Listing 9-3

A loop is iterating over each line of dynamic SQL and inspects it for potential JSON document in each column. When *ISJSON()* returns a value of 1, which means *TRUE*, then the output from that SQL is logged into a temporary table *#Result*, which is created before the cursor declaration. When the cursor is exhausted then the temporary table *#Result* returns all logged rows.

9-2. Returning a Subset of a JSON Document
Problem
You want to return an object or array from a JSON document.

Solution
The *JSON_QUERY()* function returns a subset (object or array) from a variable or column that contains a JSON document. Listing 9-4 demonstrates the query that returns the Events array objects (two of those) out of a JSON document stored in the *Sales.Invoices* table and *ReturnedDeliveryData* column. The result is shown in Listing 9-5.

Listing 9-4. Returning Events arrays

```
SELECT TOP (1) JSON_QUERY([ReturnedDeliveryData], '$.Events')
FROM [Sales].[Invoices];
```

Listing 9-5. Resulting from Listing 9-5

```
[
    {
        "Event":"Ready for collection",
        "EventTime":"2013-01-01T12:00:00",
        "ConNote":"EAN-125-1051"
    },
    {
        "Event":"DeliveryAttempt",
        "EventTime":"2013-01-02T07:05:00",
        "ConNote":"EAN-125-1051",
        "DriverID":15,
        "Latitude":41.3617214,
        "Longitude":-81.4695602,
        "Status":"Delivered"
    }
]
```

How It Works

A *JSON_QUERY()* function has two arguments:

1. Expression – a required argument, expecting a JSON document from a column name or variable.

2. Path – an optional argument, providing a JSON document path to an object part.

■ **Note** The dollar sign ($) in the path argument represents JSON context, and it could be considered as a top object.

The recipe solution demonstrated in a JSON document is stored in the *Sales.Invoices* table and *ReturnedDeliveryData* column. For example, the complete JSON document shown in Listing 9-6 has two extra key elements *DeliveredWhen* and *ReceivedBy* that are not part of the *JSON_QUERY()* result, because the path argument was set to the object *Events,* which has two child arrays.

Listing 9-6. Showing a complete JSON document

```
{
    "Events":[
            {
                "Event":"Ready for collection",
                "EventTime":"2013-01-01T12:00:00",
                "ConNote":"EAN-125-1051"
            },
            {
                "Event":"DeliveryAttempt",
                "EventTime":"2013-01-02T07:05:00",
                "ConNote":"EAN-125-1051",
                "DriverID":15,
                "Latitude":41.3617214,
                "Longitude":-81.4695602,
                "Status":"Delivered"
            }
            ],
    "DeliveredWhen":"2013-01-02T07:05:00",
    "ReceivedBy":"Aakriti Byrraju"
}
```

To return the single array object, the path argument needs to specify an array index on how it is demonstrated in Listing 9-7. Listing 9-8 demonstrates JSON output for a single array object.

Listing 9-7. Referencing a single JSON array object

```
SELECT TOP (1) JSON_QUERY([ReturnedDeliveryData], '$.Events[0]')
FROM [Sales].[Invoices];
```

Listing 9-8. Showing array output

```
{
    "Event":"Ready for collection",
    "EventTime":"2013-01-01T12:00:00",
    "ConNote":"EAN-125-1051"
}
```

■ **Caution** Unlike an XML singleton that is a *1*-based starting index, JSON arrays are *0*-based. Therefore, to reference the first array object or array value, the index must be 0, not 1.

When the path argument is not set for a *JSON_QUERY()* function, the function returns a complete JSON document.

9-3. Returning a Scalar Value from JSON
Problem
You want to return a scalar value from a JSON document.

Solution
A *JSON_VALUE()* function extracts a scalar value from a JSON document, shown in Listing 9-9. The query result is demonstrated in Figure 9-3.

Listing 9-9. Returning scalar values

```
SELECT TOP (1) JSON_value([ReturnedDeliveryData], '$.ReceivedBy') ReceivedBy
        ,JSON_value([ReturnedDeliveryData], '$.Events[0].Event') FirstEvent
        ,JSON_value([ReturnedDeliveryData], '$.Events[0].EventTime')
        EventTime
        ,JSON_value([ReturnedDeliveryData], '$.Events[1].Event') LastEvent
        ,JSON_value([ReturnedDeliveryData], '$.Events[1].Status') [Status]
FROM [Sales].[Invoices];
```

ReceivedBy	FirstEvent	EventTime	LastEvent	Status
Aakriti Byrraju	Ready for collection	2013-01-01T12:00:00	DeliveryAttempt	Delivered

Figure 9-3. *Showing the query result*

How It Works

A *JSON_VALUE()* function has two required arguments:

1. *Expression* – expects a JSON document from a column name or variable.

2. *Path* – a JSON document path to a JSON scalar value.

Unlike a *JSON_QUERY()* function that returns objects and arrays, the *JSON_VALUE()* function returns a JSON scalar value. If you attempt to return a scalar value using the *JSON_QUERY()* function, *NULL* will be returned. The *JSON_VALUE()* function is the opposite – it returns *NULL* when the path references an object or array instead of a key. For example, the query in Listing 9-10 demonstrates flipping an object and value reference between a *JSON_VALUE()* and *JSON_QUERY()* functions. Figure 9-4 shows the result when a *JSON_VALUE()* referencing a scalar value returns a *ReceivedBy* value and a *JSON_QUERY()* referencing a scalar value returns NULL. In the next two columns, the *JSON_VALUE()* referencing an array returns a *NULL* value and *JSON_QUERY()* referencing and array returns a JSON segment.

Listing 9-10. Demonstrating JSON_VALUE() and JSON_QUERY() functions

```
SELECT TOP (1) JSON_VALUE([ReturnedDeliveryData], '$.ReceivedBy')
ScalarValue
                ,JSON_QUERY([ReturnedDeliveryData], '$.ReceivedBy')
                ScalarQuery
                ,JSON_VALUE([ReturnedDeliveryData], '$.Events[0]')
                ObjectValue
                ,JSON_QUERY([ReturnedDeliveryData], '$.Events[0]')
                ObjectQuery
FROM [Sales].[Invoices];
```

ScalarValue	ScalarQuery	ObjectValue	ObjectQuery
Aakriti Byrraju	NULL	NULL	{ "Event":"Ready for collection","EventTime"...

Figure 9-4. *Showing the query result*

The *JSON_VALUE()* function returns an *nvarchar(4000)* data type for a scalar value. Listing 9-11 demonstrates how to verify a data type that is returned by a *JSON_VALUE()* function. Figure 9-5 shows the returned result.

Listing 9-11. Verifying the returned data type by JSON_VALUE() function

```
DECLARE @Value sql_variant

SELECT @Value =
(
        SELECT TOP (1) JSON_value([ReturnedDeliveryData], '$."ReceivedBy"')
        FROM [Sales].[Invoices]
);
```

```
SELECT SQL_VARIANT_PROPERTY(@Value,'BaseType') BaseType,
CAST(SQL_VARIANT_PROPERTY(@Value, 'MaxLength')as int) /
        CASE SQL_VARIANT_PROPERTY(@Value,'BaseType') WHEN 'nvarchar'
                                            THEN 2 ELSE 1 END
TypeLength,
SQL_VARIANT_PROPERTY(@Value,'TotalBytes') TotalBytes;
```

BaseType	TypeLength	TotalBytes
nvarchar	4000	38

Figure 9-5. *Resulting output from the verification code*

When the scalar value is greater than 4000 characters, the function returns a NULL. Listing 9-12 demonstrates the JSON document when the scalar value *LongText* contains 5,009 characters processed by a *JSON_VALUE()* function. The query result is shown in Figure 9-6.

Listing 9-12. Demonstrating how text that exceeds the character limit affects the JSON_VALUE() function output

```
declare @json nvarchar(max) = '
{
"RegularText":"Regular Text",

"LongText":"Long Text' + REPLICATE(' too long ', 500) + '"
}'
SELECT JSON_VALUE(@json, '$.RegularText') RegularText ,
        JSON_VALUE(@json, '$.LongText') LongText
```

RegularText	LongText
Regular Text	NULL

Figure 9-6. *Showing query result*

■ **Note** When a JSON key has an invalid character, such as a space, the key must be surrounded by double quotes (""). For example, when key is Last Name the path argument will be:

```
SELECT JSON_VALUE(@json, '$."Last Name"')
```

9-4. Troubleshooting a Returned NULL

Problem

You want to troubleshoot why a JSON a scalar value is NULL.

Solution

Implementing the *strict* mode within JSON functions raises an error when a NULL is returned. Listing 9-13 demonstrates a query in strict mode. The error message is shown in Listing 9-14.

Listing 9-13. Forcing a JSON_VALUE() function to raise an error

```
SELECT JSON_VALUE([ReturnedDeliveryData], 'strict $.receivedby') ReceivedBy
FROM [Sales].[Invoices];
```

Listing 9-14. Showing the error message

```
Msg 13608, Level 16, State 5, Line 1
Property cannot be found on the specified JSON path.
```

How It Works

The JSON functions that support the *path* argument can implement strict mode to force an error when a retuned scalar value is *NULL*. These functions are:

- JSON_VALUE()
- JSON_QUERY()
- JSON_MODIFY()
- OPENJSON()

The path argument for functions supporting the path argument can run in two modes:

- *lax* mode (default), JSON function returns a scalar *NULL* value
- *strict* mode, JSON function returns an error instead of a *NULL* value

---

▪ **Caution** Both *lax* and *strict* keywords are case sensitive; therefore, implementation is required to be in lowercase only.

Listing 9-15 demonstrates how to detect a problem for a JSON_VALUE() function scalar output when executing the code in *strict* mode. Listing 9-16 demonstrates the error message.

Listing 9-15. Implementing strict mode

```
declare @json nvarchar(max) = '
{
"RegularText":"Regular Text",

"LongText":"Long Text' + REPLICATE(' too long ', 500) + '"
}'
SELECT JSON_VALUE(@json, 'strict $.LongText') LongText
```

Listing 9-16. Showing the error message

```
Msg 13625, Level 16, State 1, Line 7
String value in the specified JSON path would be truncated.
```

The error message in Listing 9-16 notifies that the text exceeded the maximum 4,000 characters. However, the *OPENJSON()* function, which we'll cover in the next recipe, can fix this problem.

9-5. Converting JSON into a Table
Problem

You want to convert a JSON document into columns and rows.

Solution

The *OPENJSON()* table-valued function shreds the JSON document and returns a resultset in columns-rows format. Listing 9-17 shreds the JSON document from table [Application].[People], column [UserPreferences]. Figure 9-7 shows the query result.

Listing 9-17. Converting JSON into table structure

```
SELECT UserPref.theme,
       UserPref.[dateFormat],
       UserPref.timeZone,
       UserPref.pagingType,
       UserPref.pageLength,
       UserPref.favoritesOnDashboard
FROM [Application].[People]
       CROSS APPLY OPENJSON([UserPreferences])
       WITH
```

```
        (
                theme             varchar(20)  '$.theme',
                [dateFormat]      varchar(20)  '$.dateFormat',
                timeZone          varchar(10)  '$.timeZone',
                pagingType        varchar(20)  '$.table.pagingType',
                pageLength        int          '$.table.pageLength',
                favoritesOnDashboard bit       '$.favoritesOnDashboard'
        ) AS UserPref;
```

theme	dateFormat	timeZone	pagingType	pageLength	favoritesOnDashboard
blitzer	yy-mm-dd	PST	full_numbers	25	1
humanity	dd/mm/yy	PST	full	50	1
dark-hive	DD, MM d, yy	PST	simple_numbers	10	1
ui-darkness	dd/mm/yy	PST	simple	10	1
le-frog	dd/mm/yy	PST	numbers	10	1
black-tie	mm/dd/yy	PST	full_numbers	25	1
ui-darkness	mm/dd/yy	PST	full	50	1
blitzer	mm/dd/yy	PST	simple_numbers	10	1
humanity	mm/dd/yy	PST	simple	10	1
dark-hive	mm/dd/yy	PST	numbers	10	1
ui-darkness	yy-mm-dd	PST	full_numbers	25	1

Figure 9-7. Showing the query result

How It Works

The *OPENJSON()* table-valued function shreds and converts a JSON document into a rowset. Since the *OPENJSON()* function returns a rowset, the function can be used in the *FROM* clause using the *CROSS APPLY* and *OUTER APPLY* operators.

The *OPENJSON()* function consists of two arguments and a WITH clause:

- *jsonExpression* (required) – JSON valid column or variable

- *path* (optional) – JSON object or array path

- *WITH* clause (optional) – explicitly defines the output table; therefore, the name and data type is required for each column. Optionally, the *WITH* clause could reference an object or array, as shown in Listing 9-18.

Before we review the query details from Listing 9-17, we'll discuss one JSON document from the [Application].[People] table, column [UserPreferences], as shown in Listing 9-18.

Listing 9-18. Showing JSON document

```
{
    "theme": "blitzer",
    "dateFormat": "yy-mm-dd",
    "timeZone": "PST",
    "table": {
                "pagingType": "full_numbers",
                "pageLength": 25
            },
    "favoritesOnDashboard": true
}
```

The document has four key-value elements that are considered to be *first level*:

- theme

- dateFormat

- timeZone

- favoritesOnDashboard

Additionally, the sub-objects *table* contains two more key-value elements:

- pagingType

- pageLength

The *OPENJSON()* function in the Solution section (Listing 9-17) is implemented with the required argument only, which is the *UserPreferences* column, for example: *OPENJSON([UserPreferences])*. For the provided Solution, there is no need to specify the *path* argument, because all JSON keys are explicitly defined in the WITH clause, for example:

```
CROSS APPLY OPENJSON([UserPreferences])
        WITH
        (
                theme           varchar(20) '$.theme',
                [dateFormat] varchar(20) '$.dateFormat',
                timeZone        varchar(10) '$.timeZone',
                pagingType      varchar(20) '$.table.pagingType',
                pageLength      int         '$.table.pageLength',
                favoritesOnDashboard bit '$.favoritesOnDashboard'
        ) AS UserPref
```

The *OPENJSON()* function could be defined for all first-level keys by default. For example, the same output is returned for the *OPENJSON()* function when the WITH clause does not have an explicit path for the first-level keys, as demonstrated in Listing 9-19.

Listing 9-19. Shredding a JSON document with default first level keys

```
SELECT UserPref.theme,
       UserPref.[dateFormat],
       UserPref.timeZone,
       UserPref.pagingType,
       UserPref.pageLength,
       UserPref.favoritesOnDashboard
FROM [Application].[People]
       CROSS APPLY OPENJSON([UserPreferences])
       WITH
       (
               theme        varchar(20),
               [dateFormat] varchar(20),
               timeZone     varchar(10),
               pagingType   varchar(20) '$.table.pagingType',
               pageLength   int         '$.table.pageLength',
               favoritesOnDashboard bit
       ) AS UserPref;
```

There is one caveat with such an implementation; all first level keys in the *WITH* clause must match the JSON document name and the name is case sensitive. The sub-object *table* is still a required path specification, due to the second JSON level.

When the *OPENJSON()* function is used with all defaults, that is, no path argument and no WITH clause, the function returns three columns:

- *Key* – nvarchar(4000), returns a JSON key, object or array name.

- *Value* – nvarchar(max), returns a JSON property value.

- *Type* – int, returns a type of the JSON property value. The type descriptions are demonstrated in Table 9-1.

Type column value	JSON data type decription
0	NULL
1	string
2	int
3	boolean (true/false)
4	array
5	object

Listing 9-20 uses the JSON data from Listing 9-18, denoting the JSON document from a variable into a table structure. Figure 9-8 demonstrates the result from a JSON variable.

Listing 9-20. Running the OPENJSON() function without an optional argument or WITH clause

```
declare @json varchar(max) =
'{
  "theme": "blitzer",
  "dateFormat": "yy-mm-dd",
  "timeZone": "PST",
  "table": {
                "pagingType": "full_numbers",
                "pageLength": 25
            },
  "favoritesOnDashboard": true
}'

SELECT [key], [value], [type]
FROM OPENJSON(@json);
```

key	value	type
theme	blitzer	1
dateFormat	yy-mm-dd	1
timeZone	PST	1
table	{ "pagingType": "full_numbers", "pageLength": 25 }	5
favoritesOnDashboard	true	3

Figure 9-8. *Showing the OPENJSON() function result*

9-6. Processing JSON Nested Sub-Objects
Problem

You want to shred JSON with several nested levels.

Solution

To shred a sub-object you need to set the reference to the sub-object in a parent *OPENJSON(...) WITH(...)* block. The new JSON instance will stand along a sub-object JSON. The solution demonstrated is a database independent process that can run on any database with COMPATIBILITY_LEVEL = 130 or higher. The complete solution is demonstrated in Listing 9-21. The final query result is shown in Figure 9-9.

Listing 9-21. Shredding multiple JSON sub-object solution

```
SET NOCOUNT ON;

DECLARE @JSON nvarchar(MAX),
            @schema nvarchar(30),
            @tbl nvarchar(128),
            @objID int

DROP TABLE IF EXISTS dbo.Table_Info_JSON;

CREATE TABLE Table_Info_JSON (
            TableID int PRIMARY KEY,
            DBName nvarchar(128),
            [SchemaName] nvarchar(30),
            tblName nvarchar(128),
            JSONDoc nvarchar(MAX)
            );

DECLARE cur CURSOR FOR
        SELECT object_id, [Schema].name, [Table].name
        FROM sys.objects [Table]
                JOIN sys.schemas [Schema] on [Table].schema_id = [Schema].
                schema_id
        WHERE type = 'u';

OPEN cur;

FETCH NEXT FROM cur INTO @objID, @schema, @tbl;

WHILE @@FETCH_STATUS = 0
BEGIN

        SELECT @JSON = (
        SELECT db_name() as 'Database',
        [Schema].name as 'Tables.SchemaName',
        [Table].name as 'Tables.TableName',
                (SELECT [Column].name ColumnName FROM sys.columns [Column]
                WHERE [Column].object_id = [Table].object_id FOR JSON AUTO
                ) AS 'Tables.Columns'
        FROM sys.objects [Table]
                JOIN sys.schemas [Schema] on [Table].schema_id = [Schema].
                schema_id
        WHERE [Table].object_id = @objID
        FOR JSON PATH, WITHOUT_ARRAY_WRAPPER
        );
```

```
        INSERT Table_Info_JSON
        SELECT @objID, DB_NAME(), @schema, @tbl, @JSON;

        FETCH NEXT FROM cur INTO @objID, @schema, @tbl;
END;

DEALLOCATE cur;

SET NOCOUNT OFF;

SELECT db.[Database]    -- first level
       , tbl.SchemaName -- second level
       , tbl.TableName  -- second level
       , clmn.ColumnName -- third level
FROM dbo.Table_Info_JSON
       CROSS APPLY OPENJSON (JSONDoc)
           WITH
           (
                   [Database] varchar(30),
                   [Tables] nvarchar(MAX) AS JSON
           ) as db
       CROSS APPLY OPENJSON ([Tables])
           WITH
           (
                   TableName varchar(30),
                   SchemaName varchar(30),
                   [Columns] nvarchar(MAX) AS JSON
           ) as tbl
       CROSS APPLY OPENJSON ([Columns])
           WITH
           (
                   ColumnName varchar(30)
           ) as clmn;
```

Database	SchemaName	TableName	ColumnName
WideWorldImporters	Warehouse	StockItemStockGroups	StockItemStockGroupID
WideWorldImporters	Warehouse	StockItemStockGroups	StockItemID
WideWorldImporters	Warehouse	StockItemStockGroups	StockGroupID
WideWorldImporters	Warehouse	StockItemStockGroups	LastEditedBy
WideWorldImporters	Warehouse	StockItemStockGroups	LastEditedWhen
WideWorldImporters	Application	SystemParameters	SystemParameterID
WideWorldImporters	Application	SystemParameters	DeliveryAddressLine1
WideWorldImporters	Application	SystemParameters	DeliveryAddressLine2
WideWorldImporters	Application	SystemParameters	DeliveryCityID
WideWorldImporters	Application	SystemParameters	DeliveryPostalCode
WideWorldImporters	Application	SystemParameters	DeliveryLocation
WideWorldImporters	Application	SystemParameters	PostalAddressLine1
WideWorldImporters	Application	SystemParameters	PostalAddressLine2

Figure 9-9. *Showing final result*

How It Works

The mechanism to shred multi sub-object JSON data is based on a parent-child object reference set. To understand how it works, we need to take a closer look at the JSON document from the *Table_Info_JSON* table in Listing 9-22.

Listing 9-22. Showing the JSON document

```
{
  "Database": "WideWorldImporters",
  "Tables": {
    "SchemaName": "Warehouse",
    "TableName": "Colors",
        "Columns": [
                        { "ColumnName": "ColorID" },
                        { "ColumnName": "ColorName" },
                        { "ColumnName": "LastEditedBy" },
                        { "ColumnName": "ValidFrom" },
                        { "ColumnName": "ValidTo" }
                    ]
                }
}
```

The JSON document shown in Sample 9-9 has three levels:

- Top Level 1 – key "Database"

- Sub-Level 2 – object "Tables"

- Sub-Level 3 – array "Columns"

Therefore, the JSON structure reflected in the *FROM* clause is demonstrated in Listing 9-23:

Listing 9-23. Showing FROM clause

```
FROM dbo.Table_Info_JSON
        CROSS APPLY OPENJSON (JSONDoc) <- reference to the table column
                WITH
                (
                        [Database] varchar(30),
                        [Tables] nvarchar(MAX) AS JSON
                ) as db
        CROSS APPLY OPENJSON ([Tables]) <- reference to [Tables] JSON object
                        WITH
                        (
                                TableName varchar(30),
                                SchemaName varchar(30),
                                [Columns] nvarchar(MAX) AS JSON
                        ) as tbl
        CROSS APPLY OPENJSON ([Columns]) <- reference to [Columns] JSON array
                        WITH
                        (
                                ColumnName varchar(30)
                        ) as clmn
```

Reference to child-level sets in *OPENJSON* function *WITH* clause. The child object name must be in *nvarchar(MAX)* data type and set *AS JSON* object. For example: *[Tables] nvarchar(MAX) AS JSON*.

The SELECT clause delivered a result using created aliases in the FROM clause:

```
SELECT db.[Database]     -- first level
        , tbl.SchemaName -- second level
        , tbl.TableName  -- second level
        , clmn.ColumnName -- third level
```

9-7. Indexing JSON
Problem

You want to improve JSON filtering with an index.

Solution

To create an index for a JSON document, you need to add a computed column for a JSON scalar value, then create an index on this column. Listing 9-24 demonstrates how to add the index for a JSON value to an existing table. The index is created for a JSON value shown in Figure 9-10.

Listing 9-24. Creating an index for JSON key-value ConNote

```
USE [WideWorldImporters];

SET ANSI_NULLS ON;

ALTER TABLE [Sales].[Invoices] ADD ConNote AS
        CAST(JSON_VALUE([ReturnedDeliveryData], '$.Events[0].ConNote') AS
varchar(20)) PERSISTED

CREATE  INDEX IX_Sales_Invoices_ConNote
ON [Sales].[Invoices]
        (
                [ConNote]
        )INCLUDE(
        [InvoiceDate]
        ,[DeliveryInstructions]
        ,[TotalDryItems]
        ,[TotalChillerItems]
        ,[ConfirmedDeliveryTime]
        ,[ConfirmedReceivedBy]
        );
```

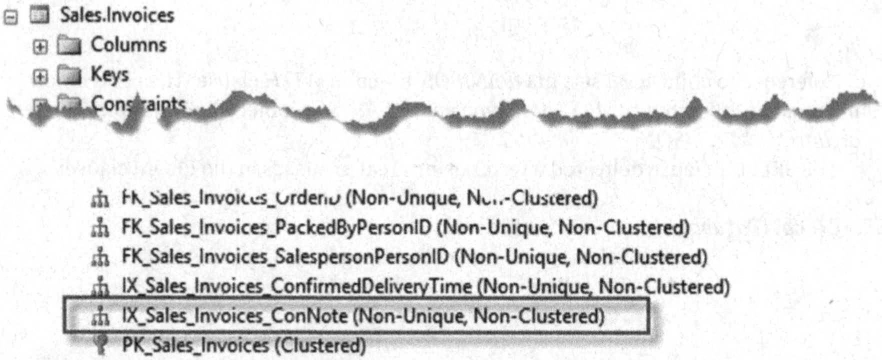

Figure 9-10. *Showing JSON index*

How It Works

JSON is not treated as a data type in SQL Server, like XML. It is more comparable to a structured string that has multiple values and stores a table as an nvarchar(max) data type (if you follow Microsoft recommendations). Therefore, a column that stores a JSON document cannot have a traditional index as a scalar value table column. However, a scalar JSON value can be obtained by a *JSON_VALUE()* scalar function, and this is the key to create an index for a JSON document.

Creating an index mechanism for a JSON document has two steps:

1. Add a computed column to a table with a *JSON_VALUE()* function that returns a scalar value from your JSON document. The computed column must use the PERSISTED option. Also, you need to keep in mind that the *JSON_VALUE()* function returns the nvarchar(4000) data type. Therefore, I recommend converting the returned data length from a *JSON_VALUE()* function closer to the original data length. For example:

    CAST(JSON_VALUE([ReturnedDeliveryData], '$.Events[0].ConNote') AS varchar(20)) PERSISTED.

2. Create an index on your computed column. When needed, the index can have an INCLUDE clause to create a fully covering index.

An index for a JSON document can greatly improve performance. Listing 9-25 demonstrates a query with a filter for computed columns over the JSON key element *ConNote*.

Listing 9-25. Filtering the ConNote column

```
SET STATISTICS IO,TIME ON;

SELECT [InvoiceDate]
      ,[DeliveryInstructions]
      ,[TotalDryItems]
      ,[TotalChillerItems]
      ,[ConfirmedDeliveryTime]
      ,[ConfirmedReceivedBy]
      ,[ConNote]
FROM [Sales].[Invoices]
WHERE [ConNote] = 'EAN-125-1051';

SET STATISTICS IO,TIME OFF;
```

Figure 9-11 demonstrates *"STATISTICS IO, TIME"* results and the execution plans for the query. Listing 9-26 is a comparison of this query before and after index creation.

Listing 9-26. Comparing a query before and after the index

```
---- WITHOUT INDEX
SQL Server parse and compile time:
   CPU time = 0 ms, elapsed time = 0 ms.
```

(1 row(s) affected)
Table 'Invoices'. Scan count 9, logical reads 8843, physical reads 0, read-
ahead reads 0, lob logical reads 0, lob physical reads 0, lob read-ahead
reads 0.
Table 'Worktable'. Scan count 0, logical reads 0, physical reads 0, read-
ahead reads 0, lob logical reads 0, lob physical reads 0, lob read-ahead
reads 0.

(1 row(s) affected)

 SQL Server Execution Times:
   CPU time = 94 ms, elapsed time = 60 ms.

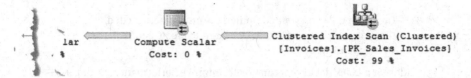

---- WITHOUT INDEX
SQL Server parse and compile time:
   CPU time = 0 ms, elapsed time = 0 ms.

(1 row(s) affected)
Table 'Invoices'. Scan count 9, logical reads 8843, physical reads 0, read-
ahead reads 0, lob logical reads 0, lob physical reads 0, lob read-ahead
reads 0.
Table 'Worktable'. Scan count 0, logical reads 0, physical reads 0, read-
ahead reads 0, lob logical reads 0, lob physical reads 0, lob read-ahead
reads 0.

(1 row(s) affected)

 SQL Server Execution Times:
   CPU time = 94 ms, elapsed time = 60 ms.

---- WITH INDEX
SQL Server parse and compile time:
   CPU time = 0 ms, elapsed time = 0 ms.

(1 row(s) affected)
Table 'Invoices'. Scan count 1, logical reads 3, physical reads 0, read-
ahead reads 0, lob logical reads 0, lob physical reads 0, lob read-ahead
reads 0.

(1 row(s) affected)

```
SQL Server Execution Times:
  CPU time = 0 ms,  elapsed time = 33 ms.
```

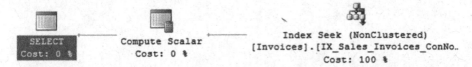

Figure 9-11. *Comparing the execution plans and STATISTICS results before and after the index is created*

As you can see, performance is improved dramatically with index filtering.

Summary

SQL Server 2016 introduced JSON integration that pairs well with the latest technologies. Chapter 9, "Converting JSON to Row Sets" covered the complete set of SQL Server functions and plenty of examples to shred and deliver the results from a JSON document.

The next chapter will demonstrate how to modify the JSON document and as a final point will compare JSON and XML performance.

CHAPTER 10

■ ■ ■

Modifying JSON

To insert, delete, and update data in a JSON document, SQL Server 2016 introduced the *JSON_MODIFY()* function that updates a JSON string value. This function, compared to XML *modify()* method, only has an *append* mode, as opposed to the *insert, delete,* and *instead of* modes provided by the XML method. Chapter 10 "Modifying JSON" will demonstrate many recipes explaining how to update a JSON document. In the final section of this chapter, I will compare the performance between XML and JSON.

10-1. Adding a New Key-Value Pair to JSON
Problem
You want to add a new key-value pair to a JSON document.

Solution
A *JSON_MODIFY()* function adds a new key-value pair when a second argument path value does not exist in a JSON document. Listing 10-1 demonstrates the query when the column InvoiceDate is modified by the *JSON_MODIFY()* function, adding a new key *"SentBy"* with the value *"John Smith"* to a JSON document. The result with both original (InvoiceDate) and modified JSON document (NewInvoice) columns is shown in Figure 10-1.

Listing 10-1. Adding a new key-value pair to a JSON document

```
SELECT CustomerName
        , PrimaryContact
        , AlternateContact
        , PhoneNumber
        , InvoiceDate
        , JSON_MODIFY(InvoiceDate,'$.SentBy', 'John Smith') NewInvoice
FROM [dbo].[CustomerInvoice];
```

© Alex Grinberg 2018
A. Grinberg, *XML and JSON Recipes for SQL Server,*
https://doi.org/10.1007/978-1-4842-3117-3_10

InvoiceDate	NewInvoice
{"InvoiceDate":"03/04/2013"}	{"InvoiceDate":"03/04/2013","SentBy":"John Smith"}
{"InvoiceDate":"03/12/2013"}	{"InvoiceDate":"03/12/2013","SentBy":"John Smith"}

Figure 10-1. *Showing the query result*

How It Works

A *JSON_MODIFY()* function returns an updated JSON document. There are three required arguments:

1. Expression – name of a column, variable, or valid hard-coded JSON.

2. Path – key path to a value. Supports the append mode only. For other actions, such as insert and update, the function works in self-defined mode.

3. NewValue – the value that replaces existing or added as new to JSON.

To add a new key-value pair, you do not need to specify a special mode. For example, to *insert* a new value, you can use the *JSON_MODIFY()* function, which is self-defined, meaning if a path contains an existing key, then the value is updated. When a key does not exist, a new key-value pair is added to the JSON string.

In the Solution section, in Listing 10-1, the column InvoiceDate is first checked by the JSON_MODIFY() function for existence of the key *"SentBy."* For example: *JSON_ MODIFY(InvoiceDate,'$.SentBy', 'John Smith')*. In the column this key was not found. Therefore, the function added a new key *"SentBy"* with the value *"John Smith."*

10-2. Updating Existing JSON
Problem

You want to change the value for an existing key.

Solution

A *Path* argument for the *JSON_MODIFY()* function must exist within a JSON document. Listing 10-2 demonstrates the query when the key "Title" and value "Team Member" are modified to "Manager." Figure 10-2 shows the original and modified JSON documents.

Listing 10-2. Modifying a JSON document

```
SELECT CustomFields
      ,JSON_MODIFY(CustomFields,'$.Title', 'Manager') NewCustomFields
FROM [Application].[People]
WHERE FullName = 'Hudson Onslow';
```

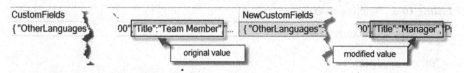

Figure 10-2. *Comparing query output*

How It Works

The *JSON_MODIFY()* function is self-defined, as explained in the previous Recipe 10-1. JSON documents in the CustomFields column contain the key "Title." Therefore, when the key path is detected with a JSON string the JSON_MODIFY() function updates the value property. This concept will be demonstrated in the Solution section, Listing 10-2.

10-3. Deleting from JSON
Problem

You want to delete a key-value pair from a JSON document.

Solution

Set the NewValue(third) argument to NULL within the *JSON_MODIFY()* function if you need to delete the key-value pair, as demonstrated in Listing 10-3. Figure 10-3 shows the original and modified JSON.

Listing 10-3. Deleting key "Title" with value

```
SELECT CustomFields
,JSON_MODIFY(CustomFields,'$.Title', NULL) NewCustomFields
FROM [Application].[People]
WHERE FullName = 'Hudson Onslow';
```

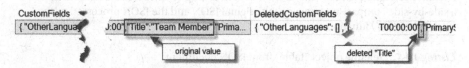

Figure 10-3. *Comparing query output with deleted key "Title"*

How It Works

When the *JSON_MODIFY()* function has a NULL listed as the third argument (NewValue), then the key-value pair is deleted from JSON. This concept applies to the key, object, and array. Listing 10-4 demonstrates how to delete the array *"OtherLanguages"* from the JSON variable @j. Table 10-1 demonstrates a side-by-side comparison between the original JSON and the JSON processed by the *JSON_MODIFY()* function.

271

Listing 10-4. Deleting an array

```
declare @j as nvarchar(MAX) =
N'{
  "OtherLanguages": [
    "Polish",
    "Chinese",
    "Japanese"
  ],
  "HireDate": "2008-04-19T00:00:00",
  "Title": "Team Member",
  "PrimarySalesTerritory": "Plains",
  "CommissionRate": "0.98"
}';

SELECT JSON_MODIFY(@j,'$.OtherLanguages', NULL) DeletedOtherLanguages;
```

Table 10-1. *Comparing the result side by side*

Original JSON	JSON Array OtherLanguages Deleted

`{`
`  "OtherLanguages": [`
`  "Polish",`
`  "Chinese",`
`  "Japanese"`
`],`
`"HireDate": "2008-04-19T00:00:00",`
`"Title": "Team Member",`
`"PrimarySalesTerritory": "Plains",`
`"CommissionRate": "0.98"`
`}`
	`{`
	`  "HireDate": "2008-04-19T00:00:00",`
	`  "Title": "Team Member",`
	`  "PrimarySalesTerritory": "Plains",`
	`  "CommissionRate": "0.98"`
	`}`

Another example demonstrates when the object *"table"* is deleted from the JSON document assigned to the variable @j, shown in Listing 10-5. Table 10-2 demonstrates a side-by-side comparison between the original JSON and the JSON processed by the *JSON_MODIFY()* function.

Listing 10-5. Deleting object "table" from JSON document

```
declare @j nvarchar(MAX) =
N'{
  "theme": "humanity",
  "dateFormat": "dd/mm/yy",
  "timeZone": "PST",
  "table": {
    "pagingType": "full",
    "pageLength": 50
  },
```

```
    "favoritesOnDashboard": true
}';
SELECT JSON_MODIFY(@j,'$.table', NULL) Delete_table;
```

Table 10-2. *Comparing the results side by side*

Original JSON	JSON Object table Deleted

{
  "theme": "humanity",
  "dateFormat": "dd/mm/yy",
  "timeZone": "PST",
  "table": {
  "pagingType": "full",
  "pageLength": 50
},
  "favoritesOnDashboard": true
}
	{
	  "theme": "humanity",
	  "dateFormat": "dd/mm/yy",
	  "timeZone": "PST",
	  "favoritesOnDashboard": true
	}

All examples demonstrate how easy it is to delete a key, object, and array from a JSON string using the JSON_MODIFY() function.

10-4. Appending a JSON Property
Problem

You want to add a new value to an existing array.

Solution

The *append* mode of the JSON_MODIFY() function specifies that the new value needs to be added to the existing list of arrays. Listing 10-6 demonstrates how to add a new language to the *"OtherLanguages"* array. A before-and-after comparison of the returned result with JSON output is shown in Figure 10-4.

Listing 10-6. *Appending Greek language to a JSON array*

```
SELECT CustomFields
        ,JSON_MODIFY(CustomFields,'append $.OtherLanguages', 'Greek') AS
        AppendOtherLanguagesArray
FROM [Application].[People]
WHERE FullName = 'Isabella Rupp';
```

Figure 10-4. *Showing new language appended to a JSON array*

How It Works

The *JSON_MODIFY()* function provides an optional *append* mode. The append mode specifies the path argument and directs the *JSON_MODIFY()* function to add a new value to an existing list. When the *append* mode is specified, but the key path does not exist, the *JSON_MODIFY()* function creates a new key-value pair. For example, the solution query in Listing 10-6 is executed when the *"OtherLanguages"* array is spelled in lowercase as shown in Listing 10-7. At this point, a new "otherlanguages" array is created by the *JSON_MODIFY()* function. The result is shown in Figure 10-5.

Listing 10-7. Appending a nonexisting array

```
SELECT CustomFields
       ,JSON_MODIFY(CustomFields,'append $.otherlanguages', 'Greek') AS
       AppendOtherLanguagesArray
FROM [Application].[People]
WHERE FullName = 'Isabella Rupp';
```

AppendOtherLanguagesArray

{"OtherLanguages": ["Turkish","Slovenian"],"HireD   ..nber","otherlanguages":["Greek"]}

Figure 10-5. *Showing JSON with a duplicated array*

To avoid such a mistake, make sure that the *JSON_MODIFY()* function path argument is provided with the correct JSON path.

10-5. Modifying with Multiple Actions
Problem

You want to apply several value changes to a JSON string.

Solution

Create several inline references with supplied arguments to the *JSON_MODIFY()* function. Listing 10-8 demonstrates multiple *JSON_MODIFY()* function calls. The following is subsequently changed:

1. Append the value "Greek" to the "OtherLanguages" array.

2. Update "Title":"Team Member" to "Title":"Manager."

3. Insert the "CommissionRate":"1.19" key-value pair.

Table 10-3 demonstrates a side-by-side comparison of the original JSON and JSON processed by the *JSON_MODIFY()* function.

Listing 10-8. Demonstrating multiple JSON_MODIFY() function calls

```
SELECT CustomFields
,JSON_MODIFY(
        JSON_MODIFY(
                JSON_MODIFY(CustomFields,'append $.OtherLanguages', 'Greek')
                    , '$.Title', 'Manager')
                        ,'$.CommissionRate', '1.19') AS Multi_Changes
FROM [Application].[People]
WHERE FullName = 'Isabella Rupp';
```

Table 10-3. Comparing result side by side

Original JSON	Modified JSON

{
  "OtherLanguages": [
  "Turkish",
  "Slovenian"
],
"HireDate": "2010-08-24T00:00:00",
"Title": "Team Member"
}
	{ "OtherLanguages": [
	  "Turkish",
	  "Slovenian",
	  "Greek"
	],
	"HireDate": "2010-08-24T00:00:00",
	"Title": "Manager",
	"CommissionRate": "1.19"
	}

How It Works

The *JSON_MODIFY()* function has the ability for continuous inline calls with multiple modifications. The *JSON_MODIFY()* function returns modified JSON. Therefore, each returned JSON string could be continuously processed for another modification.

10-6. Renaming a JSON Key
Problem

You want to rename a JSON key.

Solution

You need to create a new object or key then delete the old name. Listing 10-9 demonstrates how to rename the array OtherLanguages to SpokenLanguages with preserved original values. The renamed array in JSON is shown in Figure 10-6.

Listing 10-9. Renaming the OtherLanguages array

```
SELECT
        JSON_MODIFY(
                JSON_MODIFY(CustomFields,'$.SpokenLanguages', JSON_
QUERY(JSON_QUERY(CustomFields, '$.OtherLanguages')))
                        , '$.OtherLanguages', NULL) Rename_OtherLanguages_
Array
FROM [Application].[People]
WHERE FullName = 'Isabella Rupp';
```

Rename_OtherLanguages_Array
{ "HireDate":"2010-08-24T00:00:00", ...ber" "SpokenLanguages":["Turkish","Slovenian"]}

Figure 10-6. Showing renamed array

How It Works

SQL Server does not have a function to rename a key or object directly. Therefore, the rename mechanism has two steps:

1. Create a new object with original values, as shown in Listing 10-9.

2. Delete the old object from the JSON document.

The Solution section demonstrates that renaming the OtherLanguages array name to SpokenLanguages is a bit more complex than simply renaming a key. As you could see, the solution code calls the JSON_QUERY() function twice. This is because at first, the JSON_QUERY() function calls with a path to the OtherLanguages array to obtain original values. However, the returned values have an escape character, and to hide the escape character(s), a JSON_QUERY() function is called to fix the returned array. Table 10-4 demonstrates a side-by-side comparison between the JSON with a single JSON_QUERY() function call and the JSON with a double JSON_QUERY() function call.

Table 10-4. Comparing JSON side by side

Not Corrected JSON	Corrected JSON
```{ "HireDate": "2010-08-24T00:00:00", "Title": "Team Member", "SpokenLanguages": "[\"Turkish\",\"Slovenian\"]" }```	```{ "HireDate": "2010-08-24T00:00:00", "Title": "Team Member", "SpokenLanguages": ["Turkish", "Slovenian"] }```

When the first JSON_MODIFY() function call returns a desirable JSON result, the second JSON_MODIFY() call deletes the old name with the provided *path* arguments as '*$.OtherLanguages*' and newValue argument as *NULL*.

10-7. Modifying a JSON Object
Problem
You want to replace all values in a JSON array object.

Solution
A *JSON_MODIFY()* function replaces all values in a JSON array by specified Path and NewValue arguments. Listing 10-10 demonstrates a Solution section to replace the JSON array. Table 10-5 demonstrates a side-by-side comparison between the original and modified JSON arrays.

Listing 10-10. Replacing a JSON array

```
SELECT CustomFields, JSON_MODIFY(CustomFields, '$.OtherLanguages',
               JSON_QUERY('["Dutch","Latvian","Lithuanian"]'))
OtherLanguages
FROM [Application].[People]
WHERE FullName = 'Isabella Rupp';
```

Table 10-5. Comparing the JSON result side by side

Original JSON	Modified JSON

{
  "OtherLanguages": [
  "Turkish", "Slovenian"
],
"HireDate": "2010-08-24T00:00:00",
"Title": "Team Member"
}
	{
	  "OtherLanguages": [
	  "Dutch", "Latvian", "Lithuanian"
	],
	"HireDate": "2010-08-24T00:00:00",
	"Title": "Team Member"
	}

How It Works
To replace a JSON array, the *JSON_MODIFY()* function detects and validates an argument *path* and then applies the *newValue* argument to JSON. The *NewValue* argument must have a valid JSON array or objects part. For example, *["Dutch", "Latvian", "Lithuanian"]* is a valid array part for the *NewValue* argument used in Listing 10-10.

The Nature of the behavior for the *JSON_MODIFY()* function is that the value in the newValue argument is treated as a string. Therefore, all special characters (for example: double quotes, forward slashes, and backslashes) escape with backslash "\". That why the *NewValue* argument is surrounded by the *JSON_QUERY()* function to remove escape characters.

The Solution section provides a query for creating a JSON array. However, a similar solution is demonstrated in Listing 10-11 for replacing a JSON object. As a reminder: an array is surrounded by square brackets and contains a list of values for the same property and type. When an object is surrounded by curly braces {}, it could have a list of key-value pairs with different properties and types. Table 10-6 demonstrates a side-by-side comparison of an original and modified JSON object.

Listing 10-11. Replacing a JSON object

```
SELECT [UserPreferences],
JSON_MODIFY([UserPreferences], '$.table',
        JSON_QUERY('{"pagingType":"full","pageLength":25,"pageScope":
        "private"}')   ) AS ModifiedUserPreferences
FROM [Application].[People]
WHERE FullName = 'Isabella Rupp';
```

Table 10-6. *Comparing the JSON results side by side*

Original JSON	Modified JSON
```{```	```{```
``` "theme": "ui-darkness",```	``` "theme": "ui-darkness",```
``` "dateFormat": "dd/mm/yy",```	``` "dateFormat": "dd/mm/yy",```
``` "timeZone": "PST",```	``` "timeZone": "PST",```
``` "table": {```	``` "table": {```
``` "pagingType": "simple",```	``` "pagingType": "full",```
``` "pageLength": 10```	``` "pageLength": 25,```
``` },```	``` "pageScope": "private"```
``` "favoritesOnDashboard": true```	``` },```
```}```	``` "favoritesOnDashboard": true```
	```}```

And alternate solution could be:

1. delete the *OtherLanguages* array.

2. reinsert the *OtherLanguages* array with the new part.

The code for this technique is demonstrated in Listing 10-12. The result from the code is shown in Figure 10-7.

Listing 10-12. Demonstrating the delete and re-insert query

```
SELECT CustomFields,
       JSON_MODIFY(
              JSON_MODIFY(CustomFields, '$.OtherLanguages', NULL),
              '$.OtherLanguages', JSON_QUERY('["Dutch","Latvian",
              "Lithuanian"]')) OtherLanguages
FROM [Application].[People]
WHERE FullName = 'Isabella Rupp';
```

OtherLanguages
{ "HireDate":"2010-08-24T... ...mber","OtherLanguages":["Dutch","Latvian","Lithuanian"]}

Figure 10-7. *Showing the query output*

Inefficiency (I prefer not to use word "problematic" because the code returns a correct result) for such a technique is that:

- The *OtherLanguages* array moves to last the JSON position, so the array loses its original place within the JSON document.

- You are required to implement an additional JSON_*MODIFY()* function.

I would not recommend this technique to replace an object or array.

10-8. Comparing XML vs. JSON
Problem

You want to compare XML and JSON performance.

Solution

The solution is implemented in several steps. Listing 10-13 demonstrates the T-SQL code for the process. Table 10-7 demonstrates a side-by-side comparison between JSON and XML.

The comparison steps:

1. Create two tables, one for JSON strings, another for XML instances.

2. Create an insert process to convert the same data into JSON and XML.

3. Run XML shredding.

4. Run JSON shredding.

5. Compare results (will review in "How It Works" section)

Listing 10-13. Demonstrating T-SQL code

```
/************************ XML INSERT ************************/
SET NOCOUNT ON;

DECLARE @XML XML,
            @schema nvarchar(30),
            @tbl nvarchar(128),
```

```
                @objID int,
                @time datetime2;

DROP TABLE IF EXISTS dbo.Table_Info_XML;

CREATE TABLE Table_Info_XML (
                TableID int PRIMARY KEY,
                DBName nvarchar(128),
                [SchemaName] nvarchar(30),
                tblName nvarchar(128),
                XMLDoc XML
                );

DECLARE cur CURSOR FOR
        SELECT object_id, [Schema].name, [Table].name
        FROM sys.objects [Table]
        JOIN sys.schemas [Schema] on [Table].schema_id = [Schema].schema_id
        WHERE type = 'u';

OPEN cur;

FETCH NEXT FROM cur INTO @objID, @schema, @tbl;
SET @time = GETDATE();
WHILE @@FETCH_STATUS = 0
BEGIN

        SELECT @XML = (
        SELECT db_name() as 'Database',
        [Schema].name as 'Tables/SchemaName',
        [Table].name as 'Tables/TableName',
                (SELECT name as ColumnName FROM sys.columns [Column]
                WHERE [Column].object_id = [Table].object_id FOR XML AUTO,
TYPE
                ) AS 'Tables/Columns'
        FROM sys.objects [Table]
                JOIN sys.schemas [Schema] on [Table].schema_id = [Schema].
                schema_id
        WHERE [Table].object_id = @objID
        FOR XML PATH('TableInfo')
        );

        INSERT Table_Info_XML
        SELECT @objID, DB_NAME(), @schema, @tbl, @XML;

        FETCH NEXT FROM cur INTO @objID, @schema, @tbl;
END;
```

```
DEALLOCATE cur;

SELECT DATEDIFF(MILLISECOND, @time, GETDATE()) as XML_TIME;

SET NOCOUNT OFF;

GO

/*********************** JSON INSERT ***********************/

SET NOCOUNT ON;

DECLARE @JSON nvarchar(MAX),
                @schema nvarchar(30),
                @tbl nvarchar(128),
                @objID int,
                @time datetime2

DROP TABLE IF EXISTS dbo. Table_Info_JSON;

CREATE TABLE Table_Info_JSON (
                TableID int PRIMARY KEY,
                DBName nvarchar(128),
                [SchemaName] nvarchar(30),
                tblName nvarchar(128),
                JSONDoc nvarchar(MAX)
                );

DECLARE cur CURSOR FOR
        SELECT object_id, [Schema].name, [Table].name
        FROM sys.objects [Table]
        JOIN sys.schemas [Schema] on [Table].schema_id = [Schema].schema_id
        WHERE type = 'u';

OPEN cur;

FETCH NEXT FROM cur INTO @objID, @schema, @tbl;
SET @time = GETDATE();
WHILE @@FETCH_STATUS = 0
BEGIN

        SELECT @JSON = (
        SELECT db_name() as 'Database',
        [Schema].name as 'Tables.SchemaName',
        [Table].name as 'Tables.TableName',
                (SELECT [Column].name ColumnName FROM sys.columns [Column]
                WHERE [Column].object_id = [Table].object_id FOR JSON AUTO
                ) AS 'Tables.Columns'
```

```
        FROM sys.objects [Table]
                JOIN sys.schemas [Schema] on [Table].schema_id = [Schema].
                schema_id
        WHERE [Table].object_id = @objID
        FOR JSON PATH, WITHOUT_ARRAY_WRAPPER
        );

        INSERT Table_Info_JSON
        SELECT @objID, DB_NAME(), @schema, @tbl, @JSON;

        FETCH NEXT FROM cur INTO @objID, @schema, @tbl;
END;

DEALLOCATE cur;

SELECT DATEDIFF(MILLISECOND, @time, GETDATE()) as JSON_TIME;

SET NOCOUNT OFF;

GO

--- Shredding XML
SET STATISTICS TIME ON;

SELECT clm.value('../../../Database[1]', 'varchar(50)') as [Database]
       ,clm.value('../../SchemaName[1]', 'varchar(50)') as SchemaName
       ,clm.value('../../TableName[1]', 'varchar(50)') as TableName
       ,clm.value('@ColumnName', 'varchar(50)') as ColumnName
FROM dbo.Table_Info_XML
        CROSS APPLY XMLDoc.nodes('TableInfo/Tables/Columns/Column') as
tbl(clm);

SET STATISTICS TIME OFF;

--- Shredding JSON
SET STATISTICS TIME ON;

SELECT db.[Database]
        , tbl.SchemaName
        , tbl.TableName
        , clmn.ColumnName
FROM dbo.Table_Info_JSON
        CROSS APPLY OPENJSON (JSONDoc)
                WITH
                (
                        [Database] varchar(30),
                        [Tables] nvarchar(MAX) AS JSON
                ) as db
```

```
CROSS APPLY OPENJSON ([Tables])
                WITH
                (
                        TableName varchar(30),
                        SchemaName varchar(30),
                        [Columns] nvarchar(MAX) AS JSON
                ) as tbl
        CROSS APPLY OPENJSON ([Columns])
                WITH
                (
                        ColumnName varchar(30)
                ) as clmn

SET STATISTICS TIME OFF;
```

Table 10-7. *Comparing a JSON document and an XML instance side by side*

JSON Document	XML Instance

{
  "Database": "WideWorldImporters",
  "Tables": {
  "SchemaName": "Warehouse",
  "TableName": "Colors",
  "Columns": [
  {"ColumnName": "ColorID"},
  {"ColumnName": "ColorName"},
  {"ColumnName": "LastEditedBy"},
  {"ColumnName": "ValidFrom"},
  {"ColumnName": "ValidTo"}
  ]
  }
}
	\<TableInfo>
	  \<Database>WideWorldImporters\</Database>
	  \<Tables>
	  \<SchemaName>Warehouse\</SchemaName>
	  \<TableName>Colors\</TableName>
	  \<Columns>
	    \<Column ColumnName="ColorID" />
	    \<Column ColumnName="ColorName" />
	    \<Column ColumnName="LastEditedBy" />
	    \<Column ColumnName="ValidFrom" />
	    \<Column ColumnName="ValidTo" />
	  \</Columns>
	  \</Tables>
	\</TableInfo>

How It Works

The five-step mechanism to compare XML and JSON is listed in the Solution section as well as T-SQL code (Listing 10-13) to create the tables, establish, and run the cursors to load the table with XML using the FOR XML clause and JSON using the FOR JSON clause; and as a last step, shred both XML and JSON columns into row sets. This code should be familiar to you by now, because the code for this case is very similar to several of the previous recipes.

The comparison ran on the *WideWorldImporters* database. However, the code is database independent and could run on any database with a Compatibility Level of 130 or higher. In the "How It Works" section, I would like to compare the performance numbers between two processes. The insert runtime numbers in milliseconds are shown in Table 10-8. In both the Table_Info_JSON and Table_Info_XML tables, 573 rows were inserted. The measurement was taken by the DATEDIFF() function for both JSON and XML inserts. The start time was assigned to a variable before the cursor started, and the function call was executed after the cursor deallocation.

Table 10-8. *Comparing the insert time side by side*

JSON Insert	XML Insert
20 milliseconds	26 milliseconds

The shredding was measured by enabling STATISTICS TIME. Each shredding process ran separately, with the SSMS option *Result To Text* (Result To Grid returns slightly higher numbers).
JSON shredding record:

```
(573 row(s) affected)

 SQL Server Execution Times:
   CPU time = 0 ms,  elapsed time = 14 ms.
```

XML shredding record:

```
(573 row(s) affected)

 SQL Server Execution Times:
   CPU time = 15 ms,  elapsed time = 21 ms.
```

■ **Note**   The output on your PC could return different performance numbers.

To summarize both, in the inserting and shredding processes, JSON clearly has slightly better performance than XML. However, it does not mean that you need to implement JSON immediately! Each technology has its pros and cons. For example, JSON is lighter than XML and processes faster, so it could be a good fit for a relatively small document without a deep parent-child structure. However, as of today, JSON is in string data format and cannot compete with a solid XML data type, which is practically a language. There are many options that make XML irreplaceable: XML Schema, Attributes, and Namespaces, to name a few. I would advise against taking extreme courses of action. Any technology should be used with the best practical performance, that is, what is better for each case.

Wrapping Up

This is it! I have shared my knowledge with you, my dear reader. The recipes throughout this book came from production solutions that I faced and resolved for various clients and companies. I did my best to cover, as thoroughly as possible, recipes for XML and JSON in an SQL Server environment, and I hope that you were able to find the exact solution, or at least the knowledge and guidance to solve your XML and JSON situation.

At this point, I would like to thank you for reading this book. I hope that the content will bring useful solutions to your issues and add additional knowledge to your SQL Server skills.

Index

A

AUTO mode, JSON
    formatted result, 225–226
    JSONFormatter interface, 227
    table and column, 228–229
    XML Editor, 226

B

Binary data, 35–36

C, D

Common Language Runtime (CLR)
    command-line, 94
    creation, 95
    data type
        CAST() function, 244
        string, 242
        ToString() function, 243
    PERMISSION_SET, 98
    WriteXMLFile and ReadXMLFile,
        92–94, 96–99
Custom XML generation
    code snippet, 43–45
    EXPLICIT mode, 39–41, 45
    logical structure, 41–42
    PATH mode, 46–48

E

Element-centric XML, 31–32
exist() function, implementing, 159–160
EXtensible Markup Language (XML)
    attribute-centric, 5–6
    binary data, 35–36

    characters, 6
    clause modes, 23–24
    data settings, 25
    data type, 7–8
    element-centric, 4–5
    vs. HTML, 3
    NULL values, 33–34
    root element, 32–33
    Schema Collection, 18–20
    SSMS, 14–18
    table names, 28–30
    typed, 20–22
    untyped, 8–10
    Visual Studio, 11–14

F, G, H

Filtering XML
    empty values, 178–181
    execution, 182–183
    exist(), XQuery processes, 160–164
    multiple conditions, 175–176
    negative operator, 177–178
    range of values, 174–175
    sequence of values, 170–171
    single value, 167–168
    stored procedure, 165
    string pattern, 171–174
    Tel.Number element, 166
    T-SQL, 168–170

I

Internal ENTITY declarations
    @flags parameter, 105
    namespace declaration, 104
    @ns variable, 104

© Alex Grinberg 2018
A. Grinberg, *XML and JSON Recipes for SQL Server*,
https://doi.org/10.1007/978-1-4842-3117-3

Internal ENTITY declarations (*cont.*)
    OPEXML function, 101–102
    product model, 103
    result data, 103
    sp_xml:preparedocument, 104–105
    WITH clause, 107
    XPath, 106
ISJSON() function
    database, 245–247
    SELECT, 248
    string, 247
    WHERE, 248

■ J, K, L

JavaScript Object Notation (JSON)
    AUTO mode, 225
    benefits, 221
    blocks, 221
    brackets, 232
    built-in functions, 225
    CLR data type, 241–244
    Columns, 237–238
    escape characters, 239–241
    index
        ConNote, 264–265
        STATISTICS, 265, 267
    NULL, 230–231, 254–255
    PATH mode, 234–235
    query, 236
    ROOT key element, 233
    SELECT clause, 237
    SQL Server, 223
    sub-object, 260, 262–263
    XML, 224
JSON_MODIFY() function
    key-value pair
        add, 269–270
        append mode, 273–274
        delete, 271–273
        multiple modifications, 274–275
        object, 277–279
        rename, 275–277
        update, 270
    XML *vs.* JSON, 279–284
JSON_QUERY() function
    DeliveredWhen and ReceivedBy, 250
    returning events, 249
    single array object, 250–251

JSON_VALUE() function
    JSON_QUERY() function, 252
    LongText, 253
    returned data type, 252
    scalar values, 251

■ M

modify() method, XML
    delete
        attribute value, 151–153
        XML element, 153–156
    insert element
        attributes, 140–142
        if-then-else, 143
        multiple elements, 146–148
        namespace, 137–140
        position sequence, 144–146
        XML DML, 135–137
    update
        attribute value, 150–151
        element value, 148–149
Multiple CROSS APPLY
    operators, 132–133

■ N

Nested XML elements, 37–38
Node test, 49, 51
NULL value, 33–34, 230–231
    JSON_VALUE()
        function, 254
    strict mode, 255

■ O

OPENJSON() function
    key-value elements, 257
    tables, 255–256
    WITH clause, 257–259
OPENXML function
    CONVERT and CAST
        functions, 109
    data types, 109
    DEFAULT, 111
    nodes() method, 111
    value() method, 112–113
    WITH() method, 112
    XQuery, 109

■ P, Q

PATH type index
    creation, 194–195
    secondary path, 195–196
Primary XML index
    creation, 185–186
    PersonXML, 185, 187, 189–191
    rules, 192

■ R

Relational data, XML, 26–27
ROOT key element, 233

■ S

Secondary property type XML index, 200–202
Secondary selective XML index, 213–214
Secondary value type XML
    index, 196–199
Selective XML index
    creation
        execution plan, 209
        nested element nodes, 205–206
        query, 206–207
        statistics, 207
        tables and column, 203–205
        XMLNAMESPACE, 209
    modifying, 215–218
    optimizing, 210–213
Shredding XML
    column demographics, 113–115
    internal ENTITY (*see* Internal ENTITY
        declarations)
    legacy databases, 117–119
    multiple CROSS APPLY (*see* Multiple
        CROSS APPLY operators)
    OPENXML function (*see* OPENXML
        function)
    subset, 123–126
    tables and columns
        database, 127–129
        IMAGE data type, 130
        logical processes, 129–130
        SELECT clause, 131
    typed XML column, 120–123
SQL Server Management
    Studio (SSMS), 14–18
SSIS package
    BCP utility, 59
    Collection menu, 84–85
    configurations, 64, 66
    control flow, 60
    DelayValidation, 89
    Evaluate Expression, 67
    Execute SQL Task Editor, 83
    Expression Property Editor, 84
    File System Task property, 89
    flexibility and functionality, 79
    LoadXMLFromFile, 78–79
    Main() function, 70–71
    Mapping menu, FileName, 85–86
    OLE DB Connection, 63
    Parameter Mapping menu, 87–88
    Precedence Constraint
        Editor, 68–69, 82–83
    Script Task, 91
        Manager, 69
        variables, 81
    stored procedure, 92
    testing, 71
    Tool Box, 60
    variable list, 80
    variables, 61–62
Storing XML result
    BCP utility, 58
    file path, 53–55
    file-writing process, 55–58
    T-SQL, 72–77

■ T

T-SQL, variable values, 168–170
Typed XML columns
    creating, 20–22
    shredding
        fn, 121, 123
        query(), 122
        text(), 123
        XPath, 120–121

■ U, V, W

Untyped XML, 8, 10–11

■ X, Y, Z

XML Data Modification Language
    (XML DML), 135–137

Get the eBook for only $5!

Why limit yourself?

With most of our titles available in both PDF and ePUB format, you can access your content wherever and however you wish—on your PC, phone, tablet, or reader.

Since you've purchased this print book, we are happy to offer you the eBook for just $5.

To learn more, go to http://www.apress.com/companion or contact support@apress.com.

Apress®

Printed in the United States
By Bookmasters